P9-CLF-845

DISCARDED

SHELTON STATE COMMUNITY
COLLEGE
JUNIOR COLLEGE DIVISION
LIBRARY

JK
2316
.M27

Martin, John
Frederick.

Civil rights and the
crisis of
liberalism

DATE			
MAR 05			

® THE BAKER & TAYLOR CO.

ERRATA SHEET

Civil Rights and the Crisis of Liberalism: The Democratic
Party 1945-1976, by John Frederick Martin.

1. p. 41, line 9: "the party" should read "the government"

2. p. 141: delete "on which" from incomplete sentence at
    bottom of page.

3. p. 207, line 3 of 2nd full paragraph: "to all quarters"
    should read "in all quarters"

4. p. 225, line 1: insert comma to read "similar in another
    way, in their accent on ethnicity."

5. p. 258, last line of 2nd full paragraph: should read
    "but the abiding hatreds Americans always had had."

6. p. 273, #4: close parentheses to read: "(Oxford, 1966),
    p. 114."

7. p. 274, #6: delete "Ibid."

8. p. 283, #22: should read: "AES Papers, AES to Agnes
    Meyers,"

9. p. 285, #47: should read: "Higher Education Guidelines:
    Executive Order 11246, 1972;"

CIVIL RIGHTS AND THE CRISIS OF LIBERALISM

About the Book and Author

Civil Rights and the Crisis of Liberalism:
The Democratic Party, 1945-1976

John Frederick Martin

This book is an interpretation of our recent political past. It offers an explanation of the rise and decline of postwar liberalism, a creed that was vitally concerned with civil rights. Partly because of such special concern, liberalism inspired in many a daring vision of social justice and, by the end of the 1960s, inspired in many more a reaction of loathing and contempt.

To explain the rise of this ideology, John Frederick Martin has drawn from numerous archives and interviews and assessed the contributions of Truman, Stevenson, Kefauver, Harriman, Kennedy, and Johnson. To explain its decline, he has analyzed the reaction to the liberals' government—the sentiments aroused by busing, affirmative action, Model Cities, and the militance of blacks, Democrats, and white ethnics. Though varying in their intent, these responses shared a dislike of the liberals' treatment of minorities and a dread of government power—a dread made stronger by the antiwar movement and the Watergate scandal—and thereby discredited the very ends and means of the liberal program.

By the early 1970s, Martin argues, it was no surprise that a politics of consumerism—pivoting on the rights of the average citizen, not of the deprived citizen, and eschewing government power—had replaced the liberal ideology.

Placing this narrative in a larger context, Martin explains the importance of the race issue in previous liberal movements and composes an interpretation of the whole of American liberalism as well as of its latest stage and the Democrats' recent ordeal.

John Frederick Martin, a graduate of Harvard College, is a Ph.D. candidate in history at Harvard, where for the last four years he has been a Teaching Fellow.

DISCARDED

CIVIL RIGHTS AND THE CRISIS OF LIBERALISM

The Democratic Party 1945-1976

John Frederick Martin

Westview Press

Boulder, Colorado

DISCARDED

All rights reserved. No part of this publication may be reproduced or transmitted in any form or by any means, electronic or mechanical, including photocopy, recording, or any information storage and retrieval system, without permission in writing from the publisher.

Copyright © 1979 by John Frederick Martin

Published in 1979 in the United States of America by
    Westview Press, Inc.
    5500 Central Avenue
    Boulder, Colorado 80301
    Frederick A. Praeger, Publisher

Library of Congress Cataloging in Publication Data
Martin, John Frederick.
    Civil rights and the crisis of liberalism.
    Includes bibliographical references and index.
    1. Democratic Party. 2. Liberalism—United States. 3. Civil rights—United States.
4. United States—Politics and government—1945-   I. Title.
JK2316.M27   329.3   79-10886
ISBN 0-89158-454-4

Printed and bound in the United States of America

To my parents,

John Bartlow and Frances Rose Martin

CONTENTS

PART 2
CIVIL RIGHTS AND THE LIBERAL TRIUMPH

PART 3
CIVIL RIGHTS AND THE LIBERAL FAILURE

ACKNOWLEDGMENTS

In the course of this research I incurred many debts. At the Kennedy Library I am grateful to the director, Dan Fenn, and to the staff, principally Allan Goodrich. At the University of Tennessee I am grateful, for his friendly and patient assistance, to John Dobson, Librarian of the Special Collections.

For permission to publish quotations from their fathers' private papers, I am indebted to Senator Adlai E. Stevenson of Illinois and to Dr. D. E. Kefauver of Tennessee. For permission to publish quotations from the notes of F. Joseph Donohue (aide to Senator Kefauver), I am indebted to Mrs. F. Joseph Donohue. I am indebted also to Doubleday, and to Samuel Vaughan, Publisher, for permission to publish three quotations excerpted from *Adlai Stevenson and the World,* by John Bartlow Martin, 1977. To these people I wish to express my thanks.

For permission to quote from their own correspondence, I am indebted to Jonathan Daniels, Arthur M. Schlesinger, Jr., and Hermon Dunlap Smith. I am most grateful to them for permitting this invasion of their privacy, especially to Arthur Schlesinger, who also allowed me to quote excerpts from his diary.

Others have provided me with invaluable information. James Rowe gave me a copy of the strategy paper he wrote in 1947, when he and others were preparing the upcoming presidential campaign of Harry Truman. Joseph Rauh gave me a copy of the unpublished memoir he has written of his experiences in a series of Democratic National Conventions from 1948 to 1968. These documents were of inestimable importance to me. Moreover, both Rowe and Rauh read and criticized portions of the manuscript and answered my queries in interviews and correspondence. I am deeply grateful to them; though I should emphasize that neither they nor the others who helped me bear any responsibility for the views expressed in this book. Nor do they necessarily share these views; sometimes they have told me they do not. Others have kindly answered my request for help: Congressman John Brademas, Jonathan Daniels, Robert J. Donovan, Judge Samuel Gold, and Newton Minow. Douglas Costle gave me a copy of the study he made of the Model Cities program. And on several occasions, Milton and Lisa Gwirtzman gave me valuable advice and encouragement. To all these people, I am indebted, and I must express my profound gratitude.

In a book of this kind, on events so recent, interviews are indispensable. Those I interviewed, in the spring and fall of 1976, gave generously of their time: Derrick Cephas, witness to the Cambridge, Maryland, riot of 1967; Douglas Costle, Model Cities expert (now administrator of the Environmental Protection Agency); Richard Goodwin, Kennedy and Johnson speechwriter; Milton Gwirtzman, aide to Robert F. Kennedy; John Harwell, former official of the Urban League, Chicago; Kathy Hwang, Office of Civil Rights, Boston; Melvin King, representative to the Massachusetts legislature; James O'Hara, congressman from Michigan; Arthur Okun, chairman of the Council of Economic Advisers under Johnson; Cortney Pace, administrative assistant to Senator James Eastland; Elvira Palladino, cofounder of the anti-busing group, Restore Our Alienated Rights; Joseph Rauh, co-founder of the Americans for Democratic Action and counsel to the UAW and Leadership Conference on Civil Rights; James Rowe, aide to Roosevelt, Truman, Harriman, Johnson, and Humphrey; Herman Talmadge, senator from Georgia; Ted Van Dyk, aide to Humphrey; Robert C. Wood, under secretary of HUD and urban specialist for Johnson. These people cleared up many matters for me. I am grateful to them all.

The Mark DeWolfe Howe Fund of Harvard Law School supported me while I finished the book; to it and to its administrators I owe my thanks. At Harvard my work was also made easier by the help of the History Department and of Mather House, and by the kindness of Bernard Bailyn, John Clive, Frank Freidel, and F. Skiddy von Stade.

I wish also to express my thanks to Lynne Rienner, Executive Editor of Westview Press, who for the past several months has been most helpful and encouraging; and to Herb and Marilyn Ruben, who read an early version of the manuscript and gave me valuable advice.

Marianne and Franz Winkler have shown me unending kindness and encouragement while I worked on this book. I have also had the benefit of the advice and friendship of Dorothy Olding of Harold Ober Associates. Robert Bauer, Stephen Schuker, and Daniela Winkler each read the book and gave me their penetrating criticism, as well as their sustaining friendship. To these people I owe a special word of thanks.

And to my father, whose work has always been for me an example of honest endeavor, and who gave me during the past several years his advice and his warm encouragement. I should also mention that passages of this book could not have been written without the use of the memoranda he wrote as an adviser to Adlai Stevenson in the 1952 and 1956 campaigns. My work was also made easier by his organization of the Stevenson Papers, which he assembled while writing his book, *The Life of Adlai E. Stevenson,* 2 vols. (Garden City, N.Y.: Doubleday, 1976-77).

J.F.M.

INTRODUCTION

This book is about ideology and politics. It focuses on the civil rights issue in Democratic party politics from 1945 to 1976 but glances at a longer history to describe American liberalism. It has the limitations its topic imposes. It does not chronicle the civil rights movement or the Great Society, nor does it explain economic and demographic changes, but rather takes these events and changes into account, for they had an influence on liberal thought. And liberal thought is the subject of the book.

After World War II the Democrats seriously debated for the first time the issue of civil rights. It was a divisive issue, throwing the party into a struggle, which, by the time it was resolved in 1960, had transformed the Democrats—and liberalism too—from the ideology of property and small government to that of civil rights and federal power. Soon the liberals transformed the nation. But as they did, at the height of their success during the Great Society, they ran into trouble. They were assailed from all sides, maligned as inept bureaucrats, as the wielders of oppressive power, as the timid apologists of the white Establishment, or, more often, simply as liberals; for within a few years of their startling successes—civil rights laws and medical care for the poor and old—their name was a term of opprobrium. Why?

The answer takes us back through the history of liberalism. From the time of the American Revolution, the purpose of liberalism always had been to control power and protect people and their property, a purpose that limited liberals, often impeding their view of social problems. Another impediment was the racial prejudice of the American people. It, too, limited the reach of the liberal quest and, on several occasions, upset liberal alliances. The New Deal broke one of these limits—it dispelled a little of the fear of big government—but it did not break them all or even that one completely. The fear of power and the faith in property and racial prejudice were old, venerable beliefs. They had deep roots in the American mind. And they were not challenged, all of them together, until the civil rights issue appeared after World War II and threw the Democrats into an uproar. This issue tore the party apart, pitting the old guard of the South against the liberals of the North. Each side was adamant on civil rights; each saw that the fight would determine more than the fate of the blacks. For civil rights threatened not only white supremacy and the "solid South" but also states' rights and the laissez-faire view of government; it promised not only to make blacks equal but to do so with federal power, which the liberals thought should also protect the working man and all others made defenseless by modern industrial society. The civil rights fight thus stood as the symbol of a larger fight— the fight to determine the party's ideology.

It impinged on every Democratic decision—the choice of candidates and campaign strategy, of platforms and the party's future—and on every leader. By precipitating the fight over civil rights, Truman lost control of his party. By conciliating the sides, Stevenson maintained his influence and so did Lyndon Johnson. But others wanted to fight—the segregationists of the South and the liberals, Harriman and Kefauver—and as they struggled, the party gradually changed. By 1960, the liberals having won, the Democrats broke the restraints on liberal thought and framed a new ideology, one of civil rights and federal power. Their ordeal of fifteen years within the party was over. Their ordeal in the nation began.

This ordeal was shorter; the liberals' decline was swift. A principal concern of the Kennedy and Johnson administrations was the blacks, and a frequent demand of both was that federal power help them. Thus did Kennedy and Johnson fulfill their party's purpose, as the recent struggle had redefined it. But as soon as they did, they were attacked for their use of power and their tampering with race relations. A reaction set in from both the right and the left: the right blaming the liberals for beginning, the left for not completing a revolution in race relations; and both distrusted the liberals' power. By the end of the Great Society the liberals themselves, not the problems they tried to solve, had become the political issue. Out of office, their nerve broken, the liberals pondered their demise. They reassessed their doctrine and—this was their final defeat—retreated from their positions. Once the wielders of unprecedented power, the liberals joined their earlier foes and called for the return of small government. Once the moral core of the liberal creed, the civil rights issue faded, leaving in its stead only one fervent issue, a reminder of the past—busing, called "forced," a word to describe break-ins and rape. An old thought came alive. Born in the Revolution and nurtured since in the South, it said that power was bad, the people good. And a Georgian was elected president.

This is the history the book seeks to explain, not to take sides but to explain the recent course of liberalism in the United States. These events were swift and surprising—the Democrats' bitter fight, the transformation of liberal doctrine, the liberals' hurried achievement, even more their abrupt and bewildering failure—but none of it was by chance.

PART ONE

LIBERALISM
AND AMERICAN HISTORY

ONE

THE CONTRADICTIONS
OF LIBERALISM

Let us begin with American liberalism, that ideology which from its beginning was beset by contradiction.

To many people in the eighteenth century it appeared that the evolution of just government had reached its apex in England. The English constitution, they believed, embodied balance—the balance of estates so that none could dominate the others. It derived its authority from precedent, rather than God, contract, or the people, and therefore recognized rights as the incidents of custom and privilege and not as a quality man naturally possessed. The flower of a rich and dark past, the constitution was admired by Montesquieu and Burke and all those who rooted their rights in privilege, their freedom in restraints—including the English living in America, who believed in it no less than the English living in England. That was why they rebelled.[1]

For they thought the English were defiling the constitution. Where there should have been balance, they saw imbalance—an executive that corrupted and controlled the parliament. Where there should have been respect for rights, they saw coercion—heedless, unlimited power. And where there should have been precedent, they saw departure—a new colonial policy, which began in 1763. So, to save themselves and restore the constitution, the colonists rebelled—the first and most important event in the history of American liberalism.

The exigencies of rebellion caused the Americans, though acting in the name of the constitution, to rethink its principles and devise new theories of politics and government. The primary exigency was their subjection to superior force. It was a painful subjection, and in striving to overcome it they arrived at a set of ideas originally pronounced by Machiavelli and lately revived and given new meaning by the opposition to English government in the eighteenth century. This opposition—writers like Bolingbroke and Trenchard and Gordon, who did not always agree among themselves but nonetheless gave to the Americans a coherent political thought—had been complaining about the corruption of parliament and the concentration of executive power since the start of the century. They said that this power had upset the balance of government, denying the people their rights and proper representation. The people were the losers, as power grew, and so was the constitution: for a virtuous people were the basis of republican government, deriving their virtue from their independence, their independence from their property. When these principles ceased to serve as the foundation of government—when liberties were curtailed, property assailed, and virtue corrupted— tyranny must prevail.[2] This argument, carrying little weight in England, was particularly relevant to the colonial contest, where the Americans, coerced by imperial power, began to use it in their defense. They became haunted by power, obsessively detecting its spread. Power was everywhere. Standing armies were its instrument, plural office holding and corruption its method; these the Americans abhorred. An overwhelming executive branch was its result, conspiracy its way, and rights its victim. Power must be restrained. The colonists became equally obsessed with the virtuous people. They were the ballast of good government. They and their property must be protected, their virtue preserved. Such was the ideology that grasped the minds of the colonists and explained to them the meaning of their crisis.[3]

Such was also the beginning of American liberalism, distinguished from English constitutional thought by its emphasis on the people and on the dangers of power, and by its neglect of balance and the past. Already by 1776 this ideology had led the Americans to act in wholly new ways. First they rebelled in the name of the people; then they framed state governments, also in their behalf. They reduced the discretion of the executive, paring his appointment power, his veto, and his control of the militia. Pennsylvania did away with the executive altogether and formed a council. And they made the legislatures strong, for they were the agents of the people. The rebellion had instilled in the Americans a loathing—not just of the English, but of the ideas of the English constitution. Having once been its victim, they deeply distrusted power.[4]

But this distrust caused them trouble, as in the 1780s the

Americans discovered that a people, even as virtuous as themselves, needed strong and stable government. The confederation was incapable of regulating the military and commercial affairs of the several states, and the state legislatures were themselves erratic, failing to honor debts and inflating the currency. In recognition of this trouble, the states rewrote their constitutions and made the executive strong. But that was not enough. When Shay's Rebellion disrupted courts in western Massachusetts, fear swept the states. Something was amiss. Government was not stable; perhaps neither were the people.[5] The states convened the Constitutional Convention in the summer of 1787. By now the Americans had gone through a war, negotiated with foreign powers, put down insurrections, and seen their states write and rewrite their constitutions. Intellectually they were a generation removed from the men who had rebelled against England eleven years before. And their task was different too: rather than defy power, they had to create it. But how could they create power, when the revolutionary ideology had prepared them only to destroy it?

The delegates approached this problem uneasily. They debated the power relations of the new government—the powers and election of the president, the composition of the legislature, the means of representation—debated all summer, bothered by the seeming impossibility of making government powerful yet the people safe. At last they found a solution: they made the people the source of all power. The president, like the representatives, should derive his authority from popular election. He should not be a special or independent power in a balanced government but rather the agent of the people in a grossly unbalanced government, unbalanced because all authority derived from the same source.[6] It was a grand discovery, bringing to conclusion the logic of the Revolution, seeming to reconcile its controlling ideas—the fear of power and the virtuous people—with the necessity of strong government. As John Adams said, there had occurred a "radical change in the principles, opinions, sentiments, and affections of the people [which] was the real American Revolution."[7] This was a good people; if they had the power, power was not to be feared.

The problem of power and the virtuous people thus was solved—and also made much worse. For beneath this cool logic an ambiguity persisted. If earlier they had found that power had a tendency to expand, later Americans would find this expansion of power illimitable, for it could expand in the name of the people and not appear tyrannic. This was a difficult problem. In 1801 a

prominent scholar addressed it: "Our men in power depend on
the voice of the people, through frequent elections, for their
authority, while our manner of possessing property, the tenor of
our laws, the mode of our education, and the feelings of interest
and honour, stimulate us to love, respect and maintain our governments. The idea, that this people will not do this is inadmissible.
The thought never ought to be conceived," wrote James Sullivan.
"It may be asked, what is to be done, if the National Government
shall exceed its authority? . . . The answer . . . is, that no such
question should be asked." Thus it was an extraordinary question,
to which Sullivan gave an extraordinary answer: The question was
inadmissible. It was also a prescient answer, for how can one limit
a government endowed with the people's consent?[8]

Of course the Americans limited power. In the Constitution
they sharply limited the national government, giving it certain
duties and leaving the rest to the states; and through the nineteenth
century, into the twentieth, the states did more governing than
did Washington. But by this behavior they proved the persistence
of the problem. Notwithstanding the resort to popular sovereignty,
the fear of power was deeply rooted in the American mind. Power
was exercised with caution; when it was not, it became the center
of controversy. Debate on the national bank, the 1812 War, the
tariff, nullification, slavery—the great congressional debates con-
sisted not of social and moral arguments, even when the question
was a moral one, but of arguments about power—its control, its
users, its victims. There was the lingering sense, born in the rebellion, that somehow power was incompatible with this free and
equal people. Henry Adams grasped it, said of Pennsylvanians
(whom he considered the most American Americans) that they
behaved in 1800 "as though political power were aristocratic in
its nature, and democratic power a contradiction in terms."[9] This
is the contradiction that liberals have never escaped.

For generations to come, it and other contradictions, also
made by the rebellion, would divide the liberal against himself.
Sometimes he would find that power was needed to attain a liberal
end—to secure the rights of man—yet the rebellion taught the
liberal that power was bad, and for years he would hence eschew,
longer than the European did, the state power which alone can
regulate a modern society. Sometimes property would stand in
his way. In England it was the basis of the conservatives' power,
the thing they wanted most to protect and the tool they used to
thwart reform. But in America the liberal was taught, again in

the rebellion, that property gave a people independence and virtue, and that these enabled them to sustain a republic. This association, unique in the Western world, would tie the liberal to property, make him always defend it and consider its integrity whenever he sought reform. The dread of power, the faith in people and property—these would become limits to liberalism. They once were radical ideas, the stuff of rebellion. But later, when the task at hand was not to rebel but to govern, and the issues not political but social, they would be invoked in defense of corporate wealth and social inequity—and also of slavery and segregation, for another sentiment—racial prejudice—would join them. Then they would appear as, not the bold ideas they once had been, but the relics of a distant past.

And yet—this was the final contradiction—liberalism was flexible. From the distance of the nineteenth and twentieth centuries the thoughts of the Founding Fathers acquired an abstract quality, as if they were eternal and universal principles and not the result of a tendentious colonial quarrel. Abstractions are malleable; they may be adapted to changing circumstances. Liberalism was; it was open to interpretation from generation to generation and permitted thus to expand its concerns. Even limited by the lingering dread of power, the obsessive love of property, and the racism of the people, it thus was changeable. So if it was not always humane, and as we shall see it was not, the fault must not lie entirely with the doctrine but sometimes with the people— a fact of special repugnance to the liberal mind.

TWO

THE LIMITS OF LIBERALISM

The ideas of liberalism, remarkably resilient, controlled the important debates of the nineteenth century. Nearly everyone was a liberal, as Louis Hartz has said, and those that were not were cast as dark villains. Such were Hamilton and Biddle who, as the champions of power, monopoly, and privilege, engaged the liberals' fear of power and faith in free enterprise. They resembled the villains of the eighteenth century, parties to an old debate, given a new setting. When the slavery issue ended that debate and opened a new one, liberal ideas still supplied the arguments. Southerners argued, in eighteenth century fashion, that by exercising preponderant power the North was stripping them of their liberty. And northerners argued that they too faced a hostile power—the slave power—bent on conquering the land and destroying their republican way of life. Thus did the central ideas of the Revolution continue to dominate political debate and rouse men to action.

In a sense it was a pity they did. For they did not refer to the barbarity of slavery, and, indeed, to extol or assail its barbarity men had to depart from their liberalism and turn to other arguments. Some did. Fitzhugh and (to a lesser extent) Calhoun embarked on a quasi-feudal defense of slavery; and abolitionists employed religious and moral arguments. These men did liberalism little good, ignoring it, sometimes attacking it directly. But they had no choice if they wished to discuss slavery's moral and social aspects; for liberalism, a set of broad political sentiments, did not afford such a consideration of the issue. Most men, however, remained faithful to the liberal heritage and transformed the slavery issue, framing it as a liberal issue, one concerning property, power, and liberty. And when they did, the debate took on a racist edge. Southerners said that their republican way of life depended on slavery, that the sanctity of property (their slaves) was threatened, and that thus they stood for liberty besieged by power. Northerners said that the slave power threatened their liberty, that the threat came not just from the slaveholders but also from the slaves—a listless, unenterprising people—and that to maintain the western lands as the preserve of free and equal whites, blacks would have to go. Framed as a liberal debate, the slavery debate thus became a racist debate. In both the North and South men struggled to preserve their liberalism, which, they believed, depended on the supremacy of whites. For this peculiar similarity between Northern and Southern arguments, racism was surely responsible; but so was liberalism, which ignored the moral question and drew attention to the issues of property and liberty—property in land and slaves, the liberty of racists everywhere.

That liberalism became the hostage of racism revealed that its strengths could also be its limits, that the faith in people and property could in the time of Jackson thwart the aims of Biddle, and in the time of Lincoln deny the rights of blacks. The dread of power was another strength, and another limit. It informed the Democratic persuasion when the Democrats battled the bankers; and it prevented them from joining and leading the antislavery movement, which in turn overwhelmed them and their Jacksonian thought. And it did more. It meant that when the North amassed great power, as it did in the Civil War—centralizing the government and conquering the South—the conservatives necessarily gained ground; for the American liberal mind could not imagine the democratic, the liberal, use of power. These were limits to thought—these sentiments about people and property and power—but before dwelling on them it is only fair to look first at the Republic's early years, when they appeared as strengths.

The Jacksonian Alliance

In the beginning, liberalism faced familiar enemies. In the 1790s Alexander Hamilton proposed his economic plan, whose guiding purpose was the creation of a strong national government, and revived the fears of the Revolution—of overreaching power, standing armies, unreasonable taxation. When the Federalists passed the Sedition Act in 1798 (to end dissent from government policy), the fears were confirmed: the government intended tyranny.[1] The Republicans rose to the occasion. James Madison led the opposition in Congress, but Thomas Jefferson was the Republicans' teacher, then and later deploring the tendency to "monarchize" government. Contending that the states were "independent as to everything within themselves," he drafted the Kentucky Resolution which, with the Virginia Resolution, enunciated the states' right to nullify unconstitutional federal laws. Later he attacked the Supreme Court as subverter of the Constitution, and as an old man, likening himself to the "superannuated soldier" who has hung his arms on the post, he wrote: "It should be remembered, as an axiom of eternal truth in politics, that whatever power in any government is independent, is absolute also. . . . Independence can be trusted nowhere but with the people in mass."[2] This was a child of the eighteenth century, transfixed by the political myth of embattled liberty.

This was also the president, for the Republican opposition triumphed in 1800 and elected Jefferson president. In office he strengthened the power of the federal government, yet saw no disparity between what he did and thought—such was the grasp of ideology on a man's mind. He loosely construed the Constitution as giving him power to make the Louisiana Purchase and close American ports to English trade; he laid the groundwork for the War of 1812, carried on by his successor, fellow Virginian James Madison—and New England wailed. In a most Jeffersonian act of resistance, New England delegates gathered at Hartford in 1814 and adopted resolutions aimed at limiting the government's power to make war, admit new states, and regulate trade. Daniel Webster opposed a conscription bill and told Congress it was the duty of the state governments "to interpose between their citizens and arbitrary power"—the doctrine of the Virginia and Kentucky Resolutions and later that of Calhoun.[3] Thus did the men of New England, like the early Republicans, find refuge in the rhetoric of the Revolution.

Arrayed against these resisters was the war party in Congress, led by Henry Clay and John Calhoun. Never liking England anyway, these men wanted to expand the nation's borders and redeem national honor, which, they said, England had besmirched. They were largely a Southern and Western faction, though a handful of Southerners joined Webster and opposed the war, attacking Jefferson to uphold Jeffersonian beliefs. Among them was John Randolph, who saw issues with unblinking clarity: "You may cover whole skins of parchment with limitations, but power alone can limit power."[4] Randolph was thinking of the future—and of the South, the risk it ran by helping to create, in this time of war, a powerful national government. But for the moment his company was New England; the nation was not neatly divided yet. There was hope that a national liberal movement might emerge.

The chance came with Andrew Jackson, hero of the Battle of New Orleans, Indian fighter, and frontiersman. He was the bridge to North and South, for under him the Democrats elaborated liberalism, taking the Revolutionary thought as its core and adding to it a dose of social analysis. They took into account recent change—the growth of industry, the growing complexity of business relations, and the new urban labor force. Society was no longer, they said, an undifferentiated mass; it was composed of various groups, not all of them on the land: workingmen in the North, farmers in the South and West, and small businessmen everywhere. The Democrats appealed to these people, telling them that together they were opposed by a special interest, that of business, which sought to use state power to further its aims. To thwart those aims was the new liberal task. Thus, although liberalism matured somewhat in the hands of the Jacksonians, the liberals still had reason to fear an active government—had more reason than before, in fact, for they held that government would always be active in behalf of big business.[5]

And indeed it was. The Second Bank of the United States was a private corporation that used federal deposits, controlled credit and currency, and had a monopoly on national banking. It was an opportunity for businessmen to exploit the government; so were the public debt, the high tariff, and internal improvements—all opportunities to make government bigger and private profit, too. These the Jacksonians opposed, Thomas Hart Benton calling the bank "too great and powerful to be tolerated in a Government of free and equal laws." Jackson himself, when he vetoed the bank's charter in 1832, said that monopoly was unrepublican, a "concentration of power in the hands of a few men irresponsible to the people." Two years before he had vetoed an internal improvement because, as he said, such federal expenditures would lead to consolidated government. In these ways the Jacksonians reiterated and expanded the thought of their Revolutionary forebears— power was dangerous, especially dangerous now that it stood the chance of being exploited and controlled by business—and forged a broad alliance. A national movement emerged.[6]

And suddenly it was over. The tariff issue, and then slavery, split the liberal alliance. For several years Congress had enacted high tariffs to protect the infant American manufactures; the South, a rural land that exported its cotton and depended on free trade and low prices, protested. By its privation, Southerners said, the South was made to subsidize Northern prosperity. When Jackson signed a new tariff law in July 1832, South Carolina called a state convention and nullified it and the tariff of 1828. Jackson, though no friend of high tariffs or the interests they protected, was no friend of secession either, and he responded with the Force Bill, a law authorizing him to use troops to execute the nation's laws. In this he was supported by his erstwhile enemies, the Whigs—Webster, Justice Marshall, and John Quincy Adams. And he was abandoned by his vice-president, John C. Calhoun, who resigned his office and returned to the Senate to oppose Jackson, declaring there: "It is madness to suppose that the Union can be preserved by force"; and "Let it never be forgotten that power can only be opposed by power." Calhoun stated the issue starkly. It was "whether ours is a federal or consolidated government . . . the controversy is one between power and liberty."[7] Calhoun was discovering what Randolph had meant in the War of 1812. Liberalism meant something special to the South.

The Southern Defense

It is hard to imagine what uproar this sectional crisis caused in the minds of men. From the 1830s to the Civil War no one felt entirely comfortable with the party he was in, nor, more importantly, with the doctrines thrust upon him. Both North and South underwent an ideological crisis; both transformed their liberalism, adapting it to the slavery issue. It was a painful experience. Perhaps the agony of Calhoun best described the agony of the South.

John Calhoun grew up in the backcountry of South Carolina, and he carried from his youth till his death that fear and resentment that men of remote areas have of larger places—first Charleston, then the East, finally the North. His father, Patrick, was a Regulator, one of those men who established order in the woods where the colony government, located in Charleston, would not bother to; and it was from him, we presume, that John Calhoun learned to fear power and first heard of Thomas Paine, a man loved in the South and especially in South Carolina, which voted money for the defense of John Wilkes, chief enemy of the English government. Calhoun memorized passages from Paine's writings at the age of thirteen.[8]

But Calhoun was also a nationalist. As we have seen, he and Henry Clay led the war party in Congress. When Webster made his

interposition speech, it was Calhoun who declared that a minority
had no "right to involve the country in ruin." But his nationalism
did not end with the war. In 1815, he proposed the establishment
of a national bank; in 1816, defended the tariff and condemned
disunion. A frontiersman, he wanted the nation to expand. Against
such strict constructionists as James Madison he supported internal
improvements—they would "bind the republic together." As
secretary of war under Monroe he called for new explorations
and new roads to link the vast continent. For Calhoun believed
America had a grand destiny—"the last and only refuge of freedom." And he saw no conflict between his love of liberty, which
he never lost, and his dream of an expanding Union, but rather,
like Lincoln, found the two ideals inseparably joined. "We are
charged by Providence," he said, "not only with the happiness of
this great people, but . . . with that of the human race. We have a
government of a new order . . . founded on the rights of man,
resting on . . . reason. If it shall succeed . . . it will be the com-
mencement of a new era in human affairs." It was a pity he was
poisoned by slavery.[9]

What changed was not so much Calhoun as the situation. In
the wake of the Missouri Compromise tensions mounted between
the North and South, and Calhoun's liberalism took on a sec-
tionalist edge. (Randolph also had great influence on him; so did
his South Carolina constituency.) In 1828 Calhoun published
anonymously "The Exposition and Protest," a treatise that ex-
pounded the state's right to nullify federal laws it considered
unconstitutional. Nullification was not a ruse but a doctrine firmly
believed; not the first tactic in a secessionist strategy but, on the
contrary, a "sacred duty to the Union, to the cause of liberty over
the world." For injured states, according to this theory, could remove the injury yet not withdraw from the Union, which thus
could be saved. Calhoun's was not a rebellious spirit. But the tariff
issue put the people of South Carolina into an uproar, and Calhoun was obliged to lead them. At the Jefferson Day Dinner in
1830, a glorious scene set for confrontation, Andrew Jackson
toasted: "Our Federal Union: It must be preserved," and the vice-
president returned: "The Union: Next to our liberties most dear."
The insensible power of his dramatic role carried him further: next
he announced his authorship of "The Exposition and Protest";
resigned the vice-presidency; and, in 1833, in a reversal that
revealed the agony of the South's position and the extent of the
liberals' division, criticized Jackson's treatment of the bank. When

Jackson removed federal deposits from the bank, Calhoun said it was a usurpation and concentration of power in the hands of one man, and he likened it to the assault by the government on the rights of states. This was a liberal argument, this attack on power, but not a liberal position, for it placed Calhoun alongside Henry Clay, the Whigs, and Nicholas Biddle. But Calhoun had no choice; his sectionalism mattered more than his party. He was still a liberal, but now a Southern one.[10]

What sectionalism did to his liberal politics, slavery did to his liberal thought. Calhoun became confused.

Slavery was an integral part of Southern culture. Thomas Jefferson had opposed it until he realized, around 1786, that his opposition implied an attack on the plantation culture he lived in; then he fell silent.[11] Calhoun, though he had told the House in 1816 he was ashamed of the slave trade, was of a different generation and could not fall silent when slavery was attacked in the 1830s; he defended it till his death.

Like most Southerners, Calhoun believed that slavery was a good way to use black labor and keep the races separate. It was, moreover, the only means of handling a barbarous people: the "diversity of the races" required it. This argument was foreign to liberal thinking. Calhoun developed other arguments, not only foreign but hostile to liberalism, for there was nothing in liberal doctrine that explained or justified this racial diversity; and by the late 1840s he felt compelled to renounce much of the Revolutionary ideology and Enlightenment belief. Men were not born in freedom and equality, he said; to begin with, infants were born, not men, and they were incapable of either. Furthermore, they were born in society, not in a state of nature, and were subject to the demands of that society, which would judge if they were worthy of liberty. Jefferson was wrong—not all men were "capable of self-government"—and so were the other Revolutionaries. If they had believed in man's natural rights, Calhoun believed in his social condition; if they had hoped government would liberate men and protect their rights, Calhoun hoped it would correct and restrain them. These thoughts were not liberal; nor was his way of life. On his plantation at Fort Hill, in the large white house with columns and porticos, set on a hill and surrounded by a stand of stately oaks, Calhoun lived the life of the aristocrat. Once, in the late 1840s, he proposed a plan for an alliance between Northern businessmen and Southern planters, the better to keep down wage and slave labor. This was far from the son of the Regulator and the reader of Thomas Paine.[12]

Yet there was much of Paine in him still, and this was what confounded Southern thought. As we have seen, he framed the dispute over nullification as one strictly between "power and liberty." In the 1840s he advocated free trade. He attacked corruption, a subject often on the minds of the colonists when they launched their attack on the crown, repeating their argument that by corrupting men patronage enhanced power and hence the threat to liberty. In 1846 he worried about the effects of the Mexican War, which Southerners ardently supported (with an eye on the new domain it would create for slavery) because he feared it would require "a great national, consolidated Government . . . a military despotism." Like Randolph a generation before, Calhoun opposed a popular war to preserve a liberal principle. Off the issue of slavery, he thus was an unswerving liberal, carrying into mid-century the ideas of the Revolution.[13]

But even on slavery, he often employed liberal arguments, and this confounded not only Southern thought but liberalism as well. In curious ways, the institution of slavery long had been connected to liberal belief. It had bestowed upon Southerners the belief that they were equal. The lowest class in the South was not, as in the North, a white proletariat but a black one; so irrespective of their differences in income, rich and poor whites held something in common—superiority to blacks. This was a powerful bond. It gave rise to the belief among Southerners that they were a community of equal freeholders, and this belief led some men, such as George Fitzhugh, to denounce free and competitive society altogether and to extol the virtues of slave and feudal society—"a band of brothers, working for the common good." But most Southerners did not go so far. More simply they believed that they were specially endowed with that freedom and equality that alone can make a people virtuous and capable of republican government. Slavery was hence the basis of Southern republicanism; to attack one was to attack the other. However perverse it seems, such was Southern thinking, and it led Calhoun to employ liberal arguments in the defense of slavery, without a trace of irony. For the South to give in to the North, said Calhoun, would be to replace the Union with a "bond between master and slave," to sink "down into acknowledged inferiority." (The Revolutionaries also had portrayed the crown policy as one to enslave the colonies; for Calhoun it was a liberal, not a sarcastic, use of metaphor.) The battle, he often said, was between power and liberty, specifically the liberty to own one's property, which the North would take away. This property was protected by the Constitution, which Calhoun consistently supported (and once interpreted, outwitting Webster, as giving protection to slavery even in the territories). All these were liberal arguments. They caused abolitionists to pursue other arguments—William Seward to pretend there existed a "higher power" than the law (a notion Calhoun made light of), and William Garrison to tear up the Constitution.[14]

Thus did the South both abandon liberalism and embrace it, tainting it with the slavery defense. Had not the Southern mind been predominantly romantic, as W. J. Cash has said, perhaps it could not have contained these contradictory beliefs.[15] But it was, holding sharp and conflicting images. There was the pure and procreating white woman, a goddess invented to maintain the race and also cleanse Southern virtue, sullied by Northern charges of plantation lechery. There was the black slave, childish and sentimental, happy beyond bounds compared with the workers of the North, slaves to the wage-labor system; and also the image of a solid South, united by Anglo-Saxon blood, the absence of class, and the common superiority to blacks and Yankees. Everyone of English blood, it was said, was at least a thirtieth cousin to everyone else.[16] And yet there were also the aristocrats—the masters of Fort Hill—with land and fine culture, boundless generosity and good counsel for their lesser neighbor. Even they were confused. Rising in the frenzy of the economic boom before the Civil War, the planters forgot their debt to the cotton gin when they attacked the crass money-men of the North, and forgot also their dirt-farm fathers when they traced their lineage back to English nobles. Southerners were torn. They honored the thrift and aggressive spirit of Jefferson's yeomen but also awesome ancestry and the bluest of blood. The ambivalence about liberalism was thus just a part of a larger ambivalence. Southern identity itself was split, and no doubt slavery had helped to split it—helped to create the conflicting notions of blue blood and shared blood, feudalists and liberals, this happy band of brothers and a free and equal people. Hegel said the slave enslaves the master; he also makes him confused.

The Northern Attack

Meanwhile, the slavery crisis had a similar effect in the North. It forced some men, the abolitionists, to employ nonliberal arguments in their treatment of slavery. And it transformed liberalism, diminishing the liberals' dread of economic power, and causing them to stress the virtues of property and to associate liberalism with white supremacy. In all this, the Northerners resembled the Southerners, and together they demonstrated nothing so well as the inadequacy of Jacksonian liberalism. It disappeared, replaced by a Republican liberalism, well suited to the crisis, though, as we shall see, with limits of its own. Perhaps the crisis was proving that liberalism of any sort—whether Southern or Democratic or Republican—was not fully equal to the task before it, if the task was to be met humanely.

Reform movements are not necessarily liberal movements. Sometimes they are hostile, other times indifferent, to liberal ideals. Nativism and abolitionism, segregation and Prohibition, each a reform movement, failed to engage the principles of liberalism as they were defined by the Revolution, Jefferson, and Jackson: the dangers of power, the virtue of the people, the sanctity of property. A fight over federalism or property was a liberal fight; but it was the Southerners, not the abolitionists, who fought over federalism and property. For the abolitionists were moralists, and finding no article in liberalism that addressed the moral qualities of slavery, they like Fitzhugh departed from liberalism. They attacked sin. Their argument was biblical and moral; their tone evangelical, unbending and censorious. Neither liberals nor conservatives, they were zealots. Henry David Thoreau, a thoughtful zealot, appealed to conscience, not to ideology. William Lloyd Garrison, the leading abolitionist, was just as dogmatic. He eschewed politics, considering the nation corrupt; denounced the government as the agent of Antichrist; and called for dissolution of the Union. Even those abolitionists who split with Garrison and formed the Liberty party in 1840, even these less fanatical men relied on nonliberal arguments, on Seward's "higher power." For all abolitionists appealed to a sense of guilt, exposed sin, and asked for repentance and reformation. The train of their thought intersected nowhere with the train of liberal thought. Liberalism added nothing to the reformers' zeal, and from it had nothing to gain.[17]

Apart from them stood the liberals, the Northern and Western Democrats—Van Buren, Benjamin Butler, Thomas Hart Benton, Francis Blair, Gideon Welles, William Cullen Bryant, and others. These men were in a difficult position. They disdained the abolitionists, who were wrecking the Union and obfuscating what they thought were the more important, the liberal issues. And they had little sympathy with the Whigs, who stood for all they were against. As a result they wavered, lingering uneasily in the Democratic party from the 1830s to the 1850s, as it became the party of slavery. They tolerated Tyler and Polk; but the Mexican War, which the North regarded as a proslavery effort, exhausted their patience, and in 1848 Van Buren ran as the candidate of the new Free-Soil party. That was a fiasco; next they looked with hope to Franklin Pierce. But when in his administration the Southerners succeeded in repealing the Missouri Compromise, in 1854, the Northerners began their mass exit from the Democratic party. They became Republicans, the least obnoxious of several obnoxious choices.[18]

It is easy to see why it took them so long, why they hesitated to join Free-Soilers and abolitionists, conscience Whigs and nativists, the various groups that coalesced in the Republican party. For the evolving Republican ideology was distinctly uncongenial to the Democrats. It was, more than anything else, an ideology of free enterprise.[19] It did not recognize social classes, but rather had faith in social mobility, as permitted by equal opportunity and hard work. "Twenty-five years ago," Lincoln said, "I was a hired laborer. The hired laborer of yesterday labors on his own account today, and will hire others to labor for him tomorrow." This view owed most perhaps to the Protestant ethic, which equated economic progress with moral progress and found fault with a man's moral fiber if he failed to advance (though it owed something, of course, to the real prosperity and upward mobility of Americans). Slavery contradicted this view. It degraded labor, fostered sloth, smothered a spirit of industry, denied social mobility; and worst of all, if it expanded to the territories, slavery would take away the new land so necessary to free labor and social mobility, to the future of Northern society. Slavery hence was the central villain in this ideology, which, as the slavery controversy intensified, emerged as a powerful thought, broad and detailed, as much an explanation of Northern society as an indictment of Southern. By the 1850s Northerners began to believe that the nation could not continue half-slave and half-free but must become, as Lincoln said, one or the other.

Salmon Chase gave these ideas political force.[20] In the 1840s and 1850s this Ohio antislavery leader formulated a powerful theory—that there existed a slave power, ruling the Southern states with an iron grip, and that it conspired by devious and stealthy means to transform the nation into a slave society.

Events seemed to bear the theory out. The Kansas-Nebraska Act of 1854 and the *Dred Scott* decision three years later turned the clock back, Northerners thought, making it easier, not harder, for slavery to spread, perhaps even to the free states. The idea of a slave power rang true in another sense: it gave the North a power to fear and people and property to protect. Thus did Northern thought share with Southern thought a liberal echo of the Revolution.

Yet it was only an echo, and Democrats knew it. They did not like the emerging ideology, which, though it was in a sense liberal and had in a sense a social analysis, was not the least Jacksonian. The Republicans equivocated (in the platforms of 1856 and 1860) on the major issues—banks, monopolies, internal improvements, the tariff, and the currency. And when Lincoln ran in 1860 they stressed the part of the platform most reminiscent of Henry Clay and the American system. None of this soothed the former Democrats, who grew more nervous as war drew closer. They had begun, after all, as the party of states' rights, opposed to government and money power; now they joined a party that soon would exercise unprecedented national power to subdue wayward states. They were anxious. Gideon Welles warned that the federal government was "imperial" by nature, "the source of all power"; and power, of course, was the enemy.[21] He did not realize, nor did the other Democrats, that in the present crisis power was not the principal enemy of the North; slavery and the South were. And the principal movement was the antislavery one. All this the Democrats ignored, unable to harness their Jacksonian fervor to the new crusade. It was a pity for them—and for liberalism.

A few of them tried. A few Democrats successfully made the transit from the world of Jackson to that of Lincoln with their ideology intact. At the end of the 1830s, Ohio Senator Thomas Morris likened the slave power of the South to the banking power of the North. He described the slave power as the "goliath of all monopolies," said it and the banking power were "uniting to rule this country," and thus in a crucial connection carried Jacksonian thought into the slavery fight.[22] But no one followed. Would William Seward, Thurlow Weed, Hamilton Fish, Edward Bates, Robert Winthrop—the antislavery men, former Whigs, friends of bankers and protection, who now led the Republican party? They would not. In the minds of these men the idea of a slave power had nothing to do with the money power that Jackson had fought. Only former Democrats would respond to Morris's attack on banks, and they had little interest in the slavery issue. Thus his appeal was to a bifurcated Northern community, each half of which was receptive to one part of the proposal and cool to the other. Calhoun, as we have seen, also made the connection Morris made, though with the opposite intention, linking Jackson's assault on the bank to his assault on states' rights and condemning both as usurpations of power. Calhoun was successful, indeed the leader of the South. Who has remembered Thomas Morris?

It is not an idle question, for Calhoun and Morris faced a similar obstacle—the South too had been divided between Whigs and Democrats—yet Calhoun had surmounted it and Morris did not. While Southerners overcame their differences and shed their prior concerns, rallying around the cause of slavery, Northerners moved slowly, step by step, toward an antislavery party, always looking backward at the parties and programs they cherished more deeply. They did all they could to avoid the slavery issue. As late as 1856, Northerners gave the Democrat Buchanan his margin of victory and also gave Fillmore, the candidate of the upstart Know-Nothing party, a fifth of the popular vote—such was their desperation to defeat Fremont, the sectional candidate, and to avoid the slavery issue.[23] Northerners had trouble forgetting their past concerns, whiggish and Jacksonian, because slavery mattered little to them—less than the Union, in any case—and this was where they differed from Southerners. They were indifferent to the plight of the slaves, while the South was dedicated to slavery, and this indifference, this racism, kept them from coming together on the slavery issue, while Southerners meanwhile closed their ranks. Indeed it was only a racist argument that rallied the North at last.

The argument of the Republicans, as we have seen, was that the land should be maintained as the preserve of white labor and not overrun by black slaves. This was not a new argument. In 1846, David Wilmot, in offering his famous proviso—which would bar slavery from the conquered Mexican territory and which did much to alienate the South from the North—had described it as the "White Man's Proviso." But now in the 1850s, in an effort to rally the North, the Republicans went further and implied the removal of not just slaves but also blacks, who according to their thinking were incapable of possessing an industrious and enterprising spirit. To allow whites to mingle with blacks, free or slave, would degrade white labor and squander the land, thus deadening the social springs—the competitive and expanding force in society—that kept Americans always moving upward. In 1858 Francis P. Blair, a leading antislavery man, said it was every patriot's wish that

America "be homogeneous in race and of our blood."[24] He and others proposed colonization—the sending of blacks to Africa or Central America—an idea discarded by abolitionists in the 1830s. They made other proposals, and a new debate emerged, turning on whether or not the emigration should be compulsory. Thus was the North roused to fight; and thus did the liberal vision entail, in the North as well as the South, a vision of white supremacy.

The Jacksonians, not just the blacks and the Southerners, were slighted by this vision. Had they not been racists, they might have followed the logic of Thomas Morris and harnessed their Jacksonian fervor to the slavery cause. They might have founded their liberalism on the rights of the black man, as the South had theirs on his bondage. And had they not been liberals, had they not shunned power and cherished the rights of states, they might have led the antislavery movement; they might have saved themselves from being overwhelmed by the movement and its whiggish leaders. But they were racists and liberals and did none of these things, and did not, therefore, survive the slavery crisis. The Republicans, among them many former Democrats, did. They appealed to Northern racism, rather than trying to overcome it; and they transformed liberalism into a complacent doctrine of free enterprise, or, rather, they recognized that only as such a doctrine could liberalism be made to address the slavery issue. For when men were racists, it was impossible to interest them in the injured rights of blacks; and when power was needed, it was out of place to rant about the dangers of power. The Jacksonians' weapons were useless against slavery. The defense of enterprise and property, especially the land of whites, and the demand for an avenging war machine, made more sense. The Jacksonians were obsolete.

The war itself made sure of that. When Southerners fired on Fort Sumter, a nationalist euphoria overcame the nation, which was something of a turn in the road for American thought. Till then, probably owing to their liberal bent, Americans had not been distinguished for their nationalism or their affection for power. But the slavery debate had changed them, and all but a few, in the spring of 1861, joined in the outburst of militance. Abolitionists, who as pacifists previously had advocated the peaceful separation of the North from the South, felt the surge of patriotic zeal; so did conservative New England Brahmins and clergymen, who always had considered a war for emancipation a foolish waste; and so, too, did Ralph Waldo Emerson, who had spent his life making sure that a proper distance separated authority and society from his own interesting self. Now they all joined, for different reasons but in the same direction, the Union cause. The abolitionists rejoiced in the prospect of emancipation and also welcomed, as did the New England elite, the hardening and redemption of a materialistic people. Conservatives saw the renewal of authority and the strengthening of national institutions. And Emerson saw hope for the soul in the emotion and spontaneity of the war response. Each had a vision; all hoped for its fulfillment in war. Some were satisfied.[25]

Like all wars this war had a centralizing effect, force, not rights, being its business. The brunt of this force fell on the South, which was occupied, but the rest of the nation was not free of it. New structures appeared—from the national banking system to the sanitary commission; and new powers were used—to draft men and suspend habeas corpus. Power grew enormously, but it seemed, as the war went on, to have no higher purpose than itself. Some men worried. Moncure Conway, faithful to the abolitionist ideals of pacifism and moral regeneration, exiled himself to England, whence he attacked the North as the coercive and repressive reflection of the South it fought. James Russell Lowell and Herman Melville described the war (with varying degrees of approval) as the attainment of nationalism and patriotism, having little to do with emancipation. And Orestes Brownson said the war had put an end to the Jeffersonian ideals of rights and rebellion. At last Northern thought coalesced, though not in a liberal way.[26]

Lincoln

Standing apart was Abraham Lincoln, whose role was filled with irony. He wielded unprecedented power, prosecuted the nation's bloodiest war, and freed the slaves; yet power and bloodshed and blacks were not dear to his heart. He had one overriding purpose, as he said—to preserve the Union. Already in this purpose he differed from those who fought the war to purify the nation, punish the South, free the slaves, strengthen institutions, redeem public authority, or repudiate the revolutionary principles. But his difference went deeper, for he not only would preserve the Union but raise it (as Alexander Stephens put it) to the level of religious mysticism.[27] He believed—and Adams, Jefferson, and Calhoun had said the same—that the United States was not just a union of states but a democratic example to the world, that by threatening the Union, the Civil War threatened man's "last, best hope" for democracy. Neither God nor the world could be indifferent to the outcome. The scale was immense. So was Lincoln's part, as he conceived it, and it led him to behave as a sort of agent of Providence. When two of Lydia Bixby's sons died in battle (he thought five), Lincoln told her that the Lord had left her with "the solemn pride that must be yours to have laid so costly a sacrifice upon the altar of freedom."[28] The metaphor was not careless, nor was his expression in the wartime photographs, notably in the one taken four days before the Gettysburg Address, in which his gaze is impenetrable, set on an unworldly goal. For Lincoln had cast himself and the Union in grand historical roles, divinely appointed. His task, he said, was that of "proving that popular government is not an absurdity." Old Europe, and men of all times, had thought it was; the Founding Fathers had said it was not. The Civil War would decide. "This is essentially a People's contest," he told Congress. "On the side of the Union it is a struggle for maintaining in the world, that form, and substance of government, whose leading object is, to elevate the condition of men—to lift artificial weights from all shoulders—to clear the paths of laudable pursuit for all—to afford all, an unfettered start, and a fair chance, in the race of life."[29]

In this belief, Lincoln was almost alone. He shared the Republicans' free labor and free soil ideology—the "unfettered start" and "race of life"—but in assigning to the war itself a divine and democratic purpose he was joined by few men (among them Walt Whitman). Lincoln's view was as liberal as it could be; he worked within constraints, which perhaps he did not consider constraints. He cherished the free labor ideology of his party, lived with his racism and that of others, and led a conquering war machine. And yet, within these constraints, set by prejudice and events, he conjured up a powerful picture of a war for democracy, and also a precedent—that power, even enormous power and bloodshed, might be the last resort of rights and equality. The twentieth century would see what a liberal principle this was. But in the meantime most men were skeptical and could not conceive national power as a liberal tool. They saw it not as the shield of democracy but as the means to win a war, unite a nation, and, later, promote the prosperity of business. Gideon Welles had been right to fear power. Not even Lincoln could make it democratic. He undertook to do so, enunciated the principle, and when he was gone, Whitman mourned his passing—"For you they call, the swaying mass"; and deplored the postwar world—"nor fiercest lightnings of the war, have purified the atmosphere; let the theory of America still be management, caste, comparison."[30]

Yet in time, as his legend grew, so did the stature of his thoughts, and Lincoln got his revenge. It was his view, ironically, and not the others', that was passed down to later generations. It did so for the same reasons that it had not persuaded his contemporaries—it was a grand, apocalyptic, and democratic view— and because he was martyred, and also because before he died he gave succinct and elegant expression to his vision—the Gettysburg Address. In those 268 words, two of which—"under God"—he included only as he spoke, Lincoln linked the Revolution to the Civil War—parallel efforts to create and sustain democracy—then turned to those who had died on the battlefield and, in a remarkable piece of symmetry and driving force, found inspiration in their death for a new birth of freedom.[31] After generations have memorized his speech, after schoolteachers have embalmed it beside the Declaration of Independence and the Pledge of Allegiance, it strains one's imagination to recapture the polemical sense of these words. How hard we must strain is the extent of the irony. Lincoln has fooled us and triumphed over his contemporaries; he has jumped across one hundred years to persuade us that the war was as he saw it. It was not. In 1863 his words were not the platitudinous phrases of a revered leader, but the precise interpretation, little shared, of a hated president. When he spoke it was against uneven odds, against the men who successfully put the war to the service of a conservative resurgence. Lincoln has worked a trick. The man who often said he was the mere instrument of history, has played with history; who even in the Gettysburg Address said "the world will little note, nor long remember, what we say here," laid down for later men the meaning of the Civil War and indeed was so memorable himself that all else is forgotten, including his own isolation and the languishing state of liberal thought.

THREE

———⟨∽⟩———

THE LIMITS OF REFORM

The crisis of the Civil War revealed the limits of liberalism. The faith in property had served the liberals well from Jefferson to Jackson, and it was proof of liberalism's durability that it continued to dominate political thinking; however, with the advent of the slavery controversy—a social and moral issue—this faith helped to narrow, rather than expand, the rights of man and the action of the liberals. Their dread of power also had been useful and also had been a confining sentiment. It paralyzed the Democrats and, moreover, it meant that the Northerners' emphasis on power, a necessity forced upon them by events, could lead only to conservative conclusions. And racism, though not a liberal sentiment, had transformed a liberal attack on slavery into an attack on the slaves as well. It had become not a principle, but an assumption, of liberals everywhere. These were the limits of liberalism. They did not disappear.

In fact, their effects grew more pronounced during the second half of the nineteenth century, as social problems grew. Racism split the Populist alliance and helped disrupt the few movements of reform—Reconstruction and progressivism—movements already limited by the reformers' dislike of federal power and their faith in free enterprise. This was no surprise. For both the Reconstruction and the Progressive reformers came from the Republican party, shared its ideology of free enterprise, and differed from other Republicans only in their belief that the "race of life" could be made a better race. They established important precedents— the federal guarantee of civil rights and the regulation of business— thus beginning a revolution in federalism that has not ended yet. But they did no more than begin it; they did not explore the roots of inequality, or even question the limits of their thought. They were essentially reformers—moral, self-righteous men—quick to join a pious cause and, because of their superiority and disinterested stance, quick to leave it.

A different sort of men began to change the course of liberalism. These were the men of the machines, the bosses and the immigrants they bossed. Far from reformers, they were among the things Progressives wanted to reform. But reform, as noted before, is not always liberal; and sometimes corrupt men can lead a liberal cause. So it was with the machines. The immigrants in America presented a challenge to liberalism it had not faced—that of ethnic diversity, the tolerance of difference, the rights of minorities. The abolitionists had faced the issue, but they were moral activists, not liberal thinkers; and the antislavery Republicans had appealed to prejudice. The immigrants were different in several ways: they had the advantage of being white, and could not be so easily ignored as the blacks; they spoke for themselves, not relying on fickle patrons; and they invoked the principles of liberalism. It was this immigrant-boss network, more than the moral reformers, that expanded the liberal mind, freeing it somewhat from the grip of property and compelling it to embark upon social analysis. This was the beginning of a new liberal endeavor, which the civil rights movement brought to completion.

Reconstruction

After the North conquered the South the first item of business was to readmit the Southern states to the Union. President Andrew Johnson and the radical Republicans, differing as to the best means of bringing this about, fought for a year. Then in 1866, the Republicans won control of every Northern legislature and more than two-thirds of each house of Congress. Radical Reconstruction began. In readmitting the seceded states, the radicals designed a program to reconstruct them as well, to make them loyal to the Union, and to make them treat their blacks as citizens. Perhaps the centerpiece of this program, and the most enduring legislation, was the congressional attempt to enact federal guarantees of civil rights. Congress passed the Civil Rights Act in 1866, over Johnson's veto, and removed its main provisions from judicial review by reiterating them in the Fourteenth Amendment, ratified by the states in 1868. This amendment said: "All persons born or naturalized in the United States, and subject to the jurisdiction thereof, are citizens of the United States and of the State wherein they reside"; and went on to prohibit the states from abridging the rights of citizenship, from depriving any person of "life, liberty, or property, without due process of law," and from denying him "the equal protection of the laws." By this amendment, Congress created national citizenship—an instrument with many uses—but Charles Sumner wanted more, wanted Congress to specify the forms of discrimination proscribed. In 1875 (a year after his death) Congress passed such a bill, protecting all persons' equal enjoyment of public accommodations and conveyances, and also the equal right to jury service. (It left out, after a debate, a guarantee of desegregated schools.) This act, along with the Fourteenth Amendment and the Fifteenth Amendment (securing the vote to the black), completed the legal aims of Reconstruction and also changed the nature of American federalism and hence the constitutional theory underlying liberalism. Federal power, not its limitation, henceforth would secure men's rights.[1]

That was the idea, at least, but not the result. The laws were merely papers, and within a couple of years Reconstruction had ended. The upheaval in federalism did not have its intended effect: liberalism remained fixed in its attachment to property and small government; and blacks slid back into subservience. The several purposes of Reconstruction thus failed in several ways, each one revealing a limit to postwar political thinking.

There was the legal failure. The Supreme Court refused to accept the notion that the federal government conferred upon citizens a set of rights of a higher order than the rights conferred by the states. In the *Slaughterhouse* decisions, shortly after the ratification of the Fourteenth Amendment, it held in fact the reverse—that state protection of civil rights was paramount to any federal protection and that the latter referred only to those rights one had in his relation to the federal government, such as the right to petition Congress or to gain access to ports and the high seas. This belittlement of the rights of national citizenship ran contrary to the clear intentions of the framers of the amendment, but no matter—the Court proceeded to fortify states' rights. In 1875, in *United States* v. *Reese* and *United States* v. *Cruikshank*, the Court held that the Fifteenth Amendment did not in fact confer upon any man the right to vote—only the state could do that—and that the Fourteenth Amendment did not prevent mob action from abridging the rights of blacks, but merely prevented the state from doing so. And in 1883 the Court ruled the 1875 Civil Rights Act unconstitutional on the grounds that the Fourteenth Amendment had not given Congress power to arrange the social relations of the two races.[2] States' rights remained, and with them, for several generations, the denial of blacks' rights in the South.

But Reconstruction did not fail just because the Court adhered to states' rights. The ideology of the Republicans, even of the radicals, doomed their own program. Their faith in free labor and enterprise, their indifference—even hostility—to the blacks: these several traits of their thought, central to their ideology before the Civil War, remained central to it after the war and prevented Reconstruction, or any liberal program, from succeeding. The black man needed not merely laws but economic help. And the most obvious help Congress could give was to confiscate Southern land and redistribute it among blacks. But confiscation—even the federal purchase of land—violated the Republicans' belief in the sanctity of property and, even more, in the necessity of each man to advance in society by his own efforts. But without land reform, as Kenneth Stampp has said, the failure of Reconstruction was inevitable. In this crucial way did their thought limit their achievement.[3]

There were other ways: the reformers lost interest in the black man. Meeting in 1872, George W. Julian, Charles Sumner, Carl Schurz, Horace Greeley, Edwin L. Godkin, and others formed the Liberal Republican party. They denounced Grant and the policy of Reconstruction and called for the end of military rule in the South. The black man, his miserable plight, no longer moved them. (Only Charles Sumner, Wendell Phillips, and a few others retained their compassionate concern.) He had not performed as the free labor and free enterprise ideology said he should; to help him with federal grants was to violate the ideology even more.[4] Rather than desert their beliefs, the Republicans deserted the blacks and turned to other issues.

The principal issue was corruption. Both the Grant administration and the Southern reconstructed governments were corrupt. The reformers objected, and in 1872 made the demand for a civil service the main plank of their platform. This interest in efficient government began perhaps during the Civil War, when the war effort spawned not only a new nationalism but also a new concern for management and efficiency. Educated and conscientious men acquired a predilection, which they did not drop until the Progressives had spent their force, for reforming institutions, making them run smoothly, honestly, and fairly. To reform society was beyond their interest—and against their principles, for the reforming Republicans shared with the conservatives a basic faith in free enterprise. Their great achievement was the Civil Service Act of 1883, the same year the Supreme Court overturned the daring Civil Rights Act of 1875—an act whose purpose was no longer theirs.[5]

The failure of Reconstruction and the shallowness of reform shared the same causes—the limits of liberalism, as embodied in Republican ideology. By the 1880s at least one Republican was disillusioned (Sumner and Stevens were dead). George Julian wrote that the Republican party had been "a political combination rather than a party," and its only purpose had been "to dedicate our National Territories to freedom, and to denationalize slavery," and, that accomplished, it had little left to do.[6] What direction the Republicans got they derived from events rather than principle—the war, its effect on thought and institutions, the expansion of business and the nation, the discoveries of Darwin. Their ideology had served its purpose in 1861, but now, bereft of a cause, it was hollow; no longer probing the issues, it served rather to limit the range of government activity, though it limited the government unevenly. Congress gave enormous help to internal improvements, notably in land grants and subsidies to railroads, yet the notion of giving federal help to disadvantaged people, either workers or blacks, violated Republican thought. Republicans of all stripes endorsed the federal power that created the national financial system, yet were dismayed by the farmers' demand that federal power might reform those very banking, credit, and currency laws. The Supreme Court felt compelled to invoke the Fourteenth Amendment in behalf of business—to this extent the revolution in federalism had begun—but not in behalf of blacks. Repeatedly in the latter quarter of the nineteenth century, it invalidated state laws regulating railroads and other corporations, for in laws corporations are persons, and by regulating them states had denied them the due process guaranteed by the amendment. But the Court applied this reasoning only to fictive corporate persons, not to real black persons—a distinction symbolic of postwar thought. The forgotten Jacksonians had had a point: federal power seemed ineluctably to have only a conservative use.

Change, however, was imminent. Mugwumps and Stalwarts alike did not foresee it, but change was certain nevertheless. They had brought into being new forms of national power, yet, because of their belief in unfettered property, free enterprise, and social mobility, they failed to recognize the responsibilities of this power and the claims that all men, not just those of business, could make upon it. Soon they would see. They would grasp the irony of their having created an altogether new and powerful weapon, which would be turned against them and would, moreover, transform liberal belief. Far in the distant future, power would be democratic.

The Southern Myth

Meanwhile in the South, in the postwar years of humiliation, the Southern myth did not die but tightened its hold on the Southern mind. Southern leaders proclaimed the "solid South"— the one-party, one-class ideal—attacked big government, protected big business, and impoverished whites and blacks alike. The impulse for reform emerged briefly and then sank out of sight, drowned in racial fears.

In 1877 Rutherford B. Hayes made a deal and became president. He withdrew troops from the Confederacy, and wrote to a friend, "As to the South, the let alone policy seems now to be the true course."[7] The conservative Democrats who struck this bargain with the Northern Republican hoped to get help for Southern business—railways and iron works, cotton mills and tobacco spreads, oil companies and banks. They called themselves the redeemers, having redeemed the South, which now they called the New South. But there was nothing much new about this South; it fit the old cast of mind. The great businesses were to compensate for the great loss in war, the raging racism for Reconstruction; and the lien system and sharecropping replaced the ways of slavery. There was some change: the number of plantations increased three times in some states between 1860 and 1880, and the economy sagged badly.[8] Constantly in debt, the sharecropper fell into bondage. He lacked the money to move and seldom owned the land he tilled and sometimes not the hovel he lived in.[9] It was a condition that could not last.

And it did not. Populists, greenbackers, readjusters, silverites, and fusionists—a host of political independents rose in the 1880s and 1890s to oppose the old guard Democrats, the Cotton Exchange, and Wall Street. Not an organized movement, this farmers' revolt endorsed several scattered policies—for income tax, silver, tariff reduction, debt repudiation, inflation, usury and monopoly laws, against national banks, trusts, and wealth. The Populists were prescient. They were the first movement ever to demand that the federal government take responsibility for social welfare. The Jacksonians had not, had opposed rather than relied on government power; but times had changed. Business had grown, industrialism had come. And government had grown. If it could set up a credit and tariff system to facilitate business expansion, government could just as easily set one up to protect the small farmer. This was a new idea, and it appalled Republicans in the North and redeemers in the South. They did not admit its logic, did not acknowledge the positive role government had assumed. Instead they invoked a liberal rule that they themselves had made obsolete. The proper function of government, they said, was not to coerce men but rather to liberate them, not to put weights upon property but rather to set it free. To the sharecropper, the victim of a national economy organized by national laws, who had never been free of coercion and owned no property, this rule made little sense. And in his yearning, liberalism found its voice of the future.

But its future was not in the South. The old guard Democrats saw the peril and revived the issue of race to save themselves. They accused the independents of splitting the solid South, of giving blacks the vote and the white men's women. The Bourbons appealed to the plebians' racism, and after that, writes C. Vann Woodward, "The barriers of racial discrimination mounted in direct ratio with the tide of political democracy among whites."[10] Jim Crow—legal segregation—appeared in the 1890s and hit the South hard in the first decade of the twentieth century. Between 1887 and 1891, as the farmers' alliance overran Southern legislatures, laws segregating trains and streetcars went on the books of Florida, Mississippi, Texas, Louisiana, Alabama, Arkansas, Kentucky, and Georgia.[11] Soon ferries, steamboats, factories, hospitals, prisons, homes for the blind and aged, orphanages, parks, circuses, and residential areas—all became segregated by law.[12] Organized labor excluded blacks, Samuel Gompers saying in 1910 that blacks should be kept out of the American Federation of Labor because they lacked an understanding of human rights.[13] And it kept up with technology. During the 1920s and 1930s and 1940s legislation put blacks in separate taxicabs, waiting rooms, buses, bathrooms, parks, baseball teams, race tracks, and boxing rings; in 1944 the Virginia legislature empowered the State Corporation Commission to require separate waiting rooms in airports.[14] Disfranchisement was an even more effective way to subjugate the blacks. Mississippi's constitutional convention took away their vote in 1890, and by 1910 South Carolina, North

Carolina, Louisiana, Alabama, Virginia, Georgia, Oklahoma, Tennessee, Florida, Arkansas, and Texas had followed the lead, disfranchising their black populations either by constitutional provision or by legislation.[15] The most durable device was the poll tax, often cumulative and retroactive to the date of majority, but whatever the means, it worked: in 1897, 130,344 Louisiana blacks registered to vote; in 1904 only 1,342.[16]

Out of this Southern crisis, solidarity emerged triumphant. The key to solidarity—and to the Southern myth—was racial fear and white supremacy. Populism intensified these sentiments, for it brought the people into the equation, a people whose racial animus was exploited, a people quickly aroused to frenzy. From 1900 to 1909 lynching increased 10 percent in the South, and the number of white victims dropped by 20 percent.[17] Racism dominated politics, and a new class of leaders arose. They shared some things with the early Southern leaders—they were well off—but they were different: they were demagogues. From Ben Tillman to Huey Long to George Wallace, they brought a new style to politics. They spoke to the people—they had to, more than Calhoun ever did—and more than he they got trapped on a seesaw; the harder they pushed, the harder the people pushed back. Miscegenation was never more feared, segregation never more complete. The leader knew this, and he was brash and unabashed: "Cotton" Ed Smith, once a member of the old guard, won the Senate race in South Carolina with two issues—white supremacy and the hard-working farmer; and Carter Glass, another of the early demagogues who stayed through the New Deal, explained to Virginia's constitutional convention of 1901-02: "Discrimination! Why that is precisely what we propose; that exactly is what this convention was elected for."[18] The race issue once again had disrupted a liberal movement, this time leaving the South more committed to the myth of solidarity and white supremacy, and less prepared to face social issues, than ever before. The liberal impulse passed to the North.

Progressives and Bosses

There, at the turn of the century, the Progressive movement appeared. It was a sprawling and diffuse movement, differing from state to state and in its effect on national and state government; but, divided on many issues, the Progressives were united on one—reform. They wanted to reform business and politics, and to restore competition to both. And they wanted to reform the characters of working men and women and, especially, of the immigrants.

Their place in the history of liberalism is therefore ambiguous, for, as we have seen, the American liberal mind was not ruled by a commitment to reform but rather was ruled by a set of ideas about power and the people. The progressives nonetheless influenced this mind, both advancing and stalling the progress of liberal thought.

Thinking that capitalism and industrialism had rendered the race of life a little harsh and not quite fair, the Progressives called upon the federal government to act. They passed the income tax and banking and trade regulation, and in several states they used state government to improve the living and working conditions of the working poor. This was the advance; the Progressives found new uses for power and began a revolution in federalism that would eventually transform the liberal mind.

Yet their thought was rooted in the Republican ideology from which it sprang. They believed in property and in what Louis Hartz has called "Algerism"—a faith in free enterprise and in the illimitable advance of the unfettered individual.[19] Indeed it was because of these beliefs that they proposed reform. The power of corporate trusts had unnaturally confined the choice of individuals; to reduce this power the Progressives resorted to federal power. But they had no special fondness for government power—any more than they did for the power of unions and monopolies— and were deeply ambivalent about its use. For their aim was to unfetter the individual. In politics, therefore, they sought to break up political power, to which end they proposed devices of direct government: the initiative, the referendum, the recall, and the direct election of senators. And they wished to replace the city boss with the city manager, a nonpartisan, bureaucratic manager, skilled in the science of governing. These reforms in business and politics seemed sufficient, for the Progressives had a solid faith in the American's ability to govern and advance himself. The Progressives did not explore the deep fissures in society between races and classes, but found only defects in a system which, when made more rational and efficient, was eminently sound. They were reformers in the tradition of the Mugwumps, deeply committed to the principles of things they reformed.[20]

And like all reformers, the Progressives took the high ground of morality and looked down upon the unregenerate with pity and even a little disdain. They wanted not only to alleviate the misery of the lower classes but also to reform them after their own image. And that image was Protestant and white, well established, and usually Republican. Many in America bore little resemblance to this image, including the thirty-five million immigrants, uneducated and poor, who came to America from 1815 to 1914; and their spokesmen, the bosses of the city machines.[21]

The city machine was an old political institution in the United States—Tammany Hall as old as the Republic. In the 1890s it took on a new importance, as it began to address the issues that mattered to the growing mass of immigrants: to the Irish, who had begun their great migration in the 1840s; and to the Italians, Russians, and East Europeans just beginning to arrive. Taxes, utility rates, trolley fares, housing, rents, working hours and conditions, wages and child labor, religious and racial discrimination—these were the issues that mattered. To act on them, the Democratic machines sent representatives to the state assemblies in New York, New Jersey, Massachusetts, Rhode Island, Connecticut, Illinois, Ohio, and Missouri. In New York they had notable success. Tammany Hall, under the control of Boss Charles Murphy, sent Al Smith, an East Side Catholic, to the assembly; where he became Speaker; and Robert Wagner, a German immigrant, to the state senate; where he became floor leader. These two harnessed the powerful force of the city machine to the cause of labor, and passed, after the disastrous Triangle Fire of 1911, New York's pioneering health code reform.[22]

On this and other issues, business regulation and the income tax, the machines and the Progressives collaborated, and had they not, the state legislatures would never have passed the many reforms they did in the years just before and after World War I. Sometimes the machines wanted more than the Progressives did. Representing a poor and immigrant population, they did not share the Progressives' commitment to Algerism and were unreserved in their demand that government act to mitigate the harshness of industrial and urban life. Thus they favored union legislation that the Progressives had little use for.[23] And at all times their motives differed from the Progressives'. The spirit in which they pursued reforms was not moral but practical; health, and life itself, depended on these reforms. But on the basic issue of regulation, the bosses and the Progressives were allies.[24]

Still, the Progressives hated the machines, and not without reason, for the machines were corrupt. When immigrants got off the boats and came to the East Side of New York, the Democratic precinct captain or his lieutenant was waiting. He helped make the awesome transit from the Old World to the New a little less trying, found the newcomers housing, maybe a job and extra clothes, introduced them to the parish church—and told them how to vote. In the growing neighborhoods of the immigrants, the Democratic party was not just a political party but also a club and welfare agency; and when the party controlled the local government, government too became these things. In exchange for loyalty, the party provided jobs, municipal contracts, low property assessments, and police protection of gambling and prostitution. Graft bound the machine together, though the bosses regarded it not so much as their goal in life as the incident of a higher value— loyalty—so necessary to a struggling, minority people. To the Progressives this corruption was repugnant. They condemned it in the name of good government, a phrase which to the immigrants meant disfranchisement. But that was not all the Progressives disliked. They disliked the style of politics—the loyalty and the favors, the vice and the Irish bars—a style that violated their doctrine of efficient and honest management. Boss Martin Lomasney of Boston once pronounced his theory of government: never write anything down when you can say it, and never say it when you can nod your head. This was not the theory of the Progressives, who felt contempt for the Lomasneys and wanted to replace them with city managers.[25]

And they felt a little fear, not just of the bosses but of the immigrants, too. This fear was not theirs alone, but one that swept over all the United States, beginning perhaps with the First World War, which brought many changes. During the war, industry grew, and with it the labor movement, which became more militant. Also, the shortage of labor brought women and blacks into factories and accorded them new status. And the cities changed. From the rural outside they looked like the centers of a new hedonism—new dances and short dresses, drink and vice, the mingling of several races. Moreover, the immigration of whites from Europe and blacks from the South swelled the size of cities and gave them a foreign accent, making them suspect, even odious at a time when the United States was fighting a war in Europe—and the Bolshevik Revolution did little to abate the odium. Thus the cities and their immigrants became the special object of dislike, as Americans everywhere reacted against change. Democrats in the South responded with the Ku Klux Klan and a fundamentalist revival, the Church of Christ and the Holy Rollers. Republicans in the North responded with nativism and a somber morality. And the Progressives joined in too.[26]

Nativism, the hatred of un-American people and ideas, had a long history in the nation, and outside the South its home was the Republican party. Some Republicans, such as William Seward, had been leaders of the Anti-Masonic party in the 1830s, a party which appealed to prejudice, and many others had belonged to the Know-Nothing or American party, the most successful nativist party in our history, which served in the 1850s as a sort of bridge between the Whig and Republican parties. As the Republican party grew after 1856, siphoning off the members of the American party, the latter collapsed, though nativism survived. It was strong in the Republican National Convention of 1860, when Lincoln was chosen as the compromise candidate, the leading contenders having been the abolitionist Seward and the nativist Edward Bates. And it was strong after the Civil War, when Republicans filled the ranks of the Antisaloon League, the Women's Temperance Union, and the Immigration Restriction League. Perhaps nativism was so popular with the Republicans because, like the Republican party, its home was the small towns and rural regions of the nation and because, like the antislavery campaign, it sought to preserve America for white Americans. It was a part of the larger Republican impulse to reform the moral character of Americans, an impulse Northern Democrats did not feel, for they counted among their members Catholics, Irish, and working-class people—the sort the middle-class reformers wanted to reform.[27]

It was natural, therefore, that Progressives, many of them middle-class, Protestant Republicans, contributed to the nativist outburst during and after World War I. Their reforms appeared innocuous and unconnected to nativism—blue laws, gambling and vice squads, the city manager and penalties for graft, the restriction of boxing—but they were not. Their target was the city life the immigrants made. And when the Progressives joined the Prohibition campaign, as many did, their intention was obvious, and the rift between them and the machines enormous. The fight over Prohibition was not just a fight about liquor; it was a fight about values, the style of city life, and the ability of the immigrants to preserve their habits. Liquor became the focus of a new and large battle in America, that between the rural Protestants and the urban minorities. It was the preeminent ethnic issue.[28]

It had parallels in the past. Racism had split the Jacksonian Democrats and also the Populists, and it had perverted the antislavery movement and helped end Reconstruction. Now Prohibition was again splitting the liberals—the Progressives and the machines—in yet another example of the liberals' major problem in America—the inability to overcome racial differences. But in another sense the fight over Prohibition was a turning point, the beginning of momentous change in liberal thought. On this occasion, and for the first time, men invoked liberal principles in behalf of minority rights. The machine leaders who responded to the nativist reaction were not evangelists; they did not use, as the nativists did, the arguments of moral evangelism but turned instead to laws and precedents, and mainly to the Constitution. In denouncing Prohibition the Smiths and Wagners called it an invasion of liberty; in fighting the attempts to limit the immigrant's citizenship they spoke of due process and the equal protection of the laws. Governors Dunne and Walsh of Illinois and Massachusetts and Mayor Fitzhugh of Boston tried to ban the showing of the film *Birth of a Nation* because of its prejudiced portrayal of blacks. They made an issue of racial equality; and they made it a liberal issue.[29]

This connection was of inestimable importance. Blacks, encumbered by slavery, then by disfranchisement, never had had the opportunity to connect their discarded rights to a liberal argument. And the abolitionists and radicals speaking for them were moralists who, once concluding that the freedman was a morally deficient human being, turned to other issues. Now, on the other hand, the spokesmen of the immigrants and of the embryonic civil rights movement made the connection, and the issue of their deprivation would never go away. They might lose their fights; but they had placed themselves in the liberal tradition, and it would survive. Minorities might again be oppressed, but never again ignored.

Liberalism too would be altered by this connection. Born in a political crisis in the eighteenth century, it had received its first elaboration, a bit of social analysis, in the 1830s and had lost this elaboration in the years before the Civil War. It regained a hint of that analysis in the Progressive attack on trusts. And now, as a result of the Prohibition fight, it got a wholly new issue—ethnic rights. Liberalism still held, as it always had, that the individual's rights mattered above all else, but now it implied for the first time that the power impinging upon those rights may be not of the state, or even of business, but of a prejudiced people. This idea would alter the liberal mind.

But not for some time. The idea of minority rights did not persuade many people—Prohibition was passed and immigration restricted—not even in the Democratic party, the party of the machines. In the 1912 Democratic National Convention, William Jennings Bryan made an issue of Tammany corruption and the Catholic peril, and upon that basis struck an alliance with Democratic reformers, who, with the help of Bryan's agrarian faction, nominated Woodrow Wilson for president. Once in office Wilson segregated much of the federal government, made Carter Glass secretary of the treasury, Bryan secretary of state, and rebuffed the Japanese at Versailles when they asked for an "equality of races" clause in the peace treaty. His was not an administration partial to minorities. After Wilson, the machines gained in stature; presidential nominee James Cox at least consulted Charles Murphy at the 1920 convention, to Murphy's astonishment. But it was not till 1924 that the urban immigrants got a hearing in party councils. That year the convention was split—Southerners and old Populists and Progressives, led by McAdoo and Bryan, against the urban immigrants, led by Al Smith. The divisive issue (Prohibition having passed) was whether or not the party should repudiate the Ku Klux Klan, which, controlling several states in the 1920s, considered Catholics and Jews (the immigrants), rather than blacks, the greater threat to American life. The convention failed to denounce the Klan. Bryan, who had run for president in 1896 and would die in 1925, spoke for the past—and for the resistance that both Populists and Progressives threw up against the immigrants—when he said, "You do not represent the future of our country," pointing to the New York crowd in the convention hall. He was, of course, wrong; in 1928 Smith won the nomination. But that fall much of Smith's party defected, especially in the South, despite the vice-presidential nomination of Arkansas's Joseph Robinson. It was a mean campaign, exposing the bigoted underbelly of even such enlightened Progressives as William Allen White, who attacked Smith as the representative of the "saloon, prostitution, and gambling" and with others lamented the passing of the day when America was rural, upright, and English.[30]

With the Smith nomination, a stage of liberalism ended. The men of the machines, though fiercely opposed by their own party and the nation, made their appearance. They were different from previous liberals. Not reformers, they were the victims of reform; not moralists, they were the brokers of vice. Their habit was not to proselytize but to provide services—jobs and cheap trolley fares.

For their guiding principle was not a moral vision but self-interest: this was a central difference between them and the reformers. They would not give up their fight. The other difference appeared when the evangelists punished the immigrants for their un-American behavior, for then the urban leaders staked a new claim to America's liberal heritage and made racial tolerance a new liberal issue. But before that claim was firmly fixed, blacks would have to move North, and the New Deal would have to come and go.

FOUR

THE NEW DEAL

In search of jobs and a better life, blacks moved North during and between the two world wars; settling in the cities they gradually joined those who held a commitment to labor and minority rights and were changing the Democratic party. At the same time, the Southern Democrats controlled the party in Congress; not having changed themselves, they opposed change—social and much business legislation and all civil rights efforts. Thus in a sense the Democratic party contained the most liberal and conservative elements in the nation—those who were fashioning a new liberalism, one demanding federal action and social equality; and those of the South who cherished the antique liberalism of the antebellum world. Tension was building in the party.

It was Roosevelt's genius that he never fully satisfied, nor destroyed, the hopes of either half of the party. Both looked to him for help, and both received it only partially. For this they had to thank and blame the Great Depression. It was a crisis in the economy that produced a crisis in faith as well. Shaking the faith in free enterprise, the depression made appealing for the first time the prospect of strong and active government—Roosevelt's measures of relief and recovery. And when he went on to reform and regulate business, he brought to a climax the federalist revolution begun by the Reconstruction and Progressive reformers. This was new. At last liberals fully accepted the idea that government must protect the people from the random injustices of modern society. To this extent, Roosevelt satisfied the yearnings of the urban liberals.

But on the more controversial issue, that of racial and ethnic equality, he did not. National recovery took precedence, then the war did; and the result was, as Oscar Handlin has said, that the New Deal had the effect of "enshrin[ing] security as the preeminent social value."[1] Of course, by helping the mass of Americans—the small businessmen and farmers and workers—the New Deal helped the economic condition of minorities; but it did not plead the minorities' special case or protest their special denials. For Roosevelt could not risk losing the support of the powerful Southern Democrats, disaffected anyhow by the social and business legislation. He had to appease them, mute the party's differences, and ignore civil rights. The minorities' case was postponed till after the war, and with it too the Democrats' day of reckoning.

The Black Migration

Perhaps the most decisive event in the history of the American black man, after he was forcibly brought to this land, was that he was forced to move again, this time to the North. The event was also decisive for the future of the Democratic party and of American liberalism.

During the First World War, the Allied Powers depended heavily on American industry for supplies. This created new jobs in Northern industry, already in need of labor owing to the drastic wartime reduction in European immigration. (By 1918 European immigration was one-tenth of what it had been in 1913.)[2] For the first time blacks had an alternative to the Southern plantation system, and a well-paid alternative, one made appealing by the Southern sharecropper's worsening plight. By 1915 and 1916 the indefatigable boll weevil had spread, and crop destruction hit Georgia and South Carolina. Heavy rainfall in 1916 caused floods and made things worse—boll weevils like water. Many farmers, losing their cotton crops, switched to corn, oats, sweet potatoes, and peanuts. They bought farm machinery to cultivate the new crops and had no use for the blacks.[3]

Once economic circumstance nudged the black off the Southern farm and into Northern industry, the migration snowballed, propelled by secondary forces. New Jim Crow laws were a symptom of the growing animosity between the two races. Southern whites resented having to compete with blacks for disappearing jobs and feared that Northern egalitarianism would spread southward. In addition, more than 360,000 blacks entered military service, many going overseas, and when they returned they told of their higher social standing and higher wages in the North and abroad.[4] And, too, the illiteracy rate among blacks had dropped from 90 percent in 1865 to 30 percent in 1913, enabling them to read the propaganda of the Northern black press, chiefly the *Chicago Defender*, which urged them to come North.[5]

The effect of all this is plain. From 1910 to 1920, the North and West showed a net gain of over 330,000 blacks, with the heaviest migration between 1916 and 1918. In those ten years the number of blacks in the East North Central states increased 70 percent. Michigan showed an increase of 250 percent, and Illinois and Ohio 67 percent, while Mississippi showed a decrease of 7.5 percent. New York's and Pennsylvania's black population increased by half, Kentucky's decreased by 10 percent. Whereas in 1910 the North had 415,533 blacks, by 1920 it contained 737,423—an increase of 77.5 percent. And taken from the year 1910 to the year 1940, the percentage of America's blacks living in the North more than doubled, jumping from 10.4 percent to 23.8 percent—a total net migration from the South of 1.75 million blacks.[6]

The bulk of these blacks went where the jobs were, the cities. Of the blacks living in the North in 1910, 27.3 percent were urban, in 1920, 34 percent. Three-quarters of New York state's blacks lived in New York City. In 1910 Chicago had 44,103 blacks; in 1920, 109,458, an increase of 148.2 percent (the white population grew only 21 percent).[7] And the trend continued after the war: by 1940, 90.1 percent of all blacks in the northern and western states save Missouri lived in urban areas. In these cities, the number of blacks working in factories increased faster than the number in domestic service. In Chicago from 1910 to 1920, the number of blacks in manufacturing increased five-fold, the number in domestic service by only one-third; in Detroit the number in factories grew twenty-six times, in domestic service not quite four times.[8] Living and working together in large groups in cities, blacks by the 1930s had become a political and economic force that the North could not long ignore.

Since Emancipation, blacks in the South tended to vote, the few times they voted, Republican. When they moved North they continued that tendency, in memory of Lincoln, Reconstruction, and their Democratic oppressors. The Great Depression and Franklin Roosevelt changed that allegiance. In the first year of the New Deal, the Works Progress Administration put two million blacks on relief, or one of every six blacks. By 1935, three and a half million were on relief, one-fifth of the black labor force. The Civilian Conservation Corps alone put 200,000 blacks to work.[9] Under new guidelines, the Civil Service by 1938 employed 82,000 blacks. Some New Deal agencies, like the National Youth Administration and the U.S. Housing Authority, appointed blacks to look after black interests. In response to all this, blacks voted Democratic. In 1932, 23 percent of Chicago's blacks voted for Roosevelt, 49 percent in 1936, and 52 percent in 1940 (70 percent in Detroit).[10]

They changed their allegiance, however, not just because of the New Deal but also because of the Northern Democratic machines, which responded to their presence. Six states of the North and West absorbed 72 percent of all black net in-migration from 1910 to 1950—California, Illinois, Michigan, New York, Ohio, and Pennsylvania—states with strong city machines.[11] These machines answered the needs of these people, to a lesser extent than they had helped the white immigrants but to a greater extent than the South had helped the blacks. In the South in 1940, only 80- to 90,000 of 3,651,256 eligible blacks voted. In the North blacks got the vote, and in return for its use they got the usual favors—justice in court, police protection and protection from police persecution, patronage, and fair use of public facilities.[12] Machines also elected and appointed blacks to office and gave them low property tax assessments and a cut in the graft common to big cities. Tom Pendergast, the corrupt leader of the Kansas City machine and the patron of Harry Truman, was perhaps the first of the Democratic bosses to win over the new urban blacks, and he did so in a state where the Klan was a power in politics.[13] Blacks were votes; they mattered to the bosses—and therefore to the national party, which dared not ignore this new source of local power. It too broke precedent and began making overtures to blacks. Between 1933 and 1940, Roosevelt appointed 103 blacks to positions in the federal government, and the Democratic National Committee created a Negro Division, which in 1936 distributed a million copies of a photograph of Eleanor Roosevelt speaking to blacks at Howard University. The Democrats were changing.[14]

The labor movement helped. As late as 1927 a convention of the American Federation of Labor affirmed the exclusion of blacks; but in the 1930s the labor movement changed.[15] Congress protected the right of workers to bargain collectively, first in the National Industrial Recovery Act, which was declared unconstitutional for other reasons, and then in Robert Wagner's National Labor Relations Act, upheld by the Court in 1937. Armed with this right, the industrial unions grew. Formed to bargain with mass production industries, they organized men by the industry they worked in, competing with craft unions, which organized men by the older principle of the craft each man practiced. The two kinds of unions represented a new and an old view of work and of workers' rights, and the partisans of each view fought each other bitterly, until in 1936 the AFL expelled the industrial unions. Through that year and the next the expelled unions organized feverishly, and union strength soared—from 4 million to 7.2 million in 1937 alone. They formed a new federation, the Congress of Industrial Organizations, and tried a new kind of strike, the sit-down, to force industries to bargain with them. Several employers responded with violence, and the resulting publicity— and success of the strikes—made the militant union leaders the spokesmen of unionized America: John Lewis of the United Mine Workers, Sidney Hillman of the Amalgamated Clothing Workers, David Dubinsky of the International Ladies' Garment Workers, Walter Reuther of the United Auto Workers, Thomas McMahon of the United Textile Workers, and Philip Murray of the Mine Workers (later director of the organizing committee of the Steel Workers). These men believed that in an industrial economy the worker could not count on market forces to make his job and income secure and his prospects steadily advancing, that he must fight for his rights, employ political action, and make the parties, especially the Democratic party, earn his vote. And the party could best earn his vote if it called upon the federal government to protect the worker's security. The men of the CIO articulated a new conception of labor and politics and government.[16]

It was no surprise, then, that the labor movement began to change its attitude toward the civil rights issue. The CIO broke precedent and took blacks into unions on the same basis as whites in the steel, meat-packing, and auto industries.[17] It put blacks into national labor positions and, even in the South, held integrated meetings. It worked to win back the franchise for Southern blacks. Many unions, especially the craft unions, refused to take blacks, but the CIO broke out of the pattern. By the 1940s it began to integrate its social affairs in the South; by the 1950s it was probably the largest institutional contributor to civil rights funds there.[18] The efforts of black workers also made a difference. In 1941 A. Philip Randolph of the Brotherhood of Sleeping Car Porters pressured Roosevelt into signing an executive order creating the Fair Employment Practices Committee, a committee charged with protecting equal employment opportunity in the national defense program. Over one million blacks found new industrial jobs—a change which helped not only blacks but also labor, as George Meany explained.[19] "The first precept of our movement," he once said, "is to organize those who work for wages in the same trades and occupations under the theory that anyone who is unorganized, who is underpaid, who has substandard conditions, is a menace . . . [to] those who are organized."[20] If labor could help blacks, blacks could also help labor.

Yet there was more than expedience to the emerging relationship between the labor and civil rights movements. There was also the concept they shared, one which Walter Reuther helped formulate. It was no coincidence that he placed civil rights at its center and called civil rights a "kind of moral symbol" of the things labor fought for;[21] for both the civil rights and labor movements looked at the old struggle of power and liberty and concluded that government was not always the villain, that sometimes it was money and men. Both considered society not a congeries of atoms harmoniously working for the good of all, but rather a society of men, divided into racial and financial groups, some with power and others without. Those without were hurt, their rights ignored, and it was up to government to protect them. This was their common outlook. They were not natural allies, anymore than blacks and whites had ever been—the AFL had proved that—but in the 1930s they came to depend on one another, labor linked to blacks, blacks and labor to the Democratic party, and all three to an emerging ideology, not fully articulate, espousing the rights of the disadvantaged and the responsibility of the federal government. By the end of the New Deal the blacks at last were collecting partners.

Then came the war, which also improved their condition. War industries again drew blacks from the agrarian South to the urban North. The southeastern United States lost almost a half million blacks, while 879,000 moved to the Northeast and 336,000 to the Pacific Coast. And again they went to the cities, Los Angeles's black population jumping from 75,000 to 150,000.[22] Blacks in industrial states increased five to ten times as fast as whites.[23] And they lived better than they had: wartime jobs more than tripled their wages over those of 1939; their life expectancy rose in the 1940s from 45 to 58 years.[24] Another change, the start of integration, began in World War II. In 1940, only five black army officers commanded all-black units, the navy accepted blacks only as stewards, and the marines and air force refused blacks altogether. Black units, used chiefly for maintenance, still were formed in 1943, and segregation often applied to off-duty hours. But necessity changed all that, and the military began to integrate: in 1944 and 1945 the Battle of the Bulge demanded more men, and the only men at hand were black. They went into battle alongside whites, General George Patton telling them their color did not matter so long as they killed Germans. Two secretaries of the navy, Knox and Forrestal, made a start at integrating that branch, though by September 1945, 85 percent of the navy's 165,000 blacks still served as stewards.[25] Integration was also slow in the other services and would not be realized until Truman's administration. Nonetheless, the beginning was crucial; integration succeeded in the armed forces and it might succeed in civilian life.

Finally, World War II made the Americans of the North painfully aware of foreign parallels to America's treatment of its blacks. The war was against a power that sought to exterminate a race; and the similarity of Nazi anti-Semitism and American racism was obvious and discomforting. Later, during the cold war, it would be increasingly difficult for American leaders to deplore the Communists' lack of freedom when America itself oppressed its blacks. Northerners became eager to end overt discrimination, or at least to lessen the public disturbance it caused, so as not to embarrass American foreign policy. In 1954 the Voice of America would broadcast abroad the Supreme Court's school desegregation decision in thirty-four languages—far different from Wilson's response to the Japanese in 1919.[26]

The Southern Fear

Such enormous change in the life of the black and the society of the North—and what of the South, its whites and its party?

Francis Biddle, attorney general during the war years, invited a black friend to eat in the Justice Department and found the cafeteria segregated. To eat lunch with a black, he learned, you went to Union Station. For in the 1930s Washington was a Southern city, predominantly segregated, though like the nation it was changing. Robert C. Ramspeck, congressman from Atlanta, Georgia, was caught in the change. When he first arrived in Washington he got on a bus to go to Capitol Hill, saw the blacks sitting in the front, was startled and got off. Some years later he saw that blacks were eating in the House cafeteria. By then he was Democratic whip and slated to be Speaker next; but suddenly he quit. His friends asked him why, and he said because he had children and needed to provide well for them—an unlikely reason for refusing the Speakership. Pressed by one friend, he told the truth: Washington was changing; the civil rights movement was growing; and he, a Georgian, would have to fight it. But he was a liberal and did not want to. Instead he quit.[27]

Others did not quit, but stayed to make sure the New Deal was not one for blacks. And in their opposition to spending, social legislation, and government power the Southerners made the New Deal itself a precarious thing. But it was not easy to oppose Franklin Roosevelt: they were Democrats and so was he. During the dry years of Republican victory and prosperity, the South had remained staunchly Democratic. In 1924 the South Carolina white supremacist senator, Coleman Blease, said of the 1100 votes Coolidge got in his state: "I do not know where he got them. I was astonished to know that they were cast and shocked to know that they were counted."[28] Even in the election of 1928, when Democrat Al Smith ran, a Catholic, wet, and a New Yorker— all that was worst to the South—the Deep South, from Louisiana to South Carolina, went Democratic; for in that year the Democrats loudly warned that a Republican vote would split the solid South and help the blacks. White supremacy still outweighed religious prejudice, and still was tied fast to the Democratic party.[29] But it was hard to oppose Roosevelt for another reason: he had saved the South. The Great Depression, with its shutdown mills and foreclosed farms, made Southerners realize that their great progress did not run on spirit alone, and their faith—in themselves, their classless community, benevolent patrons, and pious life—was weakened. Roosevelt rekindled that faith, and they loved him for it. Grateful for the open banks, the high cotton prices, and the Agricultural Adjustment Administration (AAA), the Southern people cast their votes. In 1940, 76 percent of all votes cast in the twelve states of the upper and lower South, discounting border states and including Oklahoma (because it disfranchised blacks), went to Roosevelt. And in Mississippi and South Carolina he won 98 percent of the vote.[30] It was hard for a Southern man to be against Roosevelt.

But not for Southern leaders: they saw dangers in the New Deal their people did not. Southern Congressmen made the first 100 days of the New Deal possible, and later, after the urgency had passed, many Southerners—friendly to Roosevelt, loyal to

the party, or tolerant of spending—continued to help the New
Deal: Robinson of Arkansas, the Bankheads of Alabama, Barkley
of Kentucky, Patman and Rayburn and Johnson of Texas. But
many other Southerners saw the future and did not care for it,
and unlike Ramspeck they stayed to fight it. These men were stubborn and dogmatic and liked to show it: Carter Glass, their leader,
born in 1858, lived in the same Washington hotel for twenty-five
years but moved out when the lobby was remodeled. He, Harry
Byrd, also of Virginia, Josiah Bailey of North Carolina, and Thomas
Gore of Oklahoma began in 1933 what came to be known as the
conservative coalition. They saw their fight as one between "the
policy of liberty and the policy of control."[31] In their attack on
the wealth tax, the NRA, the AAA, business regulations, and
"arbitrary little bureaucrats" (the words of Glass), they prefigured George Wallace and his attack on the "pointy-headed
bureaucrats who can't park their bicycles straight"; they professed
to speak for the Constitution and Thomas Jefferson, and repeatedly defended the rights of states. One Southern propagandist later
explained that Roosevelt and "statism," the CIO and the "powerful NAACP," had conspired to thrust the "bayonet of the Welfare
State" into the heart of the South, had been bent upon destroying
Southern liberty and white supremacy.[32] The Southerners were
provoked. They saw themselves engaged in an ancient battle, one
of ideology, often of myth—Southern liberty assailed by Northern
power.

One issue that bothered the old guard was labor rights. Unions
might be bad for American industry, but they were part of an
older threat to the South, the threat to change distinctive Southern
ways. They threatened the Southern individualism, the old belief
that each man had his God-given station, the cheap labor that had
built the progress and redeemed the South, the ideal of a classless
society and Southern solidarity, the notion of hierarchy that made
blacks inferior and all whites equal. And finally, unions, like all
new things, were Northern, and the Southern mind could fantasize
in many directions except that which pointed North.[33] Neither
did the Southern Democrats like the regulation of business. In
one bit of opposition they showed that the Southern mind often
reacted reflexively, irrespective of the merits of the matter. George
Huddleston of Alabama, a congressman since 1915, by mistake
defended a version of a clause in the utility holding company bill
that would give the Securities and Exchange Commission more
and not less discretionary power; but no matter, for he attacked

the administration's version and the bureaucrats who had drawn it up, and was wildly cheered for having avowed his faith in the "old fashioned Southern Democracy of Thomas Jefferson."[34] Thus the old myths that animated the nineteenth century battles were revived for new battles and made to walk again.

Next the old guard fought Roosevelt's tax reform. He asked for legislation that would increase taxes for the wealthy—on inheritances, intercorporate dividends, corporations, large personal incomes, gifts, and undistributed profits. Southern Democrats saw this reform as oppressive to business, and they fought the president through 1935 and 1936. In some measure, they succeeded, for they forced compromises on Roosevelt—compromises he would not have won had he not also assured the South that blacks would never figure in his legislative proposals. Without this assurance, Senate Majority Leader Joseph Robinson, Finance Committee Chairman Pat Harrison, and House Ways and Means Committee Chairman Robert Doughton (of Arkansas, Mississippi, and North Carolina) would never have passed this and other reforms.[35]

But it was not only legislation that bothered the old guard. It was also the civil rights movement, which, begun at the turn of the century, was now gathering steam.[36] The NAACP increased its local chapters from 50 to 500 between the world wars. Its Legal Defense Fund began during the 1930s to attack discrimination, forcing the Supreme Court at last to apply the Reconstruction amendments to the issue they had been intended to address, white supremacy. On April 3, 1944, the Court ruled that the Southern white primary had to be opened to blacks; for the first time Democratic solidarity and, hence, white supremacy faced an uncertain future. For soon it became the dream of Walter White of the NAACP and the CIO leaders to unionize blacks and whites and campaign in the South to make the political and economic system uphold equal rights. They did badly—most Southern workers were segregationists who would later join the white citizens' councils when they appeared in 1954[37]—but nonetheless the South felt the threat, and it feared and resented the intrusion.

The old guard also disliked the change in the national party. In 1936 the Democratic convention eliminated the two-thirds rule (by which a candidate needed two-thirds of the votes to be nominated), thus ending the Southern veto on presidential nominations. When a black minister, Marshall Shepard, rose to deliver a prayer, "Cotton" Ed Smith got up, yelled, "By God, he's as black as melted midnight," and walked out. The next day, when black Congressman Arthur Mitchell rose to speak, Smith left again, taking eight South Carolina delegates with him. Later Smith described the first day's scene:

> When I came out on the floor of that great hall, bless God, it looked like a checkerboard—a spot of white here, and a spot of black there. But I kept going, down that long aisle, and finally I found the great standard of South Carolina—and, praise God, it was in a spot of whites! I had no sooner than taken my seat when a newspaperman came down the aisle and squatted by me and said, "Senator, do you know a nigger is going to come out up yonder in a minute and offer the invocation?" I told him, I said, "Now don't be joking me, I'm upset enough the way it is." But then, bless God, out on that platform walked a slew-footed, blue-gummed, kinky-headed Senegambian! And he started praying and I started walking. And as I pushed through those great doors, and walked across that vast rotunda, it seemed to me that old John Calhoun leaned down from his mansion in the sky and whispered in my ear, "You did right, Ed."[38]

The same year, 1936, also brought Franklin Roosevelt the largest percentage of popular vote ever won—and the largest black vote ever won by a Democrat. Southerners feared he would misuse the power implicit in his mandate—and he did. In 1937, Roosevelt announced his plan to reorganize the Supreme Court in such a way as to allow a president to pack the Court. The South led the fight against the plan: Glass, Byrd, Bailey, Smith, and George saw tyranny down the road; but they also feared that Roosevelt would use the Court to alter race relations, in both the North and the South. To them the Court plan resembled relief legislation (some of which they had supported but now with recovery they opposed), for they believed that each would help create a growing government bureaucracy that spent Southern money to help Northern blacks. Roosevelt's purpose, they surmised, was to win black votes. The old guard picked up strength—Robinson, Harrison, James Byrnes, and John Garner joined the conservative bloc on many votes—and attacked the 1937 relief bill and the Guffey coal bill. Ninety-nine Southern Democrats voted against the fair labor standards bill in the House. When Senator Wagner offered the anti-lynching bill, they buried it. When Roosevelt did little to stop the 1937 sit-down strikes in the steel and auto industries, they went wild. In 1936, Eugene Talmadge had called for a convention of conservative "Jeffersonian Democrats"; others had called for a conservative party, one devoted to racist and conservative fiscal policies. Nothing had happened. Now, at the end of 1937, Bailey of North Carolina repeated the call, and the conservative Democrats joined with Republicans and issued a manifesto whose guiding theme was the evil of government interference. In 1938 the Southerners led the revision of the profits tax and the next year attacked the president's housing program and the National Labor Relations Board. Carter Glass wondered whether the South would "continue to cast its 152 electoral votes according to the memories of the Reconstruction era of 1865 and thereafter, or [would] have spirit and courage enough to face the new Reconstruction era that northern so-called Democrats are menacing us with."[39] The South was rising again.

But the rise was hesitant, ambivalent. Its leaders backed Willkie in Texas and South Carolina in 1940, and Harry Byrd and others in South Carolina, Mississippi, and Texas in 1944—but the people voted overwhelmingly for Roosevelt. Its leaders said they spoke as Jeffersonians, yet they were more often speaking in the interest of Southern money, an interest that has undercut Southern liberal arguments from Calhoun to this day. Thomas Gore's rantings about the New Deal tyranny ran as freely as the Oklahoma oil he spoke for. Walter George had close ties to the Coca-Cola Company of Atlanta and the Georgia Power Company, and John Garner was equally close to Texas money. Harry Byrd, Josiah Bailey, and Carter Glass favored federal aid if it helped the large landowner but opposed federal meddling with the poll tax, which disfranchised not only blacks but also 60 percent of the poor whites. These men spoke in the Southern tradition—not Jefferson's, but the one that ignored the problems of tenantry and sharecropping and subdued class friction by arousing racial hatred. They supported government expenditures for the cotton and tobacco subsidies, for parity, and for the enormous pensions which today form perhaps the largest fixed portion of the federal budget; yet they vehemently deplored the growing federal bureaucracy. The South was the first to benefit from war industries when the nation declared war, yet was also the first to attack the government when labor legislation and relief threatened the cheapness of its labor. It resorted to terrorism, killing several union officials when they tried to organize textile workers. In the *Textile Bulletin* employers publicly urged violation of the Wagner Act. The Jeffersonian persuasion was still alive. It still opposed power and upheld liberty, but on the lips of Harrison, Robinson, and

Byrnes—three friends of Bernard Baruch—it seemed to mean the liberty to make money.[40]

Yet there was, as usual, more than money and words to the Southern fight. For the South felt, and wisely so, badly threatened. The black migration, the growing labor movement, the active New Deal government, and, most of all, the tendency of the Northern Democrats to accommodate this urban, labor, and black population—these changes brought into question a network of old and sacred beliefs, cherished by the volatile Southern mind: economic liberty and the famous progress that had redeemed the South, states' rights and cheap labor, segregation and white supremacy, and the Democratic party itself, the cradle of these beliefs for years. At the heart of the Southern concern was the black man, for he was for the first time since Reconstruction on the Northern mind, too. As the South made denial of blacks' rights the symbol of its identity, the urban liberals responded in kind, making civil rights—equal rights for all Americans and government protection of those rights—the symbol of their creed, a symbol that rallied the strength and helped define the programs of the new Democrats in the North. This was a hard, irrepressible issue, difficult to compromise; collision was certain. In 1944, Gunnar Myrdal predicted that the poll tax would be eliminated by 1954 and that the South would not unite in its opposition to equal rights for blacks.[41] He was wrong. The South united; it was the Democrats who broke apart. In the 1820s, economic forces had bound together Northern and Southern Democrats, but slavery had split them apart by the 1850s; so again, in the 1930s, depression had brought the party together and, as soon as it did, race split it asunder—the abiding issue of race.

Roosevelt

But not under Roosevelt. He was not an ideologue, and besides, to pass the extraordinary amount of legislation he did, he needed both wings of the party, especially the powerful Southern wing, which nearly dominated Congress. Under him the party's divisions grew, but the coalition held together.

Neither his upbringing nor his political experience inclined Franklin Roosevelt to ponder the injustice of race discrimination. As assistant secretary of the navy and as governor of New York, he was indifferent to blacks. And once, as a state legislator, he wrote on the margin of a speech "story of nigger" to remind himself of a special passage.[42] But in this indifference Roosevelt resembled most Americans—those who were not black or did not have black constituents. More revealing was his behavior as a presidential candidate, for in choosing his positions he had an example in his predecessor, Al Smith, whom he chose not to imitate. When, in the fall of 1930, the Democrats won their first congressional victory since 1916, Smith was worried. He feared that the Southerners would dominate Congress and smother the issues he had made in the 1928 campaign; to prevent this happening he wanted the party to affirm its liberal stance. In a meeting of the Democratic National Committee, in March 1931, Smith fought the Southerners over the platform, in which he wished to insert a demand for the repeal of Prohibition—that old issue, which for years had been to urban liberals a symbol of religious tolerance and equal opportunity (much as civil rights would be a symbol of liberalism in the 1940s and 1950s). Smith lost, and the Southerners won, largely because they had the support of Franklin Roosevelt. Roosevelt was seeking Southern votes, and he continued to do so through the summer of 1932. Making several promises to Southern leaders, and giving the vice-presidency to John Garner of Texas, he won the nomination, and the South won its greatest victory since 1912.[43]

As president of a nation thrown into depression, Roosevelt turned his attention to relief, recovery, and reform, and kept it there till the war required him to divert it. Often, as we have seen, New Deal programs helped blacks; sometimes they did not. The relief programs, the AAA, the NRA, and the TVA had the occasional effect of throwing blacks out of work or of lowering their wages, despite the efforts of Harold Ickes and Harry Hopkins to the contrary; and the Federal Housing Administration upheld restrictive covenants. But the programs' advantages and disadvantages to blacks were incidental; they did not constitute the primary intent of administration policy. Very seldom, in fact, did the administration take a civil rights position; it did on the federal antilynching bill, which it chose to oppose. In 1934, Edward Costigan and Robert Wagner framed a bill making lynching a federal crime. They did so in response to the random killing of Southern blacks whom mobs would set upon, either to intimidate the black population or to vent their rage at the increasing civil rights activity in the North—or both. Civil rights leaders thought a bill would discourage the practice; it would also bring the federal government into the civil rights field, making it a shield of those rights for the first time since 1875. Roosevelt refused to support the bill, and it died in 1935. Wagner revived it in late 1937; Roosevelt again refused to help, and without his help the Senate was thrown into a Southern filibuster, lasting six weeks— the first major civil rights debate of the New Deal—until Wagner at last gave in. Roosevelt explained his neutrality to Walter White of the NAACP: Southerners, he said, were "chairmen or occupy strategic places on most of the Senate and House committees. If I come out for the antilynching bill now, they will block every bill I ask Congress to pass to keep America from collapsing. I just can't take that risk." The exigencies of politics thus left Roosevelt little choice. For twelve years he refrained from helping the civil rights movement, except when he created the FEPC, and then it was to maintain the war effort, which the blacks threatened to disrupt. The machines and Smith had broached the issue of toler- ance; Roosevelt let it subside. Civil rights was postponed.[44]

Above all, Roosevelt was a cautious, pragmatic man. When asked if he considered himself a socialist or a capitalist, he said he was a Democrat, an American. When Benjamin Cohen and Thomas Corcoran drafted the party platform, he told them to stick to generalities and no more than two pages. He refashioned government as the guarantor of economic rights, and thus accel- erated the liberals' tendency, begun twenty years before, to turn to the federal government; yet he did so in the spirit of practical reform and was himself without doctrine. And so it was without sacrifice of principle that for fifteen years, from 1930 to the end of his life, he appeased the South.[45] He appointed its sons to the cabinet and the Court. He ignored civil rights. He vacationed in Warm Springs, Georgia, a place he loved. He would never drive the South from his party. But soon another man would.

PART TWO

CIVIL RIGHTS
AND THE LIBERAL TRIUMPH

FIVE

THE FAIR DEAL

One day in the winter of 1944/45, a friend paid a visit to Franklin Roosevelt, the last time he was to see him. The president was calm and easy, loving to talk as usual, and he talked of the previous summer, explaining the troubles he had had in choosing a vice-president. Henry Wallace, then vice-president, would hurt him with the bosses. William Douglas would "play second fiddle to no one." James Byrnes, of South Carolina, was unacceptable to labor. Harry Truman, however, had few enemies and was friendly with both the South and the labor movement. No one could help him win, Roosevelt told his visitor, so his goal was to choose the man who could hurt him least—Harry Truman.[1]

The least-harmful man: Within a couple of years this innocuous man would rank among America's least popular presidents. Leading Democrats would call for his resignation, some for the nomination of General Eisenhower. In twenty years, some would blame him for the cold war and the rise of Joe McCarthy. And in thirty years a nostalgic country would fondly recall a plain man with a straightforward manner, homespun and salty. Truman has enjoyed several reputations, none of them distinguished. In 1945 his reputation was, if anything, worse—was that of a party hack, known only for his investigation of wartime defense contracts. It is therefore something of an irony that this man formulated the first civil rights program since Reconstruction—and the first ever by a Democratic president—and by doing so released the great tensions that had been building in his party and in the liberal mind.

Truman

Truman was the first American president since Grant to have worked on a farm as an adult. He farmed for ten years, joined the

Masons and the Democratic party, then went to war, a captain of artillery. When he returned to Kansas City he went into business and, later, into politics, first as a county judge, later as U.S. senator. He had several allegiances. Born not thirty years after Appomattox, he came from a slave state which, with difficulty, had stayed with the Union. In 1924, when the Ku Klux Klan claimed five million members, and when the Democratic National Convention failed, by a narrow vote, to condemn the Klan, Truman equivocated—as few leaders of the southern Midwest did—and finally denounced the Klan. Yet he was friendly with Southern leaders, sharing a desk in the Senate with James Eastland, who became his friend.[2] A rural man, he owed his rise to the big city and to the corrupt Pendergast machine which controlled it—not the first time a city machine produced a liberal candidate. Governor Smith and Senator Wagner had similar debts; so would Stevenson, Kennedy, and Paul H. Douglas.

At the start of his Senate career, Truman spoke in the tradition of Andrew Jackson and Southern Populists. He was deeply radical: "No one ever considered Carnegie libraries steeped in the blood of the Homestead steel workers, but they are," he said on the Senate floor.

> We do not remember that the Rockefeller Foundation is founded on the dead miners of the Colorado Fuel & Iron Co. and a dozen other similar performances. . . . It is a pity that Wall Street, with its ability to control all the wealth of the nation and to hire the best law brains in the country, has not produced some financial statesmen, some men who could see the dangers of bigness and of the concentration of the control of wealth. . . . People can stand only so much, and one of these days there will be a settlement.

He was also antimodern, blaming unemployment on "the concentration of population in industrial centers, mass production, and a lot of other so-called modern movements."[3]

But Truman came not just from the farm but also from the city, and in the Senate he showed this other side. He voted with the New Deal on most matters, and went beyond it to support the civil rights movement on antilynching and anti-poll tax laws. When he supported the FEPC, Roy Wilkins praised him as a man apart from the "other fellows . . . straddling the fence" and said it was Truman's apprenticeship in the Pendergast machine that made him "politically astute" on race issues. When he ran for Senate reelection in 1940, Truman proclaimed his belief in the "brotherhood of man" and said, "In giving Negroes the rights that are theirs, we are only acting in accord with our ideals of a true democracy."[4] When he was nominated for vice-president in 1944, the big city bosses swung behind him on the first ballot; and on the second ballot it was the South that clinched the nomination. Truman was a hybrid.

Rural man and city man, Southerner and machine politician, Truman came from scattered origins and enjoyed diverse support, but on the whole as he grew, he grew more liberal, which in view of his borderstate background was unexpected. It was also against the tide.

If you traveled on a train from North to South when Truman was president, you stopped in Washington to switch to Jim Crow cars. If you were black in Washington you went to restaurants, theaters, and schools for blacks only; you lived in a segregated neighborhood because restrictive covenants kept you from the white. If you were black you could not perform on the stage of Constitution Hall, owned by the Daughters of the American Revolution, though you could sit in the audience; in other theaters you could not sit, only perform. You could dine in Union Station, the YWCA, and some government cafeterias, though not in downtown restaurants. You would probably work as a maid or laborer, the occupations of three out of every four of Washington's blacks. Your child could ride the bus but not play with white children in sports events. He could enter Washington's annual marble tournament, though it was the tournament held only for his race; if he won he was automatically designated the runner-up, for the victor of the white marble shooting contest was acclaimed the local champion and sent to the national tournament.[5] Such was the racial climate of the nation's capital.

The political climate was equally hostile to liberalism. There was, as we have seen, a conservative group in Congress during the New Deal. By 1939 this group had expanded into a coalition, and when the war came, and with it prosperity, this coalition sought to check liberal advances and perhaps repeal those made since the depression. These conservatives, strengthened by their victories in the 1942 election, drastically cut Roosevelt's tax increase (over his veto), fought his price ceilings, tried to discipline labor unions, and gave defense contracts to large industries.[6] It was amid this resurgence of conservatism, commonly associated with the 1950s but beginning in fact the decade before, that Truman assumed office, and because of it that he was to push against the tide. In his vice-presidential campaign in 1944, he called for national unemployment insurance, for a public valley authority for Missouri and the Pacific Northwest, for civil rights legislation; and proclaimed, "The Democratic Party will always be the liberal party"—a wish, he was soon to find, that others did not share.[7]

Roosevelt had battled thunder on his left and right, but he also had had help from the depression and the Democratic Congress. By 1945, the people were weary with reform and war, and Truman heard louder thunder, racist and reactionary, and faced a hostile Congress; and he drew from his past not, like Roosevelt, the ease of his position and command of his class but, like a border-state liberal, a set of conflicting claims. Yet he carried the liberal program beyond where Roosevelt had stopped.

The Presidency

The great leader dead, the war over, the tensions of a decade caught up with the nation. The South resented the advances of the blacks. The farmers complained of crop and price controls. Labor complained of prices and wages. And the consumers wanted meat. Truman had a difficult time finding his way, and in doing so he frightened the liberals. He relied at first on suspect men, conservatives, friends from Missouri. He threatened to draft striking rail workers. In 1946, he dared not denounce the Senate filibuster against the FEPC for fear of jeopardizing his economic program. Faced with a dazzling array of problems, Truman alienated every segment of the electorate by 1946; his inability to lead both the nation and the liberals seemed certain.

Yet there were signs that this was not so. If he appointed cronies, he kept some liberals—David K. Niles and Samuel Roseman in the White House, Paul Herzog at the NLRB, and David Lilienthal at the TVA. And in June 1945 he endorsed a bill to establish a permanent FEPC, to replace the wartime committee soon to expire. In September he stunned Congress and his liberal detractors with his economic message, calling for a full employment bill, increase in the minimum wage, extension of public housing programs, aid to education, increased Social Security payments and farm supports, and additional power development programs. He also asked for a national health program, a request only partially granted when Lyndon Johnson signed the Medicare Act on July 7, 1965. The following spring he vetoed antiunion legislation. Joseph Martin, conservative from Massachusetts and Republican leader in the House, reviewed the Truman program and concluded it was "just a case of out-New Dealing the New Deal." Some New Dealers thought so too.[8]

But on the whole Truman did poorly at first, and his fight with the farmers shows why. In the summer of 1946 the farming industry, especially the meat industry, wanted to end the administration's control of prices. Truman demurred, fearing inflation. He fought and lost in Congress, inflation ensued, and in August he extracted a bill that gave the Office of Price Administration meager powers. The OPA controlled meat, the farmers struck, and a meat famine spread. The farmers persisted, hoping to kill OPA and win higher prices. Consumers and labor demanded action; the New York City Council asked Truman to seize the nation's meat and distribute it fairly. By fall, the administration, up against the wall, gave in and ended meat controls. The farming industry had won, OPA was dead, and the inflation spiralled.[9] Two weeks later came the midterm election, and for the first time since 1930, the Democrats lost control of Congress. The farmers—in depression the allies of reform, in prosperity the guardians of conservatism—voted against Truman's party; and so did labor and consumers, angry with inflation. Truman had faced an insoluble situation, and he did what was required in such situations—he failed.

The 1946 election shocked Truman. He had tried to please everyone but in fact pleased no one. The adjustment to a peacetime economy, the burgeoning cold war, the social tensions concealed by depression and war—the yearnings of a black minority and the fears of a solid South: these problems divided the people and rendered Truman incapable of commanding broad support. He could not please everyone but had instead to select several issues, stake out a position, form a policy, and find his public. One of these issues, which he began to address after the election defeat and never deserted, was civil rights.

In 1946 racial violence had risen dramatically. The war, as we have seen, had improved the condition of blacks in America, and with this improvement came Southern white resistance, often aimed at the returning black veterans, just to let them know that nothing had changed. In the first year of peace the Tennessee police arrested more than seventy blacks around Columbia and killed two in jail; in Aiken, South Carolina, police blinded Sergeant Isaac Woodard, Jr., three hours after he got out of the army; and in Taylor County, Georgia, the one black who dared to vote was murdered in his yard. There were other cases. Labor and civil rights leaders protested, and in September 1946 they met with Truman and asked him to speak out against the violence and support civil rights legislation. Particularly moved by the story of Sergeant Woodard, Truman agreed, and appointed a civil rights commission on December 5, 1946, to study the problem of race relations. (He used an executive order to circumvent Congress, which he and others thought would refuse to act.)[10] Telling the committee that present civil rights statutes were inadequate, he instructed it to propose new ones—to "provide the Department of Justice with the tools to do the job." The committee—which included leading academics, lawyers, labor leaders, and businessmen—met 10 times, from January to September 1947, heard 40 witnesses, and consulted 250 organizations and individuals and 25 agencies of the federal government. When it submitted its report, thorough and unblushing, many were stunned. It gave a startling picture of the place of race in postwar America.[11]

The report began by examining the "condition of our rights," and found they were not in good shape. In the year Truman established the committee six persons were lynched in America, all black, three never having been charged with a crime; of the other three, one was accused of stabbing a man, another of house breaking, and another of stealing a saddle. The committee called for an antilynching law. It found several cases of involuntary servitude, praised the Justice Department for prosecuting these, but feared that economic depression would bring a recurrence of peonage. Next it took up voting, and found that, even without the white primary, the poll tax permitted only 18.31 percent of the electorate to vote in eight states. Turning to discrimination, the committee found that the military continued to bar blacks from command and sometimes from the service altogether; that employers had discriminated against blacks and Jews in spite of the wartime FEPC, which expired anyhow in June 1946; that restrictive covenants kept blacks out of white neighborhoods; and that seventeen states and the District of Columbia segregated their schools. It found that discrimination persisted in the South and, following the trail of blacks, was growing in the North. It protested.

And it called for action, federal action. It recommended the enlargement of the civil rights section of the Justice Department, which then had seven lawyers. It asked Congress to strengthen the Reconstruction statutes still intact and to enact new laws—against police brutality, lynching, involuntary servitude, poll taxes and white primaries, and discrimination in the armed forces. The committee called for home rule for the District of Columbia. It asked Congress to erect a permanent FEPC to guarantee fair employment. It asked that federal assistance be conditioned on the absence of discrimination. And it called for the end to segregation. These proposals, and the thinking behind them, derived from a central notion of rights and power. The federal government, said the report, "must referee the clashes which arise among the freedoms of citizens, and protect each citizen in the enjoyment of the maximum freedom to which he is entitled." The exercise of power was needed. When the committee members chose a title for their report, they went to the Declaration of Independence, where they found the phrase, "To Secure These Rights"; but then they cited a passage and made their point, stressing it with italics: "Man is endowed by his Creator with certain inalienable rights. Among these are life, liberty, and the pursuit of happiness. To secure these rights, *governments are instituted among men.*"[12] This passage is often cited for its eloquent encomium to liberty; these men cited it for the sanction it gave to power.

Unlike some presidents, Truman read his committee's report and made its recommendations his legislative program. On January 7, 1948, he said in his State of the Union Address that securing "essential human rights" was one of his five "great goals." The next month he sent his civil rights message to Congress, saying, "The Federal Government has a clear duty to see that Constitutional guarantees of individual liberties and of equal protection under the laws are not denied or abridged anywhere in our Union."[13] He called upon Congress to grant home rule and suffrage in the District of Columbia, establish a permanent commission on civil rights and an FEPC, and prohibit lynching, the poll tax, and discrimination in interstate transportation. Congress was shocked; Southerners complained, saying the president had neglected to consult them. But that was hardly the problem.

Truman did more than appeal to Congress. In December 1947, he urged his Justice Department to argue before the Supreme Court against restrictive covenants, which the Court outlawed the next year. In 1950, four years before the *Brown* desegregation decision, the department urged the Court to discard the separate-but-equal principle; and in 1952, it entered the *Brown* case with a brief that the Court found more helpful than the ten briefs filed by the litigants and that was, on the whole, supportive of the plaintiffs.[14] It was in the executive branch, however, that Truman had the advantage of discretionary power, and he used it to attack discrimination in the armed forces and in the civil service. On February 27, 1946, Secretary of the Navy James Forrestal ordered all commanders to lift restrictions on the assignment of black personnel. The policy spread to the other branches after Truman received the civil rights report in October 1947. In November, A. Philip Randolph and Grant Reynolds organized the Committee Against Jim Crow in Military Service and Training, and the following spring, while considering a draft bill, the Senate Armed Services Committee heard Randolph warn them that a Jim Crow draft bill would result in "massive civil disobedience."[15] Congress balked at the threat and passed the draft bill without a desegregation proviso. On June 24, Truman signed the bill, but the next month, urged by the Urban League, the NAACP, the ADA, and such leaders as Adam Clayton Powell and Jacob Javits, he ordered that the armed services provide equal opportunity to its personnel, regardless of race. Executive Order 9981 decreed equality of treatment and opportunity in the "National Military Establishment" and authorized a Committee on Equality and Treatment and Opportunity in the Armed Forces, with powers to investigate rules and procedures and make recommendations to the president and the military authorities. Randolph dropped his plans for civil disobedience (though not until the Korean War did the president's order take full effect). The same day, July 26, 1948, Truman issued a similar order regarding the civil service: he barred discrimination by race, religion, or national origin in the hiring and treatment of all federal officials.[16]

Truman appealed to the public as well. He told a press conference that by his executive order barring discrimination in the armed forces he had intended to end segregation as well. And he became the first president to address the NAACP. Speaking in June 1947 before 10,000 people at the Lincoln Memorial and a worldwide radio audience, Truman explained as clearly as anyone the significance of his civil rights program. "We cannot be content with a civil liberties program which emphasizes only the need of protection against the possibility of tyranny by the Government. . . . We must keep moving forward, with new concepts of civil rights to safeguard our heritage. The extension of civil rights today means not protection of the people against the Government, but protection of the people by the Government."[17]

Here Truman, like his civil rights committee, was twisting liberalism in new directions, for he stressed that half of American liberalism that found benevolence in strong government. Few leaders in the American past had stressed this half. As we have seen, the Founding Fathers themselves had equivocated—had created a democratic power potentially illimitable, then sharply divided and controlled its exercise. In the expectant first two decades of the nineteenth century, Calhoun and other Southerners had placed their hope in nationalism and blessed the government as the agent of democracy; then came the sectional crisis and their retreat to states' rights. Lincoln too had charged the Union with the sacred obligation of spreading democracy, but few had shared his view, and though Whigs and Republicans, before and after the Civil War, had endorsed strong government, they did so to spread business rather than democracy. Both Reconstruction and Progressive reformers had turned to the federal government, but their efforts were hesitant and their movements short-lived, undercut by the Republican ideology they had in common and a moralism gone sour. Populists had turned to federal power, but their movement was drowned in racism. And the spokesmen of the immigrants, though fighting for racial tolerance, did not successfully use federal power but rather, as they discovered in the Prohibition and immigration fights, became its victim. Thus were the liberals until the New Deal. Never did they successfully, enduringly wed the power of government to the cause of spreading democracy.

They did not because of a set of attitudes which were forever reappearing and limiting the reach of their thought. The fear of power, present at the beginning, recurred in the minds of Calhoun and all later Southern leaders, of the Reconstruction and Progressive reformers, and even of the immigrants who saw in Prohibition how the state could make men conform. The obsession with property also began with the Revolutionaries and went on to dominate the thought of the Republican party, and especially limited the antislavery movement and the reform of Reconstruction, the Mugwumps, and the Progressives. And finally there was racial prejudice. It perverted the liberalism of both the South and the North—of Calhoun's precise and logical liberal mind, and of the antislavery movement. It helped split the Jacksonians and the Populists. And it kept the Reconstruction radicals from understanding the freedman's plight and helped transform Progressives into bible-banging reactionaries. Such were the three attitudes, which up to the New Deal took the form of barriers, continually preventing liberalism from reaching its logical goal, the enhancement of liberty for all men.

Franklin Roosevelt went a long way toward upsetting these attitudes. He did more than anyone else had to diminish the fear of power in the liberal mind—the depression was more fearsome. But Roosevelt kept his distance from ideology, as we have seen, and made it appear that government evolved more by accident than design—as a result of depression and war—into a massive center of power and decision. And in part this was true, for the New Dealers, especially Roosevelt, were not given to systematic social analysis: they repaired what they found broken. Truman and the postwar liberals, on the other hand, found not something broken but something wrong—racism, deeply rooted in American society. It was so rooted that only strong federal action could overcome its effects, and thus they made big government a point of ideology. A thought began to emerge under Truman, reflected in his civil rights report, that justified this huge government and built an ideology around it, that found some goodness in power and some badness in people, and that, in response to the renascent conservatism, embraced a new liberal crusade. Simply by taking this step—by making an ideology of what the New Deal had done in practice—Truman and the liberals went a step beyond the New Deal.

But surely the more daring step was the espousal of civil rights itself. Roosevelt had addressed himself to economic security, not to civil rights, did not break down the barrier of racism and in some ways built it up. In this he was no different from his predecessors. Truman, however, was different. He took up the cause of blacks, and thus not only called for federal power, in defiance of the liberal tradition, but also defied the powerful tradition of racism—a double defiance of the past. Perhaps it was natural, even necessary, that the two traditions be overthrown at once, for surely civil rights needed federal protection, and perhaps, too, liberalism needed civil rights. For more than a hundred years racism had limited the liberal impulse; maybe only by directly assaulting race prejudice—by endorsing civil rights—could liberalism find its own liberation. Racism had divided the liberals, prevented them from probing the social origins of inequality, and excused them from exercising federal power. Now civil rights might liberate them, permit them as they never had been permitted before to form alliances irrespective of race, to probe deeply into social inequality, and to demand unabashedly the use of national power. Racism always had stood as a barrier, but after 1945, and through the 1960s, civil rights would stand in the center of liberalism, the symbol of a new and vigorous creed.

Such a change in doctrine did not go unnoticed in the South. At a White House luncheon for the executive committee of the Democratic National Committee, an Alabaman committeewoman said to the president, "I want to take a message back to the South. Can I tell them you're not ramming miscegenation down our throats?" Truman reportedly read her the Bill of Rights and explained he was "everybody's President." In all, fifty-two congressmen attacked Truman for his civil rights message, and a movement began in the South to deny the Democratic party its usual place on the ballot. (South Carolina's Democrats let blacks vote in the 1948 primary only if they took an oath, vowing to uphold segregation and oppose Truman's FEPC bill.) Moderate Southern leaders, however, said that while they opposed Truman's program they had no intentions of deserting the party. Sam Rayburn, always nimble in honoring both his Southern and national commitments, said, "I am not going to vote against the Democratic ticket just because I don't agree with President Truman on these matters." Maybank of South Carolina said the same, declaring that the Republican party never had been a friend to the South.[18] Southern opposition was nonetheless formidable, and it strained the South's relations with the party and the administration. On June 29, 1945, the *Congressional Record* had cited Truman's friend James Eastland as saying that the Negro race was inferior; later Eastland would go further (also in the *Record*): "The mental level of those people renders them incapable of suffrage." And now he and his colleagues planned to filibuster—as they did in Truman's first year when he pressed for an FEPC—if any portion of the program reached the floor. But they saved their breath. The two principal bills, for the FEPC and against lynching, they killed in committee.[19]

Still, the Southerners were shaken. The integration of the armed forces particularly worried them. Senator Richard Russell of Georgia said he preferred "patriotic Negroes" to A. Philip Randolph. General Eisenhower joined the protest, announcing that one could not make "somebody to like someone."[20] But it was Representative William M. Colmer of Mississippi who summarized the South's reaction, when, on April 8, 1948, he spoke to the House and compared Truman's message to Lincoln's rescue of Fort Sumter. Truman had "raised anew the issue of the rights of the sovereign States as against a strong centralized government and driven a devastating wedge into the unity of the Democratic Party." The South "has ever been a strong believer in and contender for the Jeffersonian theory of democracy," and never had it seen "such a devastating, obnoxious, and repugnant program to the people of that section and their Jeffersonian conception of democracy as this so-called civil rights program." Colmer predicted the destruction of the Southern way of life and principles of government; and he blamed racial disturbances and the arrogance of blacks, including Randolph's threat of civil disobedience, on Truman's espousal of civil rights.[21]

There was truth in all this. The Southern mind foresaw the end of an era. Their party, offices, schools, and jobs—all was at stake. And there was truth in the attack on Truman. For it was in the climate of civil rights, shaped in part by the prestige and power of the president's leadership, that the NAACP gained new members and great influence, that the Supreme Court, in *Morgan* v. *Virginia* and in *Shelley* v. *Kraemer,* began to assail the laws and patterns of segregation, and that the number of voting blacks in twelve Southern states increased, in seven years, by six times.[22] It is impossible, and also unnecessary, to link every advance of civil rights in the 1940s to Truman's leadership; sufficient it is to know that the greatest civil rights advances (up to that time) came during the tenure of the president most committed, by word and deed, to civil rights—and he a Baptist of a border state, once a farmer, and a Democrat.

Even so, Truman was not the liberals' idol. His treatment of the rail workers and coal miners prompted the New York CIO to label him "the No. 1 strikebreaker of the American bankers and railroads."[23] The resignation of Harold Ickes and the firing of Henry Wallace intensified the dislike the New Dealers had conceived for Truman simply because, as after President Kennedy's death, the inner circle of friends and advisers felt the successor a poor substitute for the lost and mourned leader. His loyalty program frightened many liberals, and this and his containment policy in foreign affairs have since led some to portray him as the father of McCarthyism. And, too, many would say he was not a committed liberal because he failed in Congress, never passing his civil rights or health insurance bills.

Whether or not any of these sentiments are grounded in fact is not a question that must concern us; though it bears pointing out that many of Truman's problems were not of his own making.

In reconversion he faced a baffling task—5,000 strikes in one year alone—and though he was not a strikebreaker by inclination, he broke some strikes and seized several industries. He could not avoid winning the hatred of not just labor but business too. In foreign affairs, Truman also inherited problems—an ambiguous policy, which, because he lacked experience, he made more ambiguous, on the one hand deploring the Communist menace, on the other professing his affection for "old Joe" (Stalin).[24] Such vacillation did him no good. At home the Communist issue was becoming a point of conflict between a revived conservatism and a defending liberalism. Atomic espionage and Communist activity in Turkey, Greece, and China gave new life to the old fear of bolshevism, which the Republicans and Southern Democrats exploited, likening the "Reds" abroad to the liberals at home. For their part, the liberals rallied around Henry Wallace, who defended unions and civil rights and pled for rapprochement with the Soviets. Truman was caught in the crossfire, the indecisive man in the middle. But in 1948 the situation changed. Communists staged a coup in Czechoslovakia and the Russians blockaded Berlin. Rapprochement lost its advocates, and a sort of consensus developed around the policy of containment. Increasingly, the issues separating conservatives from liberals were domestic ones, and on these, in the same year, with his State of the Union and civil rights messages, Truman grew more liberal. The Americans for Democratic Action, founded in early 1947 to meet the conservative resurgence, supported him when he vetoed the Taft-Hartley Act, which prohibited the closed union shop (it was passed over his veto), when he pushed for civil rights, and when he attacked Joseph McCarthy, from 1950 on. These facts must be borne in mind—the complexity of postwar problems, the sharply divided opinion—and also the fact that ideologues, when they attack a less dogmatic ally, overlook the opposition he faces, the available alternative—the Republicans, in this case, and their leaders, Robert Taft and, later, Joseph McCarthy.

But if Truman inherited some problems, others he alone created. He had risen in politics as a party hack, had no patience for contemplative thinking, was not an intellectual—indeed was the first president since Cleveland not to hold a college degree—though he liked reading books, especially those on history. He disdained what he called (in his diary) "professional liberals."[25] Their style offended him, and his offended them. He once told

Harold Ickes that he hoped the Democratic party would become a "liberal party" and that the South would join the Republicans, the party of its natural inclination; yet he failed to communicate this sense of conviction. Rather he was regarded as an impulsive man without firm principles. He had a tendency to shoot from the hip, to make a decision quickly, on the basis of his intuitive sense of right and wrong, without regard for the conservative or liberal implications. Sometimes he was rash. In the spring of 1946, coal and rail strikes together dragged on for weeks, stopping relief shipments to a hungry Europe and causing industries to cut production and almost a million men to lose their jobs. Truman lost his temper. In May, he went before Congress to ask for a law inducting recalcitrant railworkers into the army—certainly not a liberal law, probably unconstitutional as well. Liberals were aghast. It was this sort of decision, and this sort of style, that put a distance between them and Truman.[26]

Yet in spite of this distance, Truman became in 1948 the foremost proponent of the new liberalism, if not the best friend of the liberals; and what remains is the problem of motive. What moved Truman to add civil rights to the litany of liberal causes and champion them all in this unfavorable time is hard to tell. Certainly after 1946 he learned he could not please everyone. But his reasons for choosing this particular program were another matter; perhaps they were what he said they were. He set up the Committee on Civil Rights on December 5, 1946, because, as he said, violence done to blacks had increased since the war. Two years later he mentioned the violence again. "My forebears," he said to Democrats who asked him to endorse a weak civil rights plank at the 1948 convention,

> were Confederates. I come from a part of the country where Jim Crowism is as prevalent as it is in New York or Washington. Every factor and influence in my background—and in my wife's for that matter—would foster the personal belief that you are right. But my very stomach turned over when I learned that Negro soldiers, just back from overseas, were being dumped out of Army trucks in Mississippi and beaten. Whatever my inclinations as a native of Missouri might have been, as President I know this is bad. I shall fight to end evils like this.[27]

His intuition led him to undertake the conscription of railworkers; it led him, too, when he heard of the blinding of Sergeant Woodard, to endorse civil rights.

Politics also pushed Truman left. Like other liberals, he bristled when the stubborn Eightieth Congress buried liberal programs and enacted antiunion laws. Another source of political pressure was Henry Wallace, who, announcing for the presidency in December 1947, flanked him on the left. And his staff, adept at politics, more so than he was himself, pushed Truman left. They were mostly liberals, some with experience, such as Leon Keyserling, who had served as assistant to Robert Wagner; James Rowe, who had clerked for Justice Holmes, been an assistant to Roosevelt, and would go on to have a distinguished career as a lawyer and as advisor to Harriman and Johnson and other liberal leaders; and David K. Niles, who, having been Roosevelt's assistant for minority affairs, held the same post under Truman and probably had more influence than anyone else on Truman's civil rights policy. Clark Clifford, as special counsel to the president, had considerable influence in the White House; he would later become Johnson's defense secretary. Richard Neustadt, just beginning his career, would advise Kennedy and become a professor of government at Harvard. David Bell later would help run Adlai Stevenson's first campaign for the presidency and serve as Kennedy's director of the budget. These men—and there were many more—pushed Truman left when he wandered in a conservative direction; and sometimes they restrained him, as during the rail strike, which Truman had planned to meet with a speech even more violent than the violent one he gave.

They also planned his 1948 campaign, which had some bearing, no doubt, on the measures he took as president. In the fall of 1947 Rowe wrote a memorandum on strategy, which, when it was circulated confidentially, became the outline for campaign operations. In 16,000 words, Rowe looked at the conditions of American politics and suggested how Truman should meet them.[28] He said it was "inconceivable that any policies initiated by the Truman Administration no matter how 'liberal' could so alienate the South in the next year that it would revolt. As always, the South can be considered safely Democratic." Instead, Truman should worry about Wallace. He should make a liberal campaign, concentrating on winning the West, the liberals, and the blacks:

Unless the Administration makes a determined campaign to help the Negro (and everybody else) on the problem of high prices and housing—and capitalizes politically on its efforts—the Negro vote is already lost. Unless there are new and real efforts (as distinguished from mere political gestures which are today thoroughly understood and strongly resented by sophisticated Negro leaders) the Negro bloc, which, certainly in Illinois and probably in New York and Ohio, *does* hold the balance of power, will go Republican.

This was Rowe's analysis.

His advice was to move left. Truman should establish better relations with labor—invite its leaders to the White House. He should attack Wall Street, an attack, Rowe recalled, belonging traditionally to the Democratic party, from Jackson to Bryan to Wilson and Roosevelt. But Truman had to do more: he had to fashion programs specially designed to meet the needs of farmers, blacks, and labor. He had to appeal to the groups that since the New Deal had become dependent on government help—labor for wage laws and price controls, farmers for supports, the West for power projects, and blacks for everything. In the politics of the depression these groups turned to Roosevelt, who exerted little effort to win their support, but Truman faced a different politics, and he had to work for their support.

It is likely that Rowe's memorandum was the blueprint for Truman's liberal program of 1948, for the month after he got it Truman called on Congress to enact many of its proposals. In his January 1948 State of the Union Address he demanded expansion of unemployment compensation, more social security benefits, national health insurance, federal aid to education, a housing program, tax revision, rent controls, and federal power projects. And in February he presented his civil rights program. All these were suggested by Rowe and others on Truman's staff. Yet it would be inaccurate to say that Truman's liberalism wholly derived from Rowe's or anyone else's memorandum. His civil rights program, after all, embodied the recommendations of the Committee on Civil Rights, which he had appointed a full year before Rowe advised him. He had called for an FEPC in his first year in office; and he had announced the national health insurance program in November 1945. More than the coming campaign lay behind Truman's program.

Politics always is on a president's mind—and well it should be— but it is not the only thing on his mind. It was not on Truman's mind when he attended the funeral of Tom Pendergast, a prisoner in a penitentiary, and it probably was not his only consideration when he submitted his civil rights program just before meeting Southerners and the rest of the Democrats in the national convention in Philadelphia. If it was a consideration, he had considered poorly; for surely he knew that the South, though perhaps remaining loyal to him, would not like him for his espousal of civil rights. All this evidence leads one to believe that in framing his liberal program Truman was lucky. What was politically desirable happened to be what also he believed, for he believed that discrimination was wrong; in fact, it had turned his "very stomach."

But however one assesses Truman's motives, what is clear, and more important, is his effect. By speaking out on civil rights, and making it an issue of national importance, Truman had broken with the past and started a momentous chain reaction; and like many before him he soon lost control of the events he set in motion. He had scared the Southerners—more than Rowe had predicted— and encouraged the liberals; and when the two met in Philadelphia they would fight and divide over Truman's program, despite his efforts to stop them.

The Convention

In the months before the convention Truman's chances of being nominated and elected looked slim. Walter Reuther, David Dubinsky, and CIO President Philip Murray withheld their endorsement, though AFL President William Green and A. F. Whitney of the Brotherhood of Railway Trainmen (his antagonist during the rail strike of 1946) endorsed him. A switch in the U.S. position on the partition of Palestine temporarily cost Truman some Jewish support, such as that of machine leader Jacob Arvey of Chicago, who joined Franklin Roosevelt, Jr., and the New York and New Jersey political machines in floating Eisenhower's candidacy. This speculation gave Southerners their chance to launch an anti-Truman campaign. Senator Richard Russell spoke with Eisenhower several times and assured his colleagues that the general was acceptable to the South, a "states' rights man." South Carolina's Strom Thurmond also came out for Eisenhower.[29] For a few weeks in the spring of 1948 it seemed that most Democrats were against Truman and that for varying reasons they were turning to Eisenhower—liberals, the machines, and the South. But then on July 5 Eisenhower withdrew, and the Chicago and New York machines came out for Truman. Only the South held back, wondering how it could stop the president.

One way was with the party platform. If the Southerners could shape the platform so that it repudiated Truman, they might deny him the nomination. It was a plausible plan. Democrats always had taken the platform seriously—in 1924, when the issue was the Klan, as we have seen; in 1931, when it was Prohibition. For the platform revealed the posture of the party, expressed its principles and direction, and bound it together—not only to win elections but also to stand for certain things. And it influenced the choosing of a candidate, who almost always reflected the positions adopted in the platform. The platform battles thus serve as a window thrown open on the party's fight over ideology and candidates. But in 1948 the platform was especially important, and so was the choice of candidate, for this was the first time the party had assembled since the death of Roosevelt, and the Democrats knew they stood at a crossroads. If Truman was nominated and his programs endorsed, the party was certain to continue in a direction inimical to the South. If Truman could be ousted, however, perhaps the South and its conservative economic and racial ideology could dominate the party for the foreseeable future. But for the moment, in the spring of 1948, these designs were hidden, and the Southern leaders promised Frank Myers, chairman of the platform committee, they would not make an issue of the civil rights plank.[30]

Others made no such promise. In March the ADA, in one of its first national political acts, sent a letter to party leaders urging that the convention adopt a strong civil rights plank; Hubert Humphrey, mayor of Minneapolis and vice-chairman of the ADA, signed it on behalf of himself, James Roosevelt of California, and Jacob Arvey. When the delegates began arriving in Philadelphia, the ADA set up headquarters in a fraternity house on the campus of the University of Pennsylvania, a few blocks from the convention hall, and spent their hours there preparing a fight on civil rights.[31]

But even before the ADA could force a fight on the platform, one had broken out on credentials. On the second day of the convention, the credentials committee met to hear testimony bearing on the credentials of several Southern delegates. A challenger to South Carolina said there were ten million blacks living in the South and not a single black delegate to represent them. Strom Thurmond said if the challenging delegation was seated, his delegation would walk out, and the meeting grew tense: "I will answer you nothing," said Thurmond. They argued more, the public meeting adjourned, and the executive session of the credentials committee decided, as it had in the past, to seat the challenged delegations.[32]

This should have been the end of the matter. That night, however, when the credentials committee chairman presented her report that all delegations be seated, George Vaughan, delegate from
Missouri, submitted a minority report in protest, charging that the
state convention of Mississippi had passed a resolution on June 22
requiring her delegation to withdraw from the convention unless
it upheld states' rights and repudiated Truman's program, and
requiring it furthermore not to pledge the support of the state
Democratic party if Truman was nominated, if anyone supporting
his program was nominated, if the platform advocated his civil
rights program, or if the convention failed to adopt a states' rights
plank. Vaughan called for unseating Mississippi. Adlai Stevenson
and Hubert Humphrey, among others, supported him, and though
he tried to speak heckling stopped him. The minority report was
rejected and the majority adopted by voice vote. Alben Barkley,
temporary chairman of the convention, ignored the Illinois and
California delegates' demand for a roll call and went on to other
business.[33]

Meanwhile, the ADA fought for a strong plank. The administration had sent a moderate civil rights plank to the platform committee, hoping not to offend the South. ADA members Hubert
Humphrey, Andrew Biemiller (ex-congressman from Wisconsin,
later lobbyist for the AFL-CIO), ex-Senator Hugh Mitchell of
Washington, and Esther Murray of California served on the platform committee and opposed the administration plank, calling it
a "sellout to states' rights over human rights." They demanded
that Frank Myers, chairman of the platform committee, add a
sentence calling on Congress to guarantee "the right to full and
equal political participation, the right to equal opportunity of
employment, the right of security of person, and the right of equal
treatment in the service and defense of our nation." But Myers,
a senator from Pennsylvania and friend of Truman, controlled the
committee, and a majority of its 108 members defeated the
minority plank; they hoped to prevent a row with the South.
That was Tuesday, July 13. The liberals planned to bring their
fight to the floor on Wednesday afternoon.[34]

But that night the liberals ran into trouble. Hubert Humphrey,
presumed to be the floor leader in the civil rights fight, wavered.
Mayor of Minneapolis, candidate for senator, Humphrey feared
for his campaign that fall. Some let him know that he threatened
to split the party and ensure defeat in November if he went along
with the ADA fight; he would not be popular with the party

organization. The liberals beseeched him through the night, until at 5 A.M., Wednesday morning, Eugenie Anderson, ADA chairman of Minnesota, thought to include this in the minority plank—"We highly commend President Harry Truman for his courageous stand on the issue of civil rights"—and thus at a stroke took the anti-Truman sting out of the liberal plank. Humphrey agreed. The next problem was to get Rayburn to call the roll, for the chair had refused to call it on Tuesday night when credentials was the issue, and it could do so again. Jack Shelley, a large man, a teamster, chairman of the California delegation and later mayor of San Francisco, warned Rayburn that if, on Wednesday afternoon, he refused to call the roll, Shelley and his delegates, seated in the front of the hall, would storm the rostrum. This was one way of forcing the issue. But another would appear later in the day.[35]

Wednesday morning the liberals lobbied for their plank. Jonathan Bingham, later congressman, got the support of Bronx boss Ed Flynn. Richardson Dilworth and Joseph Clark, later governor and senator of Pennsylvania, then with the ADA, persuaded David Lawrence, state party leader, to go along with the plank. ADA Chairman Leon Henderson went to Illinois leader Jacob Arvey, who promised to support the plank. Joseph Rauh of the ADA, floor leader of the liberal forces that day, went to several state delegations and was told he and his comrades were tearing the party apart. David K. Niles, Truman's assistant for minority affairs, told him, "You won't get 50 votes on your minority plank; all you'll do is ruin the chances of the number one prospect [Hubert Humphrey] for liberalism in this country." The Missouri and Kentucky delegations spurned Rauh, and said the fight was hopeless. Truman, through his emissaries—David Niles, Howard McGrath, Alben Barkley—and through such party leaders as Frank Myers and Sam Rayburn, put pressure on delegates to kill the minority plank, for the sake of party unity. He felt that his liberal programs of the last two years had punished the South enough—enough at least to split the party.[36]

He was right. When the delegates filed into the hall that afternoon there was in the air a sense of excitement and dread, the sense that comes before a confrontation whose outcome is still unclear. Senator Myers rose and presented the majority platform to the convention, including the bland civil rights plank asking Congress simply to work for protection of equal rights. Suddenly, Dan Moody, former governor of Texas, submitted a plank calling for endorsement of the principle of state sovereignty. Two other states' rights planks followed. The South, insulted by two years of Truman's civil rights pronouncements and threatened again in the last twenty-four hours by the liberals' rally, overplayed its hand, and in a rash miscalculation, broke its promise to Myers not to touch the civil rights issue. Speeches followed, one by Cecil Sims of Tennessee, ominously prophetic, who said: "If we from the South, having extended the hand of friendship to this Convention, if we are defeated, then I say to you that you are witnessing here today the dissolution of the Democratic Party in the South." Andrew Biemiller then submitted the liberals' plank and Humphrey spoke:

> Friends, delegates, I do not believe that there can be any compromise on the guarantees of the civil rights which we have mentioned in the minority report. In spite of my desire for unanimous agreement on the entire platform . . . there are some matters which I think must be stated clearly and without qualification. There can be no hedging. . . . My friends, to those who say that we are rushing this issue of civil rights, I say to them, we are 172 years late.

And, "The time has arrived for the Democratic Party to get out of the shadow of states' rights and walk forthrightly into the bright sunshine of human rights." He ended by demanding that the convention state "in unmistakable terms that we proudly hail and we courageously support our President and leader, Harry Truman, in his great fight for civil rights in America." A wild parade followed, lasting fifteen minutes, led by Paul Douglas of Illinois, in jubilant support of the civil rights revolt.[37]

The South had erred in presenting its planks—they were defeated three to one. Then the convention adopted the liberals' plank. The vote was 651½ to 582½. It was a startling victory.

Truman's position in all this was ambivalent. He opposed the minority planks, both Northern and Southern, for fear the fight would cost him the election. His Missouri delegation voted against the Biemiller plank; so did the Rhode Island and Kentucky delegations, controlled by his men, National Committee Chairman Howard McGrath and Senate Minority Leader Alben Barkley. But Truman himself was not opposed to the position of the Biemiller plank: on the contrary it endorsed his programs. He considered himself a staunch civil rights supporter and did not publicly denounce the plank. He thought that by his pronouncements in the last two years he had offended the South and strained the party enough and that, anyway, he could do more as president than as the defeated candidate of a broken party. Even the ADA leaders understood that Truman's opposition in Philadelphia was simply a matter of politics.[38]

But the fight was more than that: it was a matter of ideology. This was the first gathering of the nation's Democrats since the death of Roosevelt. The issue at stake was no less than what the party, in the post–New Deal, postwar era, should stand for. The reform of the New Deal had touched blacks only incidentally; and the 1940 and 1944 Democratic platforms had given affirmation to the right to live, develop, and vote equally, with no mention of specific proposals or congressional action. Truman had begun the new era by soundly committing the presidency to a spirited liberalism. Congress had begun it differently. It was up to this convention to decide what the Democrats wanted—a retreat as happened after the last war, when progressivism died, or an advance, which would carry the party, and perhaps the nation, beyond the New Deal. The party officials wanted neither; they wanted to win in November. The South wanted retreat, the liberals advance, and the latter won, not because the ADA controlled the convention, which it did not, but because of labor and the city machines. Jack Shelley epitomized the massive labor force, unionized and recognized during the New Deal, which saw the cause of labor linked to that of civil rights; he would storm the rostrum if Rayburn faltered. And Chicago's political leader, Jacob Arvey, a Jew, then launching the careers of Paul Douglas, Adlai Stevenson, and Richard Daley, epitomized the Northern big city politician, the machine man who was perhaps more sensitive than any other kind of politician to the rights and needs of minority peoples. (Arvey himself backed the Biemiller plank, though Chicago's black congressman, William Dawson, vice-president of the Democratic National Committee, stuck with the administration.) This was the sort of men who voted for the liberals' plank. They came from the same states that had absorbed three-quarters of the black migration, that had strong unions and city machines. They formed a slight majority of the convention, and when the ADA appealed to them, they defied the president to endorse the president's program, and stamped on the platform the title, "A Program of Progressive Liberalism."[39]

They also put the South in an intolerable position. A number of its delegations were bound by instructions similar to Mississippi's. All resented being associated with a party that not only applauded the president they had come to hate but also called for congressional action to protect the right of blacks to political participation, equal employment, personal security, and equal treatment in the armed services; they had fought this program in Congress already. Inimical to Southern white supremacy, these rights the party now declared to be "fundamental American principles." So later on that Wednesday day, in the convention's sixth session, when Alabama was called, its delegation chairman, Handy Ellis, rose to speak. He explained that, in the recent Democratic party convention held in the "Sovereign State of Alabama," a portion of the electors pledged themselves not to vote for Harry Truman and to walk out of the convention should a platform like this be adopted. Said Handy Ellis: "At this time in view of the platform as written, without hatred and without anger, and without fear, but with disillusionment and disappointment, we are faced with the necessity of carrying out our pledges to the people of Alabama. . . . we bid you good bye."[40]

Most Southerners stayed, uncomfortable and disheartened, including Lister Hill of Alabama. He yielded to Georgia, which put Richard Russell's name in nomination for president. J. Strom Thurmond seconded the nomination and said, "We believe that State sovereignty is a principle which transcends parties and personalities and cannot be surrendered under any circumstances." But that night Truman was nominated, and he gave a rousing speech, denouncing the Republicans and announcing his call for a special session of Congress to meet after the convention to enact his program. The liberals rejoiced, Joe Rauh saying later that at last the "Democratic Party became the party of commitment to equal opportunity for all citizens." But there was no motion to make Truman's nomination unanimous; the party was deeply split. Thirty-five delegates had walked out. Strom Thurmond explained the problem: the difference between this convention's avowal of equality and previous declarations was that Truman "really means it."[41]

After the convention, Truman returned to Washington, signed his executive orders banning discrimination in the military and civil service on July 26, and the next day sent again to the Hill his priority bills on price controls and housing, education and the 75-cent minimum wage, increased social security and federal power projects, and civil rights. Strom Thurmond returned to the South, and in Birmingham, Alabama, was nominated the presidential candidate of the States' Rights Democrats, or Dixiecrats, who, in the fall elections, carried four states—Alabama, Mississippi,

Louisiana, and South Carolina. These were among the first states to secede in 1860-61. They were the Deep South; their politics turned on race. They were states that did not go for Hoover in 1928, when much of the greater South did, because they feared the effect of Republican rule on white supremacy, or, put differently, they responded to the dictates of the Southern mind, which linked the Democratic party to all Southern things, especially solidarity and white supremacy. They would split again in 1964 and vote for Goldwater, in 1968 (with Georgia but without South Carolina) and vote for George Wallace—they were intractable. They responded reflexively, their race nerve was sensitive, and in 1948 Truman had touched it.

But in the fall campaign, Truman did not address himself to the Dixiecrats, nor to Henry Wallace, who flanked him on the left, nor even to Dewey on the right. For Truman was in an odd position. The Dixiecrats could only gain by his attack, so he left them alone. And Wallace posed little threat. In style he seemed left of Truman, but he went no further nor could become more liberal than Truman. On social issues the Democratic platform spoke a liberal line, partly because labor and the city bosses had Wallace in mind when they framed it. And in foreign affairs, Wallace stood for appeasement, not a popular position in the year of the Czech coup and the Berlin blockade. Dewey, on the other hand, was a cautious man, thus not an easy target. Truman waged his campaign, then, against the Republican Eightieth Congress. He attacked its attempt to repeal the New Deal, ran on the Democratic platform, and got the help of its backers—the CIO, the Liberal party, the ADA, and the Farmers Union.

His appeal was to those who relied on the beneficence of the federal government. On October 24, at a rally in the Chicago stadium, Truman warned against the "dangerous men" who made war on democracy and on "Catholics, and Jews, and Negroes." Four days later he carried his attack on Congress into Harlem, where he defended his civil rights program.[42] He went to the Midwest, where he told the farmers that the Republicans planned to end price supports. In Los Angeles he said: "The Democratic Party is the party which truly expresses the hopes of American liberals"; and in St. Paul, "Now, I call on all liberals and progressives to stand up and be counted for democracy in this great battle. I call on the old Farmer-Labor Party, the old Wisconsin Progressives, the Non-Partisan Leaguers, and the New Dealers to stand up and be counted in this fight." Battling three opponents, two of them former Democrats, Truman rose to the occasion. Never able to deliver a speech well—partly because his sight was so poor he could not read the page—he spoke extemporaneously and at last came across (sometimes as a demagogue): "I am on a crusade," he told a Missouri crowd, "for the welfare of the everyday man." "All over the country they call me Harry. I like it. I believe when you speak to me like that you really do like me—and I want you to like me because I'm trying my best to serve you with everything I have."[43] He did, in short, what Rowe had suggested the year before—he made a bid for the votes of labor, blacks, farmers, the old, a bid to those who needed help from Washington. It was a liberal bid—as liberalism had changed—and it worked.

After the election, in January 1949, Truman gave his State of the Union message and announced the Fair Deal, the package of legislative requests he had been presenting for almost four years, now given a special name. But the name helped some, and liberals recognized as they had not before that Truman was their leader, committed to social reform. Now he worked more closely with the ADA and made friends with its leaders. The administration's liberal accent became, in short, more pronounced. At the same time, liberals began to define their creed, and as they did they placed it in the mainstream of American reform; they believed, as Arthur Schlesinger, Jr., said, that they were the "vital center" of American politics. Truman himself said he stood "between the reactionaries of the extreme left with their talk about revolution and class warfare, and the reactionaries of the extreme right with their hysterical cries of bankruptcy and despair"; there between lay "the way of progress."[44]

But the politics of Truman's second administration, and indeed of the years after, seemed to belie this judgment. For the center was not overly broad, nor was it vital but to a handful of liberals. In 1948, after all, more Americans voted against Truman than for him. And in Congress he had no command. The administration won a victory early in 1949, when Democrats ended the House Rules Committee's power to strangle legislation, but that was almost the last one. In February, when Congress faced Truman's civil rights program, important for its symbolic meaning as well as its substance, the South began to filibuster, blocking a change of the cloture rule, which required a two-thirds vote of the Senate to cut off debate. The South won by wearing down the administration's resolve, and in March cloture by two-thirds was kept. Truman later denounced the Dixiecrats and expelled from the national committee those who had endorsed Thurmond the year before, but this only revealed—and sharpened—the fracture in his Democratic base. The Southerners caucused separately and joined the Republicans to defeat not only civil rights but also the health insurance plan and the repeal of the Taft-Hartley Act. Truman continued to plug for the Fair Deal—more veterans' and social security benefits, expanded unemployment compensation, and higher minimum wages—but got little of it. He had no mandate.[45]

Some would blame the Korean War and the loyalty fights for submerging the liberal program. But Communists were hardly the problem. The Republican and Dixiecrat alliance, which had stalled Truman's efforts since he first took office, continued to run Congress during his second term. When Truman appointed a committee to fulfill his pledge to integrate the armed forces, he met resistance on the Hill and then in other quarters, mostly those of the army. He succeeded in forcing the army to end its racial quota but terminated the committee when Defense Department pressure mounted. He appointed a black judge to the federal circuit, the first such appointment, but met resistance in the Senate Judiciary Committee, which finally gave in after intense lobbying by the ADA and the White House. On fair employment practices, Southerners offered to compromise with a voluntary FEPC, hardly a compromise. Truman rejected it outright and stuck to his bill for a strong commission, which succumbed to a filibuster in May 1950. And things got worse. That spring Congress deregulated natural gas, but Truman vetoed the bill. That fall Everett Dirksen defeated Senate Majority Leader Scott Lucas, and Robert Taft survived a strong labor campaign to oust him from his Ohio seat. And the incoming Eighty-second Congress proved no less stubborn on social issues, passing in 1951 a bill (which Truman vetoed) permitting segregation in federally financed schools in the South. Korea was not the problem—not even an issue until June 1950. The problem was rather one of votes, for though the Democrats controlled Congress, the liberals did not; and though assuredly there was a vital center, the liberals did not compose it.[46]

Truman ended his years in office as be began them—with little support. The Korean War was unpopular. A cloud of corruption befell his administration; recession and inflation and strikes rocked the economy; and loyalty hunts unsettled everyone. By February 1952 one magazine said that only the blacks supported Truman, and indeed their support may provide a clue to the source of Truman's troubled leadership.[47] Truman had altered the lines of liberal dogma, had gone beyond the New Deal to make active government and civil rights articles of the liberal faith. And the tide was against him. Little of his program was passed—though it would not be forgotten. In the years ahead the measures he fought for, especially civil rights laws, would dominate Democratic politics, until Congress enacted them in Johnson's Great Society.

Through the spring of 1952 he spoke for his Fair Deal and searched for a liberal successor, who, once found, was overwhelmed that fall by the champion of the vigorous, if not vital, center, Dwight Eisenhower. In May, Truman addressed an ADA dinner and gave a rousing liberal speech. Listening was his wife, whom he had met when he was a boy. Over dinner, when Francis Biddle told her proudly that Groton Academy was integrated, she turned to a companion and said, "they [blacks] should have their schools and we should have ours."[48] Truman's background never left him; it sometimes pulled him up. But when it weighed him down, as it must have on civil rights, he overcame it, and committed the Democrats to a program and a struggle.

SIX

THE TRUCE OF 1952

In 1952 the intention of the party was to forget its troubles, its program and its schism. The 1948 convention had jolted the South, which had not expected such harsh repudiation of its ways, and whose bolt from the party had accomplished little. Now, in 1952, it wanted to get along. Northern Democrats sensed Republican resurgence and also wanted peace. Everyone wanted the calm that comes with blandness; few wanted discord. Everyone wanted to win.[1]

The 1950s was a time, so the story goes, when America was complacent, happy with peace and prosperity and a rising birth rate, when the government's greatest contribution to the quality of life was the interstate highway system, and when the people, weary of war and reform, asked for nothing more. Whether accurate or not, this picture of apathy leaves something out—the unceasing struggle over the liberal program left by Truman. Conservatives dominated Congress and the Republicans; liberals, by a hair, had won control of the Democrats. The future was uncertain. The fight continued. It was an ideological fight, often centering on civil rights, and it took place in the Democratic party, where the Northern and Southern wings embodied in purest form the nation's competing ideologies. The Democrats fought each other at every opportunity and made every decision—candidates, platforms, jobs, and Senate office space—a contest of ideology. In a sense, they grappled with the issues the nation at large ignored. For the people may indeed have been complacent—a recent study of voter attitudes has shown that they were, that in the 1950s they had little sense of the issues, little interest or understanding. But it has also shown that they identified with the parties and voted along party lines, much more than they would in the 1960s and 1970s.[2] The people let the parties do their thinking for them, let them sort out the issues and form an ideology. The Democrats performed their chore. They struggled throughout the decade, and let the nation sleep.

For them, it was anything but a complacent decade, as from 1952 to 1960 they gradually became the liberal party that Truman had wanted. It was a slow and painful transformation, resisted by the South. The first step, in 1952, was to compose the differences that had split the party in 1948, for the party could neither decide its future nor win elections if it did not hang together. So when the Democrats went to Chicago to write a platform and choose a nominee, they went looking for a compromise, which explained why, of the two principal candidates, Adlai Stevenson and Estes Kefauver, one was inexorably right for the time and the other inexorably wrong.

Stevenson

Contrary to popular belief and unlike most northern Democratic leaders of the 1950s, Adlai Stevenson had a basically conservative bent. He was more inclined to inaction than action, and when confronted with the growing liberalism of his party, an activist creed, he became uneasy, sometimes ambivalent. Yet his ambivalence was not the sort that derived from the opportunistic attitude of a calculating politician. It was a queer wavering. Sometimes Stevenson seemed unsure of himself and of the importance of the issues. Other times, thinking they were so important, he saw all sides of the issues and would not take a stance. During the four years of his governorship, he exhibited the qualities of a firm, directed leader; and after that he led almost alone the battle against McCarthy. But on issues other than civil liberties, and most specially on civil rights, in 1952 and beyond, this uncertainty and constant vacillation returned to plague him—and aid him. Never an ideologue, Stevenson felt remote from his party's raging ideological storm; and by staying clear of it, he kept himself afloat.

As a child Stevenson grew up in the quiet midwestern town of Bloomington in downstate Illinois. As an adult he lived off the substantial profits of the family newspaper, the *Pantagraph,* and enjoyed the company of his Lake Forest friends. Like most white rural midwesterners growing up in the early twentieth century, he lived amid racism and did not entirely shed its vestiges in later life. In Bloomington his family had a black servant, Sambo, who slept

on the basement's dirt floor in the winter and under the trees in
the yard in the summer. One warm night Stevenson's father put
a sheet over himself and went out under the trees to scare Sambo.[3]
As a young administrator in the Roosevelt administration, Adlai
Stevenson wrote to his wife Ellen of the many Jews in Washington, explaining that their "racial characteristics" were more pronounced in some than in others.[4] On the night that John Kennedy
failed to win the Democratic nomination for vice-president, Stevenson's sister, Buffie Ives, said to a table of guests, "Oh, those poor
little Catholics."[5] Stevenson was by no means a racist; he was too
intelligent and thoughtful a man to subscribe to the vulgar racial
theories that gained so much currency in the years of his youth.
But neither was he wholly free of the prejudice that inhered in
American society. Even his closest advisors realized that he never
appreciated the civil rights of minority groups so fully as he
appreciated civil liberties.[6]

Stevenson saw himself as a conciliator, not a partisan. He said
on one occasion in 1952:

> I would urge in these fields and in many others that affect national
> policy, that all of us resolve to take a fresh look. There has been too
> much freezing of positions, too much emotion, too many dogmatic
> statements of irrevocable attitudes. We are dealing with human situ-
> ations, with human emotions, with human intelligence; our purpose
> must be to reason together for a common betterment of us all; our
> interest must be, not in controversy, but in results.[7]

Laudable and rare as this conciliatory spirit was, Stevenson seemed
seldom to freeze a position, seldom became emotionally immersed
in his work, seldom adhered to a consistent dogma. This temperament suited the times, when passions were too aroused and division
too deep for a man to rule by imposing dogma from above; it
was Stevenson's ambivalence that enabled him to rule, or, better,
preside, over the Democrats in the 1950s, and inherent in his rule
was the ability to be swept along by forces he neither liked nor
fully understood. Yet inherent also was the inability to commit
himself to issues.

At times he displayed almost a frivolousness, as if the business
of public affairs were a lark. During his governorship of Illinois,
from 1949 to 1953, he wrote to intimate friends—he loved to
write by hand to his friends—of his mood: "I suspect my political
fortunes are fading. But I don't mind and I'm having fun. If only

somehow, sometime I could get the day cut from 16 to 10 hours I'd really be happy in this job at last."[8] Other times he forced a show of earnestness. During a television broadcast, the "Governor's Open House," Stevenson told several jokes, chatted with his secretary, and then spoke extemporaneously, in contrived, dull fashion, of the Cicero race riot, an episode of particularly nasty violence. The impression was one of a man who enjoyed himself while entertaining an audience with eloquence and wit and who also felt obliged to perform the uninteresting, onerous tasks expected of a leader.[9]

All this—his childhood and conciliatory temperament—rendered Stevenson unsuited to lead the civil rights fight. And he did not take an interest in the issue until forced by political necessity. "He began to care about civil rights in the 1950s," one aide recalled, "when he was confronted with it as an issue."[10] It is doubtful, however, that he ever cared deeply about the movement. Political machine leader Jacob Arvey observed that Stevenson disliked addressing Catholic, Jewish, and black groups; he found it trying to say what they wanted to hear, but if he did not the situation became awkward. Once in a conversation he complained that the NAACP was bothering the mayor of Atlanta. And on another occasion he spoke ill of then civil rights lawyer Thurgood Marshall, who was, according to Stevenson, "stirring up racial trouble in Cairo, Illinois." As for the South, Stevenson praised it often in speeches, mentioning sometimes his Southern forebears. Southern Democratic leaders returned the compliments, saying he was their only Northern friend. One said that at first Stevenson reminded them of Woodrow Wilson.[11]

Perhaps more than anything else Stevenson simply did not understand the civil rights issue. He expressed dismay that blacks should attack him and his party when both had done so much for them. During the 1952 campaign, when Stevenson and his advisors feared that blacks and the press would make an issue of Stevenson's staff staying in a segregated motel, where black reporters were barred, Stevenson, irritated, asked his advisors, "Why can't they go somewhere else? Are they just trying to embarrass us?" The advisors explained that the issue was delicate and some felt strongly about it. This blunted perception and indifference to civil rights may have been abetted by the sanguine notion that blacks were permanently Democratic. An intimate friend told him once that Truman had captured the black vote forever and that if Stevenson took a less liberal position on civil rights it would not affect blacks' Democratic allegiance.[12] Perhaps this thought entered Stevenson's calculation; or perhaps he had no calculation and acted instead on instinct: it was always hard to tell. In the 1948 convention he had voted for the ADA civil rights plank (as did all the Illinois delegation, controlled by Arvey); but that night, when Truman and Barkley were nominated, he seconded Barkley's nomination and spoke highly of "Southern courage"—the same courage, of course, which had inspired several delegations to bolt the convention earlier that day.[13] Either Stevenson was carefully placating both sides in the dispute, or he failed to see the meaning of his words, and hence the meaning of the civil rights fight. In any case, neither then nor later did he evince deep sympathy for black Americans.

There was one exception, an important one. In the most eloquent speech on civil rights in his career, delivered September 6, 1948, in Brooklyn, Illinois, he praised Harry Truman, called for an Illinois FEPC, and ended: "Day in and night out, month in and month out, we shall lay brick against brick, plank against plank to form the structure of life which will bring us a bit nearer to the society of our dreams." His speeches always were inspiring.[14]

But Brooklyn was an exception. Here he spoke to an all-black audience in a town founded for blacks. Although he mentioned the FEPC, his emphasis was on education, a lifelong concern. And he never gave a civil rights speech so strong as this during his next two campaigns. Brooklyn was an exception in another way, for there he praised Harry Truman. Stevenson and Truman differed in several ways. Truman was dogmatic, Stevenson was not; Truman, judging by his public utterances, had overcome whatever prejudice he grew up with; Stevenson had not. Truman understood the civil rights movement; Stevenson did not. They never got along very well. One Truman aide thought Stevenson felt uncomfortable, perhaps embarrassed, "in the company of Truman politicians," as if he considered them beneath himself.[15] There were political problems, too. Truman was unpopular, and Stevenson considered him a liability in 1952, and therefore dissociated himself from the president by locating his headquarters in Springfield, instead of Washington. (Truman would not forget.) Even before this, in 1948, when Stevenson ran for governor and Truman for president, the former kept his distance from the latter. When the president toured Illinois on September 30, the major Democratic candidates accompanied him, but not Stevenson.

And, speaking at the Chicago stadium on October 24, the campaign windup, Stevenson said of Truman, in his presence: "They have called him an impulsive blunderer. Of course he has made mistakes—human mistakes, mistakes of the heart." In his speech, Truman spoke of the dangers of religious and racial prejudice.[16] Stevenson was always to have trouble with Truman.

Yet despite all this—his preference for conciliation, his indifference to civil rights, his troubles with Truman—Stevenson established a reputation as a liberal. Intellectuals and liberals misunderstood him for several reasons, but first because of his actions while governor of Illinois. Stevenson took strong stands on the FEPC, military desegregation, and, the "Governor's Open House" notwithstanding, the Cicero race riot. The Republican Senate in the Illinois legislature defeated the FEPC in 1949 but could not keep him from desegregating the National Guard. In 1951 Stevenson sent the Guard to the Chicago suburb of Cicero when its largely East European workingman population rioted against a black family trying to move into town. These actions were not radical, but they were new; an Illinois governor had never done such things. (In view of his victory by a half million votes, Stevenson by no means risked his political future.) But it was his opposition which most of all built up his liberal credentials. When he pushed for the FEPC, as when he brought Louis Armstrong to play at the Illinois inaugural ball, a furor arose, especially among business groups, and Stevenson, by comparison, appeared a fighting liberal.[17] He further endeared himself to national liberals by vetoing the Broyles bill, an anticommunist loyalty bill, and by giving a deposition attesting to the good reputation of Alger Hiss, on trial for perjury.

This record, and also the attack from the right, prompted liberal groups in Illinois to ally themselves with Stevenson. In 1949, the Illinois State Federation of Labor announced that it supported him and the FEPC, and furthermore pledged members of Illinois unions affiliated with the AFL behind the legislation. In Chicago, the City Club's race relations committee wrote Stevenson that it would do everything possible to help him pass the FEPC. Gilbert Gordon, regional attorney for the Commission on Law and Social Action of the American Jewish Congress, wrote an article urging Stevenson to join with the CIO unions, the Federation of Labor, the League of Women Voters, the Independent Voters of Illinois, and minority group organizations in support of the FEPC.[18] Following a corrupt and ineffectual Republican administration, Stevenson easily won the backing of Illinois' liberals.

Stevenson impressed liberals for one final reason—his style. He was not himself an intellectual (and had trouble enough in Harvard Law School to drop out, finishing at Northwestern). He loved to talk but disliked reading books; one aide had difficulty getting Stevenson to read the position papers and reports drafted for his use. Yet he was quick, he spoke with charm and intelligence, and he was funny. In the low world of glib and dull politicians, Stevenson raised political discourse to a new and high level, and stood apart from the others—not only as a thoughtful man, dedicated to educating the public, but as a fresh and lively presence. And, though not an intellectual, he had the ability to gather about him a herd of intellectuals—Harvard professors Arthur Schlesinger, Jr., John Kenneth Galbraith, and Seymour Harris; Oberlin's professor Robert Tufts; Northwestern's professor Willard Wirtz; and writers Archibald MacLeish, Bernard DeVoto, Robert Sherwood, and John Bartlow Martin. From them, he got his ideas and his speeches. What he lacked in commitment, especially in commitment to liberal programs, they—and Stevenson himself, occasionally—made up for in words, words like those he spoke in his November 1951 Gettysburg battlefield address, typical for its sparkling phrases and typical, too, for its treatment of civil rights, which was brief. On the eighty-eighth anniversary of the battle, he spent one minute on blacks and equality: "In making slavery the foundation stone of their government, the Confederacy was renouncing the doctrine of the equal rights of man in favor of the creed of the master race, an idea that Lincoln abhorred. . . . [The] Declaration of Independence . . . affirmed that all men are created equal, that they are endowed by their Creator with certain inalienable rights, among which are life, liberty, and the pursuit of happiness." Another, more important speech, was his address to the National Urban League at the Waldorf-Astoria Hotel in January 1952. He spoke of the immorality of prejudice and discrimination, yet avoided specific proposals, praised the South's progress, and approached civil rights from a side angle, not directly— Cicero was bad because it helped the Communists abroad. And he dwelt, as usual, on the need to educate the public. His detachment was plain.[19]

Yet liberals across the country responded to his intellectual tone. They overlooked Stevenson's absence of emotion and bold reforms—the FEPC bill was his only major civil rights issue as governor, and by 1952 it was not so bold—and it mattered little that he rarely cracked a book. He was an intelligent, sensitive man, seemed an intellectual, and sounded liberal. (Truman, on the other hand, an avid reader of history and advocate of far-reaching civil rights legislation, had a different style and, though he collaborated with liberals, never shook the image of party hack.) Stevenson impressed people immediately as a liberal and, moreover, as a strong, determined leader. In 1948, when he had just been elected to his first office, Arthur Krock suggested Stevenson might be the Democrats' presidential nominee in 1952. After the Cicero riot, Ralph Bunche congratulated Stevenson, saying Illinois and the nation were in debt to his courage; later he said the Governor would make an "excellent President." Harold Ickes also complimented Stevenson on his action in the Cicero affair. And after the Urban League speech, Jim Farley congratulated him, and the assistant superintendent of New York City's Board of Education told Stevenson it would be "an inspiration for a long, long time."[20]

Adlai Stevenson did not dupe the American intellectual community: rather, it misread him. He was not an intellectual but felt comfortable among them, not a liberal but worked with them, and not an ideologue but could with effort get along with them too. Above all he was flexible, a bridge to both sides, a healer rather than a warrior. As the 1950s passed, as the ideological struggle within his party intensified, and as in the end the liberals won, Stevenson, pushed by his advisors, became increasingly what the liberals thought he was all along. And Southerners, as time wore on, got worried. But all this was not his doing, neither the struggle nor his movement, for throughout his life moderation remained his goal: to understand, educate, appease, and moderate were the duties he recognized as his. He was indeed an "inspiration for a long, long time," but never a crusader. Yet, for his style and his moderation, for his overseeing the party in the years of the liberals' struggle and triumph, he may have been if not the spokesman then perhaps the caretaker of modern liberalism, justly claimed by liberal heirs and justly maligned by the South.

Kefauver

Near the corner where Tennessee meets Georgia and North Carolina, rise the Unico Mountains, a spur in the Appalachian Range, and on their slopes rests the county of Monroe. Monroe, like other Southern uphill country, unsuited for large plantations, supported small farmers who seldom owned slaves, and during the Civil War it joined the rest of eastern Tennessee in sending 30,000 sons of her state to fight on the Union side. Kentucky also split down the middle, and even in the Deep South, in Mississippi, Jones County refused to secede. After the war the wounds of division lingered on, and these counties stayed loyal to the Union cause; they voted Republican. Pockets of dissent scattered about the South, they remained a sore to the eyes of Southern orators, who preached the romance of a solid and Democratic South. An ugly fact is a hard thing for men of romance, and these orators did what they could to treat it with humor, although an uncertain humor, edged with contempt—they named Jones the "Free State of Jones," and today the name still sticks. Any Democrat who dared to succeed in one of these wayward counties was a brave politician and a loyal Southerner, breaking out of the local pattern, which itself had broken free from the Southern pattern; and so it is of interest that, born and raised in Monroe County, in the town of Madisonville, the grandson of a Baptist preacher, Estes Kefauver was early on a Democrat.

Kefauver was a big man. He was six feet three inches tall, weighed 215 pounds, and had overly-large features and an unbridled ambition. He was a man bent on doing battle. Pugilistic in the way Stevenson was not, he upset the Crump machine in Tennessee and later bucked Truman's leadership in the nation. In high school he announced he wanted to become president, in college he headed the Southern Federation of College Students (the first such president from the University of Tennessee). In public he was untiring, known for his relentless handshaking. In private he was, like most politicians, impenetrable and reserved, perhaps, as some have said, because of the horror he felt at the age of eleven, when he and his brother went swimming and he saw his brother drown. (Stevenson also had a childhood trauma: when he was twelve he accidentally shot and killed a girl.)[21] Kefauver was charming and ebullient, possessed of a grand style—dramatic congressional hearings, an instant smile, slashing attacks and quick denials, and, in the 1952 campaign, the coonskin cap and Kefauver coonskin cap clubs. Many in his party despised him.

It was difficult to like a Southerner whose ambition it was to become the president, and Kefauver had a powerful ambition. It had strung for him a thin wire that made uneasy walking. On the one hand pulled the rigors of Southern politics, on the other the rigors of national politics, and these last became, as time went on, more rigorous. For if Kefauver was to succeed, he had to present himself, a Southerner, as more committed to civil rights than any other Northerner. As he did so, he got caught like any popular leader in the demands of his own ideology; he could never retreat on civil rights but had to be ever more strident. He became desperate, sometimes shrill, in his effort to prove his commitment, and the louder he proclaimed it the more it seemed but a necessity of his ambition. Walking this unyielding wire Kefauver became known among his Southern confederates as not only a man "strong as a bull" but also a "selfish man," "a renegade of the South," and among many Northern liberals as a phoney and a playboy.[22]

Like Huey Long before him and James Carter after him, Kefauver had to be several things to several regions. Upon becoming congressman, an achievement he dismissed by saying, "They're a dime a dozen, but you know it might just lead to something," he voted for civil rights legislation intended to protect the black man's right to vote.[23] Later he voted with liberal Democrats to eliminate the poll tax and other disfranchising devices. But here came the end of consistency, for this was the only civil rights position that he reached early in his career and stuck to for the rest of his life. Even on this issue, his valor was less than met the eye: he knew that Southerners had many ways, should they choose them, of keeping the vote from the black. And on other civil rights issues, Kefauver shifted to fit the year and locale.

When Tennessee was on his mind, he was a Southerner. On March 17, 1949, Kefauver voted with Southern conservatives for the Wherry Rule (later Rule 22), which said that sixty-four senators were required to limit debate and which allowed a handful of men, primarily segregationists, to prevent civil rights measures from ever coming to a vote. Ten years later, in 1959, after two presidential campaigns, he again helped defeat a cloture bill. In 1949 he wrote a constituent: "I do feel that the enactment of an anti-lynch law now would be a mistake. We are making voluntary headway in solving lynching problems—only two were reported last year—and I believe an anti-lynch law would do more harm than good."[24] He opposed a compulsory federal FEPC and supported a voluntary one, but said in 1952 that if his party adopted a plank calling for the FEPC he would support the party. He was cagey on Truman's civil rights program. On June 8, 1951, Kefauver wrote to a correspondent: "I am opposed to all the civil rights program except the provisions to repeal the poll tax, and to reform election laws to prevent fraud." And once he made a broadcast on the subject to his constituents: "I have stated time and time again and restate now, that I am opposed to all of the President's civil rights bill as now written except that I favor preventing election frauds and favor repealing the poll tax."[25]

To the nation, however, he said the opposite. "I have supported most of the President's civil rights program," he wrote to a councilman in Los Angeles, California, where he planned to enter the primary. "I led the fight for Home Rule for the District of Columbia, which is part of the Civil Rights program. . . . I have joined in opposition to the filibuster."[26] He supported civil rights in the nation because he had to: He came from the South. He knew that his only hope was to take strong civil rights positions and try by them to split the party and win the nomination. He employed this tactic in 1952 and 1956, and in the process did more than any other Democrat to push his party left. Thus in 1956 he greatly influenced Stevenson by accusing him of taking an equivocal position on the Supreme Court's school desegregation decision. Yet still Kefauver could never escape his constituency, and two years later, about the same decision, he wrote to a constituent in Memphis, "There is no doubt that relations between the two races have seriously deteriorated since the hasty and somewhat unfortunate action of the Supreme Court."[27]

Kefauver's difficulty was understandable. His people were Southern, ruled by Southern fears. One exhorted him not to become a "niggers' politician." Another, deploring the effects of the *Brown* decision, warned him: "Now as I understand the South, the South says Caucasian marries Caucasian—not Mongolian anymore than Negroid."[28] Having to heed this constituency, Kefauver compromised himself with his national constituency, and the effort to reconcile the two sometimes drew him into intricate explanations of his behavior. Such was the case in 1956, when his aide Jiggs Donohue compiled a list of bad votes—those that would hurt Kefauver in the Northern primaries—and possible excuses for them. One concerned the Selective Service Act of 1950: Kefauver voted against an amendment to eliminate a provision for voluntary segregation in the armed forces if a majority of the personnel expressed such a preference. The aide advised: "This seems to be a genuinely bad vote. No other liberal Senators voted with the Senator on this; the amendment was passed 42 to 29. Best way to handle this is to . . . describe it as a rider to 'good legislation,' and to argue that passage of the rider would have

endangered the necessary passage of the selective service act."
(Inasmuch as both the amendment and the bill passed, this seemed
shaky advice.) On the Selective Service Act of 1951, Kefauver
voted to kill another civil rights amendment, and Donohue coun-
seled the same defense, adding that the amendment violated
states' rights. He concluded that, "Voting with Senator Kefauver
were almost all Senators considered liberal on civil rights questions—including Martin, Chavez, Wherry, Taft, Tobey, Williams,
Smith (of Maine), Monroney, and Nixon."[29] If one were looking
for liberals, this was a desperate choice of company.

But Kefauver was a little desperate, after all, as any man would
be who tried to reconcile his Southern and Northern constituencies
in the 1950s. Perhaps it was this desperate quality which prevented
him, though be became the strongest advocate of civil rights in
the Democratic party, from ever being a friend to many liberals.
There were other qualities. He had a reputation for drinking and
promiscuity,[30] proclivities which represented no inability to hold
liberal convictions, but which, when combined with his political
behavior, suggested a driven or frantic man—acting the racist to
become congressman, the statesman to become president, employ-
ing such devices as the coonskin caps and clubs and sometimes
reckless campaign remarks, leaning on Donohue to straighten
things out when the press bore down too hard. Kefauver gave the
impression not of probity and conviction but of rashness and
ambition, and it may be for this reason that liberal intellectuals
were not, as they were with Stevenson, among his close associates. Yet he also lost his Southern friends, who never forgave his
apostasy and believed he did what he did only to win black and
Northern votes. A liberal when liberals needed friends, Kefauver
often stood alone.

Alone he must have been in 1952, when, after campaigning
for months, he lost the nomination to Stevenson, who campaigned
not at all. Kefauver wrote himself a note. A strange note, written
by hand, with eccentric grammar, it said:

> S.[tevenson] would loose if election held today. . . . K.[efauver]
> wants to help in every appropriate way but aid can be substantial or
> less so depending on way S. wishes to use help. . . . [I have] over
> 3000 clubs or committees composed of loyal, crusading, idealistic
> people. . . . These people largely look to K as leader. Most will help
> but not with enthusiasm unless they are told their cause will be fur-
> thered. At present they feel a) S. has been put in by bosses and
> T.[ruman] in a somewhat controlled convention b) They are leary of

S. and will carry on T. group and T. will have great say so. c) They
are leary of S. efforts to clean out corruption, palace guard and
Crime. D. They fear S. will recognize and do business with same old
worn out bosses the states. . . . K. can help greatly (especially
in Calif-Oregon-Wash-S.D.-Neb-Ohio-Mich-Penn-N.Y.-N.J.-Mass-N.H.-
Ariz-N.M.-) if able to effectively and consciently persuade my followers. . . . K. can be very effective if statements and action show
these things will be done. Also it is necessary that there be transition links and letters K to Nat. Comm. and that K. groups be recognized in Nat. Comm. . . . K. be given important place in campaign.[31]

A power in politics, a mover in ideas and shaper of opinion,
a threat to his colleagues who felt less sure of issues and saw some
gray, Kefauver was also, it seems, a somewhat lonely man, who
had become persuaded himself by the image he created to persuade
other people.

The Convention

By early 1952 the party had grown restless under Truman's
rule. Leaders announced their candidacy for the presidency every
few weeks, sniped at one another, and staked out hard positions
on race and labor. This went on all spring. Then at Chicago they
met and composed their differences and settled on the one who
never announced, Adlai Stevenson.

Kefauver announced his candidacy on January 23 and promised
to clean up government, a promise embarrassing to Truman, whose
aides had recently fallen under suspicion of corruption. Moreover,
the president had not yet taken himself out of the race, and to
announce as Kefauver did was to insult Truman, to appeal to those
Democrats who disliked Truman personally but approved of his
liberal policies. Said Paul H. Douglas, "Estes Kefauver is a Southerner we Northerners go for"—though some Northerners, most
Democrats, and certainly Truman bristled when Kefauver brought
his congressional crime committee into Illinois and helped defeat
Senator Scott Lucas, Truman's majority leader, for reelection.
Soon Truman announced his decision, made two years before, not
to run.[32] He thought Stevenson the right man to carry on the
liberal standard and summoned him to a meeting on January 22,
1952. Stevenson came but declined to run, citing his unfinished
business in Illinois. Others urged him. In early spring Joseph Rauh
and James Loeb of the ADA went to Springfield and pressed him;
Stevenson cited his work. In March, Truman tried again but Steven-

son again demurred. Truman grew uneasy: he did not abandon this unusual governor from Illinois, but he was unsure of him, and also of the Democrats' plight.[33]

Alben Barkley and Richard Russell rose to represent the moderate and conservative wings of the party. Barkley of Kentucky, a New Deal Southerner, announced May 29 and attracted people that liked Truman but not his policies. A moderate favoring calm in a time of stress, he spoke for party unity; but labor would not have him. Russell of Georgia announced in February and left open the possibility that he and the disgruntled Dixiecrats might bolt the party if provoked. When Averell Harriman of New York announced on April 22, this was not a distant possibility, for now with two candidates claiming the New Deal–Fair Deal heritage— he and Kefauver—the competition in liberal professions might move so fast as to provoke the South. Kefauver won the New Hampshire primary on March 11 and appeared to be gathering steam; Truman distrusted him. Stevenson formally withdrew on April 16, and Harriman's attempt to head off Kefauver was foundering. Truman grew anxious. Meanwhile, as Kefauver gained, so did Russell, who was the first candidate to break the Kefauver string of primary victories when, in the May 6 Florida primary, he beat Kefauver by almost 100,000 votes. The party was polarizing, a leader was lacking. For a moment, Truman thought to run again but decided against it.[34]

On May 17 he again implored Stevenson to enter the race. Stevenson responded: "My life is undiluted anguish," a characteristic response, which did little to allay Truman's anxiety.[35] But the response did not reveal all of Stevenson's thinking, for although he formally withdrew on April 16, he already had begun making speeches outside Illinois and did not stop. He sought advice all spring, and liberals and intellectuals gave it, urging him to make concrete proposals on civil rights and other liberal issues. For they, like Truman, were distressed by the turn of events: Kefauver was divisive; Harriman, who himself had urged Stevenson to run, never had held elective office and had a narrow base; the Southern old guard might control the convention. Arthur Schlesinger, Jr., wrote Stevenson on April 8: The liberals must head off the Southern attempt to capture the party, he said; they must rally around a liberal candidate. If they could not have Stevenson they would settle for Kefauver, but they preferred Stevenson. Schlesinger urged him to take "strong Fair Deal positions on these issues. . . . The important thing is not to be outflanked on the left by

Kefauver." (The fear of being outflanked by Kefauver would be a continuing concern for Stevenson, affecting his and his party's positions for the next several years.) "What you must have," Schlesinger said, "is the crusading enthusiasm of the labor and independent groups. I don't think that people like Reuther and Humphrey want you to be 'active' in a geographical sense. What they want is clear and militant leadership on issues. What they care about particularly is that you seem firmly opposed to the southern attempt to go back to the days of John J. Raskob and Jouett Shouse."[36]

Militant liberal leadership, crusading enthusiasm, firm commitment to the issues—these were the things Stevenson lacked. Just a week before, he had told Harriman and Schlesinger, when they pressed him to run, "This will probably shock you all; but at the moment I don't give a god damn what happens to the party or to the country." Harriman thought Stevenson tired, confused, and suffering from a cold, but whatever the ailment, it was clear that if Stevenson became the party's nominee, he would do so on his own terms, not as the pawn of Truman or the liberals.[37] When Stevenson withdrew, liberal sentiment moved to Harriman, though the votes moved to Kefauver. Schlesinger wrote him again, "In view of everything, I am going to do my best to get Averell the nomination. He is a fine man, who represents the best in the New Deal–Fair Deal tradition. He would make an honorable candidate whom we could all support with enthusiasm." Stevenson, meanwhile, flaunted his independence from that tradition. In a speech five days before work began on the Democratic platform in July, he praised the South's progress and chastised "some of us in the North" who were "more intemperate than informed about the South and the rapid evolution of its racial problems."[38] He was not helping the liberals' fight.

Yet in a curious way he was. When the delegates streamed into the amphitheater by the stockyards on Chicago's South Side, they were badly split over candidates and principle; but they also badly needed to mend their fences. Truman was unpopular and the Republicans looked strong; Democratic schism would make them only stronger. It might also, should it happen for the second successive Democratic convention, destroy the party. Stevenson avoided the divisive issues; he blunted their edges and muted their squawk. He might hold the party together so it could ease into a liberal posture, not in 1952 but off in the future, without violent disruption. No one designed this plan at the time—but this was what began in Chicago.

The convention's first duty was to write a platform, and in it the civil rights plank revealed the party's mood. The resolutions committee, as the platform committee was called, began its hearings on July 16; party leaders forced a compromise draft in the early morning hours of Wednesday, July 23; and after midnight that evening the convention approved it.[39] The week between gave evidence of the Democrats' continuing troubles. Walter White, chairman of the Leadership Conference on Civil Rights and executive secretary of the NAACP, introduced leaders of groups advocating a strong civil rights plank—the ACLU, American-Jewish Committee, B'nai B'rith, ADA, AFL, CIO, United Auto Workers, and United Steel Workers. The Chicago Federation of Labor urged the committee to adopt planks for the FEPC, antilynch law, and anti-poll tax law. Walter Reuther attacked filibusters and urged the nomination of "candidates true to the spirit of the New Deal and the Fair Deal." Appearing July 21, he spoke first on civil rights, praising Truman, then against the Taft-Hartley Act—labor rights and civil rights still made the crucial nexus for the liberal movement.[40]

A handful of party leaders joined these outside groups. Adam Clayton Powell, in 1946 the enemy of Truman, in 1956 the supporter of Eisenhower, appeared to speak for the standard civil rights measures, then attacked the House Rules Committee and John Sparkman and praised Harry Truman. Senators Benton of Connecticut and Lehman of New York argued for abolition of the filibuster. The issue was, as Emmanuel Celler of New York said, a plain one: The committee could write a plank that abided by the "progressive . . . principles of the New and Fair Deal" or it could retreat from 1948; "the same needs and demands that existed in 1948 now exist."[41] But these leaders were not in control of the party and so not in control of the platform.

There was a stronger bloc of Democratic leaders—primarily moderates from the North and South—Kentucky's Lawrence W. Wetherby, Massachusetts's John McCormack, Washington's Warren Magnuson, Texas's Sam Rayburn, Alabama's John Sparkman, Arkansas's Brooks Hays, Georgia's B. D. Murphy, and Chairman Frank McKinney of Indiana. They favored compromise. McKinney told the press on July 14 that the major aim of the platform committee was to "remove the disunity that existed in 1948."[42] Of the major party leaders only Herbert Lehman insisted on a federal FEPC clause, and his judgment of the party's mood was amiss. He told Harriman (who was assured of the District of Columbia), that if he wanted to hold the New York delegation he should take the strongest possible position on civil rights. Rowe countered, said Harriman should be moderate on the plank, but Harriman followed Lehman's advice and, partly owing to his civil rights position, lost the nomination by a long shot. Even Hubert Humphrey, the fighter of 1948, felt the pull for unity and agreed not to initiate a civil rights floor fight.[43] In 1948 the convention, in adopting the minority report, implicitly had supported the FEPC: It had commended Truman's work and urged Congress to guarantee the "right to equal opportunity of employment." In 1952 the platform commended no one but included the phrase "right to equal opportunity of employment"—far from endorsement of a federal FEPC. The filibuster issue had arisen in the last four years, but the 1952 civil rights plank made no mention of it; instead the committee slid the issue into a separate section of the platform, entitled, "Improving Congressional Procedures"—diminishing thereby its ideological importance—and asked only that steps be taken so that "majority rule prevails." The convention adopted the plank and, in titling the platform, pointedly omitted the words of four years before—a "Program for Progressive Liberalism." This was a different bunch of delegates.[44]

But the path to unity was not smooth yet. For next the party faced a fight over credentials. A vastly complex issue, the credentials issue had its origins in a rather simple fact: Southern Democrats had kept Truman's name off the ballot in four states—Louisiana, Mississippi, Alabama, and South Carolina—and had enabled Strom Thurmond to carry those states. Now, four years later, those delegates were back, and they presumed to be seated as regular Democrats. Others disagreed. There were three positions on this "loyalty" issue. Some Democrats thought each delegate had the obligation to support the candidate of the national convention. Others, the moderates, saw merely an obligation to help the candidate appear on the ballot. The third group, mostly Southerners, recognized no responsibility to the national party, for they regarded state rights and individual conscience, as always, supreme. These were the three positions; they were held or opposed largely depending on which candidate one supported and which ideology one espoused. There was of course the question of merit, of principle and conviction, and Joseph Rauh found himself doubting his own, the liberals', position, which was the most rigorous, because he thought it inappropriate for the party to force the conscience of any man.[45] The South also believed that in supporting the third position it was waging yet another battle in its century-old war against Northern attempts to rule the South and usurp its rights. But on the whole, apart from Rauh's concern (chivalric in a time of conflict), the various positions on rules and credentials and candidates reflected the various positions on ideology.

The hopes of the liberals, Kefauver and Harriman, and of the liberal wing, looked dim at the outset of the credentials struggle. After confrontations and compromises in the credentials subcommittee of the Democratic National Committee, in the national committee, and finally in the convention credentials committee, from July 18 to July 22, the two delegations whose credentials were contested, Texas and Mississippi, got seated, and their challengers got thrown out. This was a Southern and moderates' victory, coming after Wright Morrow, the Texas national committeeman and counsel to the Dixiecrat delegation, refused to answer whether he would "abide by the majority vote of the convention"; the threat of a bolt had quieted the agitators.[46] Yet a handful of liberals, led by Senator Blair Moody and Franklin Roosevelt, Jr., persuaded the convention to adopt a loyalty resolution, stating that no delegate would be seated unless he indicated he would use every "honorable means" to get the names of the party's nominees, under the heading of the party, on the election ballot in his state. Roosevelt was working for Harriman. His aim was for the convention to chastise the South, perhaps anger it, perhaps enough to push it into a walk-out, thus brightening the prospects for Harriman's nomination. But the South protested vehemently, and after a day of fitful fretting Chairman McKinney and Senators Hill and Sparkman worked out a compromise to modify the resolution to keep the party intact.[47] The convention passed the new rule, which read in part: "That for this convention only, such assurances shall not be in contravention to the existing law of the state, nor of the state Democratic governing bodies."[48] This was something of a travesty, for the only delegations that might not support the decisions of the convention were those Southern delegations instructed explicitly by their state parties not to be bound by the national convention's decisions. The moderates prevailed, the liberals failed.

But this was not the end of the issue. By July 23, the day the convention adopted the committee reports, all believed that Texas and Mississippi had taken the loyalty pledge or been properly exempted by the revised Moody resolution.[49] South Carolina,

Louisiana, and Virginia, also jittery about challenges, had filed statements with the credentials committee explaining that their state parties had bound them not to be bound by the convention's decisions; all assumed these states were also properly seated. So Governor Byrnes of South Carolina was not alone in his vexation when the convention chairman declared, on July 23, that he and his friends were not permanently seated yet.[50] But nothing more was done, presumably in the absence of certainty, until the next day, when after the nominating procedure began, Governor John Battle of Virginia asked on behalf of himself and South Carolina and Louisiana whether they could vote. Chairman of the credentials committee Calvin Rawlings inexplicably answered that these states "do not meet the requirement" of the Moody resolution and therefore "are not properly qualified to vote." Confusion followed. Chairman Rayburn called the roll on the seating of Virginia, and by the end of the first reading it was apparent that most delegates did not know what they were voting on; some were caucusing still. The Illinois delegation had a special problem. Suddenly it realized that it had voted against seating Virginia when Pennsylvania, guided by ex-Senator Myers, Stevenson's floor manager, had voted for seating Virginia. Panic broke out among the Illinois delegates. Its leaders were called back from dinner, and they found that at 8:46 p.m. Virginia had been unseated. At 8:50 Illinois declared its "confidence in the governor of Virginia" and changed its vote. Thirteen states followed, and by 10:00 Virginia, South Carolina, and Louisiana were declared seated.[51]

It was a near thing. Illinois had almost killed the chances of its governor to be nominated but changed its vote in time to seat the segregationist delegations and permit Stevenson's nomination. Here the questions of civil rights and ideology, credentials and nominees, all became entangled, each affecting the others. Throughout the convention, Kefauver and Harriman had urged the adoption of strong civil rights measures, in committee and on the floor. Harriman the previous week had reiterated his demand for a progressive civil rights plank, and on July 17 he and Kefauver had agreed to work together to seat the delegations challenging Mississippi and Texas. Having failed in these endeavors, they voted on the night of the 24th to unseat Virginia. But during that confusing vote, when some thought the issue already settled and others thought to unsettle it, Chicago leader Jacob Arvey caught the pattern amid the disorder. He recalled:

It suddenly dawned on us what was happening. The strategy of the Kefauver backers and the Northern liberal bloc was to try and make impossible demands on the Southern delegates so that they would walk out of the convention. If the total convention vote was thus cut down by the walkout of delegates who would never vote for Kefauver, then the Tennessee senator would have a better chance of winning the nomination.[52]

The Stevenson forces voted to hold the party together, and to hold it for Stevenson.

The link between Stevenson's nomination and the drive for compromise was yet more explicit. On July 21 McKinney and party leaders worked out an arrangement to seat the contested delegations temporarily and verify loyalty later. This was bound to provoke a credentials storm at some point, and the convention would polarize, as it did three days later. That afternoon, on July 21, the "Draft Stevenson" movement first became a serious effort; his partisans chose Governor Schricker of Indiana to nominate Stevenson and Myers to run operations on the floor.[53] When it became clear, then, that the initial civil rights credentials decision would not last but would break down and split the convention, a moderate candidate became appealing. That night Barkley withdrew, leaving the moderate field to Stevenson alone. That day also was the opening day, when Stevenson gave his welcoming address, stirring the delegates with his eloquence. He told his audience that until he assumed office Illinois had elected but three Democratic governors in one hundred years, and of them he said, "John Peter Altgeld, my friends, was a Protestant, Governor Dunne was a Catholic, Henry Horner was a Jew. And that, my friends, is the American story, written by the Democratic party here on the prairies of Illinois." He won the respect of the liberals, who had wandered between Harriman and Kefauver; but then three days later, when the liberals threatened to force the South out, his delegation switched to keep it in, and he won the gratitude of the South. He was a candidate suited to the mood of compromise, one who had stayed far from the platform committee when it considered the civil rights plank, one regarded by liberals as in the center or even "right of center."[54] In a time of imminent divisions, Stevenson stayed aloof from the struggle, only joining it indirectly—when Arvey extended a hand to the South. He stood for compromise.

Russell was unacceptable to the North, Kefauver and Harriman to the South, and Barkley to labor—Stevenson was nominated. The South seemed pleased with the convention results. It liked Stevenson (until in later years he appeared to move left) and also Sparkman of Alabama, the vice-presidential nominee, though even with his home in his favor the old guard thought him susceptible to labor and New Deal influences. The South also felt content not having to bolt the convention. The last walkout had not helped Southerners much, and anyway they thought Republicans as fickle on civil rights as Democrats. Liberals also seemed pleased: They liked Stevenson, though not Sparkman, and could tolerate the platform; 1952 for them was a "partial victory."[55] Everyone seemed fairly pleased with the unity, and everyone had his misgivings.

One was Harry Truman. Stevenson made clear his independence of the president, and after watching him all spring and all week of the convention, Truman grew to dislike Adlai Stevenson. Partly he disliked Stevenson's hesitation, so unlike his own manner of quickly making hard decisions. But he also feared what Stevenson's oldest and closest friend saw and did not mind but in fact liked in the candidate's posture. Hermon Dunlap Smith wrote that week to his daughter:

> Adlai is certainly a moderate. You may recall that when *Newsweek* referred to him last Spring as an 'extreme Fair Dealer' I wrote a letter stating that that was an incorrect statement and supporting it with evidence from both his speeches and his actions, and also discussed this with Raymond Moley, who finally agreed with me. . . . Of course, there are going to be strong pressures on him from the left wing, but I feel sure that he will resist them. Many of my conservative business friends have expressed concern that some of Adlai's old friends with Republican backgrounds like mine, might be influenced by party considerations to leave him at this time. They point out that the result of that would be to create a vacuum into which the left wing groups would move into. . . . I would stay with him on the grounds of personal loyalty alone.[56]

Smith knew Stevenson well, knew he was not a Fair Dealer, and knew he hated pressure. This Truman saw, as did the *Wall Street Journal,* which declared, "Last week there came . . . the end of a revolution. The Democratic Party itself called a halt to the militant movement that for 20 years has been known as the New Deal or Fair Deal." And, "It was merely the possibility—not the assurance—that Mr. Stevenson . . . might be the nominee that pulled back the hot-headed young Turks, threw doubts on the determination of the solid south and compromised a threatened platform fight out of existence."[57] Stevenson was acclaimed the peacemaker.

Yet peace is a misleading word, for it implies harmony reached through accords. The Democrats' division was such that they could never be a harmonious bunch, and though Stevenson's moderation suited the mood of compromise, such a mood could not last. Even that week there were hints of discord. When Eleanor Roosevelt addressed the convention, and received a standing ovation, Governor Shivers and his Texas delegation remained seated, and Harry Byrd walked out of the hall.[58] Neither were the liberals entirely content: Stevenson was the beneficiary of a convention rigged by Truman and the bosses, said Kefauver; and FDR, Jr., called him the "Northern Dixiecrat." "The platform they have constructed," wrote one reporter, "serves the useful purpose of blurring and glossing over the deep divisions within the party."[59] The gloss was thin and the blurring temporary. Neither convinced Southern conservatives nor convinced Northern liberals could long live with the peace that only nonideologues cherished.

That fall nonideologues might again have liked Adlai Stevenson, for in the campaign he was flexible and undogmatic. He was ambivalent, too, on occasion, and his ambivalence heightened the sense that the party had lost direction, that the convention compromise had satisfied neither wing of the party, and that the Democrats were wandering, divided, and aimless, together only in their defeat. He cut himself loose from Truman by making Springfield instead of Washington his campaign headquarters, a rebuff to the outgoing president. Truman disliked him more. The running mate, John Sparkman, assured newsmen that the Republicans had a stronger civil rights plank than the Democrats. Liberals complained.[60] Stevenson, as always, might give stirring speeches: In St. Louis he prefigured John Kennedy, saying, "I would speak to you of America's new frontier." But on several issues he fumbled and lost his way. In Evansville, Indiana, before a crowd of 10,000 CIO workers, as he reached his attack on Senator Taft, Stevenson departed from his text and blurted: "I say to you, my friends, that we don't want [pause] —No labor bosses are ever going to boss me, and I think that goons and violence and property damage is as wrong and intolerable in labor disputes as it is anywhere else."[61] A stubbornly independent man, he had trouble pleasing liberals. But neither could he please conservatives: He lost four outer South states; three Deep South Democratic governors endorsed

Eisenhower; and Harry Byrd stayed neutral.

He was especially erratic on civil rights. At Harlem on October 27, after an enormous crowd gathered in the street and waited in the rain late at night, Stevenson at last arrived. He threw away his speech, an elegant discourse on the Bill of Rights and the equality of men, and delivered an improvised five minute chat, mentioning the FEPC, foreign affairs, natural resources, and his Alabaman running mate, whom he defended. The crowd was miffed, his staff was stunned. James Reston wrote that Stevenson during the course of two months of campaigning changed his position three times on the filibuster issue.[62] In Richmond, Virginia, candidate Stevenson blamed harsh Republican rule, from 1865 to 1912, for the South's lean years; praised Sparkman and Russell and the Constitution of the Confederacy for its political genius; and ascribed Southern economic conditions—which largely had created "many of the lamentable differences between Southern whites and Negroes"—to the "long years of Republican neglect and exploitation." Elsewhere in the South, Stevenson linked his family and his attitudes to the Southern heritage and, by subtle allegory, mocked Republicans and Sherman's march to the sea. In New Orleans, when he stayed in a segregated hotel barring black reporters, Stevenson refused to issue a statement or move out of the hotel. One advisor, borrowed from Truman's staff, said Truman in such circumstances would have moved out. Later in the campaign, in Dallas, Stevenson faced the same problem, and spent the night on a train.[63]

1952 was a terrible year for Democrats. There was certainly the continuing conservative and Republican resurgence in the nation, natural after twenty years of Democratic and liberal leaders. But there was also a Democratic party which, though united, lacked direction. A man who carried the trappings of an intellectual liberal, carried in November only Southern and border states. He carried, indeed, the same four Deep South states that went for Smith in 1928 and Thurmond in 1948—states that voted for reasons of race and for Stevenson because he was a Democrat who stayed off civil rights. Victory was elusive, and so was the party's purpose. Having been brought together that they might win, the Democrats lost, and still had their differences to settle, their purpose to define.

SEVEN

THE RESUMPTION OF CONFLICT

When all eyes were turned elsewhere—to Korean peace and McCarthy's hearings, to the unleashing then releasing of Chiang Kai-shek—the Democrats, out of office, quietly began again to split apart after they had contrived to come together. By habit, now, they fought over the filibuster and FEPC during the primaries, but even when no election beckoned, from 1952 to 1956, when no pressure acted but their own, they fought among themselves for control of the party. Again they fought over civil rights.

In the party there was a power vacuum. Adlai Stevenson, defeated and bereft of a power base, could not and would not impose his will on Democrats; the congressional leadership, Southern and conscious of Eisenhower's popularity, was cautious; Truman was retired; and the presidency, for twenty years a center of party influence, was Republican. Ideology raged below, yet there was emptiness at the top, and people rushed to fill it: For the first time in twenty years the chairmanship of the national committee was important; an advisory group sprang up to push Stevenson in a liberal direction; the CIO, NAACP, and ADA vied with the national committee and the congressional leadership for influence; the South tried to lead in the Congress and the national committee. The struggle was sharpening.

In this contentious climate, the aftermath of the 1952 compromise, when no one ruled and nothing was resolved, the Supreme Court's school desegregation decision, the *Brown* decision, was handed down. It had an extraordinary impact on Democratic politics. When the Court decided that separate schools were inherently unequal and ordered them desegregated, it resolved, in the long run, the question of Northern interference in Southern society, a question that went to the heart of the liberals' struggle. But *Brown* had another effect, more immediate and searing: it brought into sharp relief the struggle over equal rights, integration, white supremacy, and states' rights. It compressed all these monumental and general questions into one stark issue—you supported the law or you did not. This cut the ground out from under the South, unless of course the South wished to find new ground—the ground of illegal defiance—which many Southerners did. Their position then became untenable. Frantic in defense of segregation, they trapped themselves in extreme isolation, beyond the pale of the law, where liberals could not reach them to make a compromise, even if they wanted to. Relations in the party grew worse—and worse still when, in 1955, the Court handed down its implementation decree—a vague decree, open to interpretation—for to each candidate fell the task of giving a timetable for desegregation. It was a hard task, forcing men to speak precisely, leaving little room for elegant rhetoric; and the more precisely they spoke the more distance they put between themselves and the old guard, who rejected timetables altogether. Far from removing civil rights from politics, the Court thus made a sharp conflict even sharper and brought it closer to resolution.

Party Squabbles

Just after the 1952 convention, Adlai Stevenson, intent upon dissociating himself from the unpopular Truman, had fired Chairman of the Democratic National Committee Frank McKinney, friend and appointee of Harry Truman, and replaced him with Stephen Mitchell. Mitchell was a moderate. In 1953 he prevailed upon Stevenson to conciliate the South, and Stevenson went to speak in Alabama and Georgia. But while Stevenson mended fences, the ADA was breaking them. It attacked the congressional leadership, especially Lyndon Johnson, Senate minority leader. Mitchell disapproved, considered this disloyal, and, with Stevenson's apparent approval, told the ADA to desist from such attacks or break its ties to the Democratic party.[1] The congressional leadership, which was Southern, was not mollified. Men like Russell, Rayburn, and Johnson thought Stevenson was unduly influenced by the ADA, and although Stevenson tried to stay out of the fray, his friendship with such ADA men as Schlesinger, Rauh, Allard Lowenstein, and James Loeb tainted his indistinct coloring. Johnson once said of him: "That fat ass, Stevenson—he's the kind of man who squats when he pees."[2] The divisions ran deep.

In this unsettled atmosphere, the national chairman, as controller of party functions, including the convention, took on additional importance. In 1954, Mitchell decided to resign, and the office became even more important. Each power center—Stevenson, Southern conservatives, and liberal groups—wanted its own man. Paul Butler of Indiana was the candidate of Mitchell and soon became the candidate of the South. Mike DiSalle, Ohio leader and once the head of Truman's Office of Price Stabilization, was the candidate of Truman, McKinney, and the liberals. James Finnegan, leader of reform forces in Philadelphia's machine, was the candidate of such party leaders as Jacob Arvey and David Lawrence. Stevenson decided he could get along with any one of the three leading contenders and resolved to stay out of the selection process, knowing it would become, just like the platform, credentials, and the loyalty issue before, fraught with ideological conflict. On December 4, 1954, at a meeting of the national committee in New Orleans, Butler was elected chairman.[3]

The events leading to Butler's election were murky. Congressman John Brademas, also of Indiana, believed Butler won because he campaigned hard; and in fact Butler called many members of the national committee, asking for their support.[4] Another view has it that he won because of a deal with the South. Jacob Arvey said: "At New Orleans Rayburn said that Finnegan is a little too Irish-sounding but Butler is okay. At the time we didn't know why Rayburn took that position. I found out two years later when a certain person showed me an envelope and showed me that Butler had written on the back of it: 'If elected I will not consider it my duty to go into the question of civil rights—that's a matter for Congress.' "[5] Arvey favored Finnegan, whom big city leaders could trust not to divide the party by taking an extreme Southern or liberal stand, and the night before the balloting he and David Lawrence of Pennsylvania went to see Rayburn. Butler had the election sewed up, said Rayburn; Arvey did not understand. But the next day things became clear: Hale Boggs of Louisiana nominated Butler; an Alabama committeewoman seconded; and Butler won all of the Southern votes save one (of Florida's two votes). Later, Arvey understood: "Butler won on the Southern deal."[6]

That Butler won on a Southern deal testified to the continuing force of the civil rights issue in the party. During the next few years, his behavior did, too. Early in 1955 Butler made good on his deal, predicted a mild civil rights plank in the 1956 platform, and announced that the loyalty oath had been thrown "out the window." Later Butler switched on civil rights, made it an issue, and won the admiration of such liberals as Schlesinger and Joseph Rauh. He betrayed the South, Arvey believed, because he "wanted to establish himself as a vice-presidential or presidential candidate. He thought civil rights would do it."[7] This may be harsh. But there is no doubt that Butler recognized, as Kefauver did, the cutting edge of civil rights, and used it first to win the South and then to wean himself away from it. In both he was successful. By 1957 Strom Thurmond declared: "The national Democratic Party should be called upon to dismiss the present National Chairman. He has made it absolutely clear that he is not interested in the views of the South."[8] Until Kennedy dismissed him, Butler pushed civil rights hard, to further the ends of his ambition and of the liberal wing.

Liberalism nonetheless was waning. Truman's program had vanished. The Democratic leadership in Congress was lumbering, "trying to smother issues," as one liberal Democrat noted, yet adamantine in its power, recruiting such erstwhile militant liberals as Joseph Clark and Hubert Humphrey, whose eyes stretched beyond the Senate and who therefore worked with Johnson. Eisenhower also smothered the social issues and busied himself to no avail with reducing the size and expense of government. Stevenson proved unwilling to exert liberal leadership on labor issues and civil rights, though he spoke eloquently in defense of civil liberties and against Joe McCarthy.[9] The liberals cast around for a base, and for a while they found it in the Finletter group. Thomas K. Finletter, secretary of the air force under Truman, was a liberal on economic and civil rights issues. On the first weekend in October 1953 he met with George Kennan, Adlai Stevenson, and Chester Bowles (in Bowles's house) to discuss issues and organize a reasearch and discussion group. "The Congressional leaders were not leading," Finletter later put it; and for three years they met to try to fill the gap. Attendance varied and the group grew, including among its members Seymour Harris, Arthur Schlesinger, Jr., John Kenneth Galbraith, Paul Samuelson, George Ball, Alvin Hansen, and Roswell Gilpatric. Their purpose was to discuss major issues and prepare position papers, sometimes with an eye to influencing Stevenson, who seldom read them but responded gratefully. One member said: "We thought that Stevenson would be President and that he was a marvelous man. We thought that he should be educated."[10] Part of that education was to counter the influence that his downstate Illinois and Lake

Forest background had had on him. But the aim was also larger: It was to maintain liberal thinking on a national level, to withstand the onslaught of conservative Democrats and Republicans, to prod those who smothered issues and provide direction to a fractured party. The party was torn and its doctrine unclear. Democrats groped for direction.

Others groped as well. Walter Reuther told the founding convention of the AFL-CIO in 1955, "I believe that this labor movement of ours will make a great contribution in the field of civil liberties and civil rights," and the promise was not empty: By then the AFL had eradicated discrimination from its union constitutions in all but one union. The constitution of the AFL-CIO held that one of the purposes of the merger was "to encourage all workers without regard to race, creed, color, national origin or ancestry to share equally in the benefits of union organization." It further established a committee on civil rights, and the founding convention passed resolutions supporting an end to discrimination, an amendment of Senate Rule 22, a federal FEPC, abolition of the poll tax, and a federal antilynching law. Thurgood Marshall, noting the link between labor and civil rights, said at the time: "We in the NAACP salute the merged AFL and CIO. . . . we can now depend upon an even stronger support from this new consolidated arm of organized labor."[11]

But other events portended something different. The merger of the AFL and the CIO, while seeming a boon to organized labor and thus to the liberal movement, in fact hurt the liberals badly. David MacDonald, head of the Steelworkers, for his own reasons, threatened to secede from the CIO and join the AFL. Walter Reuther, head of the Auto Workers, resisted the merger, knowing that it would subordinate the CIO and mute its liberal voice. But Reuther had no choice. MacDonald hated him and would split the CIO if it did not merge. The CIO merged, and with the merger came its submergence, for it was engulfed in the parent organization, the AFL, which outnumbered the CIO by three million members. The AFL was always less activist than the CIO, and so for liberals the merger was a debilitating blow—"one of the worst things to happen this country," said Joseph Rauh. "It hurt liberalism badly."[12] But this was not the only problem. All of labor was becoming less liberal, less concerned with the rights of disadvantaged people; for as working people shared with the rest of the nation the fruits of the phenomenal postwar economic growth, winning higher wages, they grew less responsive to the

demands of others. This shift did not complete itself in the 1950s:
It continued into the 1960s and defies careful calibration; the
precise effect of the merger likewise remains unclear. Certainly
labor still relied on the federal government to regulate the economy, still gained new black members, and still called for the repeal
of Taft-Hartley. But a shift nonetheless set in, slowly arresting
the reforming spirit that swept the workers in the 1930s when
they were out of work and in need of a helping hand. Perhaps it
was that while labor still opposed corporate power and called for
federal action it became itself a massive and sprawling center of
power.

Labor was not alone in its transformation. Farmers shifted
earlier, moving from the farmer-labor movement of the 1930s,
when they voted for Roosevelt and the AAA, to the reaction of
1946, when they enjoyed high profits and took a dim view of
Truman's price ceilings. After that, the farmers voted liberal or
Democratic only twice—in 1948 and 1964—and then only because
they were persuaded that the Republicans were bent on repealing
the New Deal. They voted two times for Eisenhower and three
for Nixon. Like labor, the farmers relied still on government support and thus in theory still were liberal, but that support was so
assured that it figured little in their political calculation. Other
things mattered more. After the war technology improved, and the
farmer's productive capacity increased 84 percent—three times
faster than the industrial worker's. The number of farms dropped
by a million, the number of farmers by five million: those that
remained were large farmers, with advanced machinery and high
profits—an interest group pressing for advantages, not the masses
striving for protection. The National Farmers' Union, once the
spokesman for poor and foreclosed farmers, lost its army, and like
the CIO lost its influence. The masses underlying the liberal movement slowly were shifting their interests.

But on the surface the leaders carried on. Patton for the farmers and Reuther for the workers stayed on a liberal course, and
they and the ADA and blacks and intellectuals spoke in the early
1950s to keep alive their ideology in the party and nation. They
met trouble not only with prospering constituents but also with
Stevenson and the Democrats in Congress, who would not speak
out, and with the South, which openly betrayed the party. Harry
Byrd visited Eisenhower to persuade him not to follow Truman's
example in urging the Supreme Court to integrate public schools.[13]
But he, the president, the Democrats—all were overwhelmed, each

forced to take a side, when the air was cleared by the Supreme
Court's decision on civil rights.

The Supreme Court Decides

On May 17, 1954, a Monday—in certain places soon to be
known as "Black Monday"—the Supreme Court outlawed segregation in the nation's public schools. For a decade the Court had
been undermining the constitutionality of racial discrimination—
in 1944 the white primary, in 1948 the restrictive covenant. But
the Vinson Court, though it made state educational institutions
admit blacks where black schools were proved inferior to white,
never challenged the separate-but-equal doctrine set down in
Plessy v. *Ferguson* in 1896. Neither had the lawyers of the NAACP
Legal Defense Fund, led by Thurgood Marshall, made integration
their goal, though they had been attacking discrimination for more
than twenty years. In 1950, they changed their mind. They
brought *Brown* v. *Board of Education* to the Court and sought the
reversal of *Plessy*. They said that state laws requiring segregation
in public schools were unconstitutional, for such laws fostered a
belief in one's inferiority, hence created unequal conditions, and
were thus a violation of the equal protection clause of the Fourteenth Amendment; moreover, these laws created an unreasonable
classification, one by race, and hence also violated the equal protection clause. Such was the legal argument, but perhaps the more
compelling argument was that summarized by James Nabrit, in
oral argument in 1952: "The basic question here is one of liberty"—
liberty denied by states, liberty which it was the government's
duty to protect. This was a most liberal argument, as Truman and
the postwar Democrats had redefined liberalism. The power that
threatened was not that of the federal government but that of
the states and the people, if they were prejudiced, and it could
be overcome only by federal action. It was also a persuasive argument. The Court agreed unanimously that, in the words of Earl
Warren, "separate educational facilities are inherently unequal."
An hour after Warren read the opinion, it was broadcast by the
Voice of America in thirty-four languages.[14]

The Supreme Court, in May 1954, did not decree how or when
its decision should take force. It did so a year later, on May 31,
1955, but in the meantime deep resistance swelled in the South,
and in the North, hesitation. President Dwight Eisenhower helped
set the mood of ambivalence: for three years, he refused to endorse

the Court's decree. When, in February 1956, Autherine Lucy was denied entrance into the graduate school of the University of Alabama, he said, "I would certainly hope that we could avoid any interference."[15] On another occasion his spokesman said the president would make no assumption that the Court could not enforce its own orders—a polite way of repeating Andrew Jackson's dictum that the Court had taken its decision and now could itself enforce it. Eisenhower refused to deny the rumor that privately he deplored the *Brown* decision and thought that integration ought to go more slowly. Another time he said, "I don't believe you can change the hearts of men with laws or decisions." It was a distinctive attitude, antigovernment in nature, and one which the South shared and, as we shall see, expanded into a philosophy.[16]

The leader of the Democrats was hardly more decisive. When the Court made its 1954 decision, Adlai Stevenson was scheduled to deliver a speech in the South. He delayed making a statement until May 27, when from Jackson, Mississippi, he announced his sentiment:

> It seems to me that much of the talk since the Supreme Court decision has missed the most important point: The South has been invited by the Supreme Court to share the burden of blue-printing the mechanics for solving the new school problems of non-segregation. . . . The rest of the country should extend the hand of fellowship, of patience, understanding and assistance to the South in sharing that burden. We should harness the resources of the Federal Government, the United States Office of Education, all the technical skills of our great universities—in short our brains and hearts north and south—to help one another work out this problem, even as the Constitution governs us all.[17]

The Court might be inviting all to work out a solution, as Stevenson said, but even such men as himself hesitated to accept. This was a deadly issue, and people ran for cover.

Stevenson stayed under cover for the next two years, eschewing a strong stand on *Brown*. Perhaps he believed that by keeping quiet he had more to gain—the Southern vote—than he had to lose. For what he had to lose was the black vote, and Stevenson did not think he would lose it. Millard Tydings, fearing he might, urged Stevenson to issue a forthright endorsement of *Brown*, but, perhaps recalling what a friend had told him years before—that on account of Truman's work blacks would remain Democratic—Stevenson responded: "I believe the rank and file [blacks] know where their enduring friends are."[18] The Southerners, on the other hand, had once before proved that their allegiance to the party was not so strong as their attachment to white supremacy; Stevenson was reluctant to offend them.

Thus when Jonathan Daniels urged Stevenson to exercise strong liberal leadership and purge the party of Southern racists, Stevenson demurred. A newspaper editor and Democratic National Committeeman from North Carolina, Daniels had served as Roosevelt's press secretary, then as advisor to Truman during the 1948 campaign. (His father had been Wilson's secretary of the navy, under whom Stevenson's father had worked.) A lonely liberal voice in the South, Daniels looked to Stevenson for leadership, writing him in 1955:

> I note your statement, "While I don't have any aggressive notions myself." That may be true as regards the specific candidacy of Stevenson. It cannot be true—and I know it isn't true—as to the direction of the Democratic Party. . . . the party cannot go far in appeasing those arrogant 'Democrats' from the South. . . . I am for Stevenson. Even more, I think, I am for Stevenson as party leader now who in himself or somebody else can make possible a candidate who will never sell the party down the river for the benefit of the Byrds, Kennons, Shiverses who now demand the right to dominate the party which they eagerly betrayed. This is a time for 'aggressive notions' by those of us who are not willing that Ku Kluxers in pleated bosomed robes, run the party down here or anywhere else.

Daniels wanted action; Stevenson, responding graciously, did not: "How you can write! It was a grand letter and my blood is hot. But I worry about too much 'loyalty [oath] emphasis' just now when we are in better and better shape in much of the South and some of the gentlemen you mention are losing ground I am told." Later, in preparation for the 1956 campaign, Stevenson called together Southern Democratic leaders, excluding Jonathan Daniels, who might have offended the conservatives. Instead he summoned from North Carolina the man who led the state's resistance to school desegregation.[19]

Several people, giving him advice that was consistent with this conciliatory bent, asked Stevenson to befriend the South and leave civil rights alone. Harry Ashmore of the *Arkansas Gazette,* later a campaign aide in 1956, told Stevenson that the Court decision had ended the legal battle, that civil rights had lost its political significance, that the issue would no longer divide the Democratic party.

He was happy to report that, with this issue out of the way, it would become clear that the South was not so medieval as some suspected, and that it was in fact sympathetic to Stevenson's brand of moderation. The party's future lay in such moderation, Ashmore said, and thus Stevenson could help both himself and the party by cultivating good relations with the South.[20] Another correspondent, a professor from North Carolina, told Stevenson that miscegenation was not desirable, that Harriman was not liked in the South, and that Stevenson was the South's only Northern friend. He said Southerners had confidence in Stevenson, who he hoped would give some sign of his confidence in the South. Stevenson responded eagerly: "As to what can be done about giving the South assurance as you suggest, I should certainly welcome your suggestions."[21] When it came to civil rights, the liberal Finletter group were not the only ones wielding influence on Stevenson.

It is likely, however, that Stevenson had more than the coming campaign in mind and that he was truly divided on the merits of rapid integration. Years later he told a friend that had he been president when the Court decided *Brown* he would have begun a campaign to educate the people and prepare them for integration. It bothered him that liberals accused him of timidity and thought him "old-womanish." Integration was a bigger problem than they realized; it would take time to work it out if the nation was to avoid violence.[22] And he had a point, borne out in the coming years by the resistance to integration. Stevenson was a sensitive man. He sensed the trouble looming ahead, and also had a sense for his present political situation; and he accordingly became, in the eyes of one friend, more resistant to civil rights pressure during these years, from 1954 to 1956, than he had been in either 1948 or 1952.[23]

As such he disappointed the liberals, who hoped that the Democrats might use this momentous decision to rally Northerners and point the party in a liberal direction, punish the Southerners and end segregation. The Washington director of the NAACP said that although Eisenhower was no great friend of the civil rights movement, he was more outspoken on civil rights than all the Democratic leaders, except Averell Harriman.[24] Indeed civil rights leaders were among the few to give vehement support to the Court's decision. Labor did, too. The AFL adopted a resolution urging affiliated unions to "join hands with law-abiding government officials . . . in the local communities in the South in helping to bring about full and complete implementation of this decision."

In his keynote speech to the first constitutional convention of the AFL-CIO, George Meany spoke of civil rights:

> We have had striking evidence in the last few days, if we needed any such evidence, that the Constitution of the United States and Bill of Rights and the civil liberties that we all like to boast of do not prevail in certain parts of our country for people whose skin is a little different in color than that of ourselves. We have men who call themselves statesmen who are public servants, elected by the people, and still who, in the interest of white supremacy, defy a decision of the United States Supreme Court in regard to desegregation.

The chairman of the Committee on Civil Rights said that "a united, democratic labor movement of 15 million Americans can be the greatest single force in our society for the swift expansion of civil rights."[25] Few politicians went so far. Excluding labor and blacks, there was no concerted political effort, no common front in support of the Court.

One who could have led the front was Kefauver. When the Court outlawed school segregation Estes Kefauver found himself in an awkward position. In 1952 he had worked with Harriman and Paul Douglas for a strong civil rights plank; now, in 1954, he ran for reelection to the Senate against a segregationist named Pat Sutton. This was the sort of situation that enlivened Kefauver's life throughout his political career. On June 12, 1954, he said that it was significant that the Court had not issued implementation decrees, that when the Court did he was confident it would consider the "varying problems and traditions of local communities." Sutton went for the jugular. He produced a Harlem newspaper article quoting Kefauver as saying that if elected president he would work to ensure "that there will be no segregation." Kefauver scrambled. He had never advocated an end to segregation, he said. Then on July 23 he reached a position he held until 1956. The Court's decision was the law of the land, the Senate could not reverse it (as some had urged), and anyone who said that it could, including his opponent, was mistaken or lying.[26] It was a bold move, hardly that of the fighting civil rights liberal he professed to be but nonetheless one that supported the Court, prodded the hesitant leaders in the North, and infuriated his colleagues in the South. Kefauver was pursuing the presidency, and in his pursuit he helped draw the line between those who upheld and those who defied the law. If Eisenhower and Stevenson illustrated the failings of democratic politics—public pressure is insistent—Kefauver showed its virtue.

But not even Kefauver or labor, and certainly not Eisenhower or Stevenson, rallied the North behind the Court's decision. No one could and no one dared—no one save the South. And the South could do it because it dared too much.

The South Decides

On July 11, 1954, not two months after the *Brown* decision, Robert Patterson, a red-faced plantation owner, founded the first citizens' council, in Indianola, Mississippi, and by October he had helped found thirty other councils, which together formed the Association of Citizens' Councils, joined soon by the first council outside Mississippi, in Selma, Alabama. They began to purge libraries and magazine racks, edit television and ban films, harass teachers, and drive the NAACP underground. Then they went after the state houses. From 1955 to 1957 Southern states enacted 120 pieces of racial legislation: This was not a movement of a handful of rednecks. It was a movement of the South, the aim of which was, according to Patterson, to prevent the "mongrelization" of the Caucasian race.[27]

To understand this fearsome uprising, we must pause to explore a pocket of the Southern mind. We have said, borrowing from W. J. Cash (who died before *Brown*), that there was a Southern mind, which lived in the embrace of a myth. This myth, though surely not the same throughout the South, was, in the influence it bore, unparalleled by any comparable thought in the North. It recognized certain virtues—individualism and honor, purity and Southern solidarity, and a curious blend of aristocracy and egalitarianism. It inculcated a fear of inferiority; its purpose was one of daring and supremacy. Its crux was race. The Civil War put a strain on this myth. Slavery had amounted to the legal and social recognition of white supremacy; and the impossibility of mingling the races was an assumption established beyond doubt. But when emancipation made blacks putatively free and equal, the assumption was somewhat weakened, and the need to keep blacks from whites became more urgent than ever before. The South, therefore, became obsessed with racial purity. Its mind spat out in its direct and surreal fashion the image of the pure Southern white woman, gentle and fair, for whom the war was fought; the caste system and Jim Crow sprang up to keep the black man from her body. "Amalgamation" and "mongrelization" were the dreaded prospect, contrary to nature and human instinct, beastly in the act and pernicious in its effect. Raped by the North in the Civil War and unnerved by the threat of dying culture, the South lynched its alleged black rapists to save what it had left. Sex was the bottom issue. On this point the South was hysterical.

Desegregation touched this point, raised in the Southern mind the possibility of miscegenation, and hence provoked a hysterical reaction. (The South, it should be noted, was not unique in having this reaction. In Ireland, the one untouchable issue since the 1920s has been school integration: Catholics and Protestants reluctantly discuss collaboration in government and civic affairs but not in their schools. In Quebec, where the English and French communities fear that each is attempting to control the culture of the province, the two fight most bitterly over the education of their children. For it is by one's offspring, and by the schooling of one's offspring, that one's heritage is passed on; if the schools are altered or if the children interbreed, one fears that one's heritage may come to an end.) Southerners, whose identity largely was based on their separateness from blacks, were especially determined to keep themselves separate.

To justify segregation, they concocted a set of reasons, a rationale, which was a sort of historicism. Jim Crow laws they regarded as the "final settlement," the "return to sanity," and by this they meant that legal segregation merely affirmed relations which at heart were natural. They adopted William Graham Sumner, the Yale sociologist writing at the start of the twentieth century, as their hero for having asserted, in *Folkways,* that patterns of behavior were such because they were inherently correct: Laws could not change them, though laws might affirm them.[28] Now, this was not a new idea but one which was, ironically, first directed against the world of myths and legend. When Giovanni Vico searched for a science of history, he meant to discard romance and to see how the events of history were made of a piece, how things of the moment sprang from early origins and grew, tempered by the mind and habits of man, to become what they are. The discipline of history began. Later in the eighteenth century, Montesquieu related social life to racial types and climates; Herder devised an evolutionary theory of culture; and Burke produced the English variant, finding in the slow accretion of precedents, of customs and experience, an organic growth that produced the England of today.

Historians of the nineteenth century elaborated this theme, sorting out the ways the past always burdened the present. Hegel's notion of the dialectic presumed the organic development of society, and so did Marx's theory of revolution. Revolution would come not when an idea decreed it or a man declared it but when the working class and the productive functions of capitalism both had reached such a state that revolution needed no urging—it was inevitable. Michelet, subscribing to a more cultural historicism, recalled a peasant revolt and wrote, "The souls of our fathers still throb in us for pains that have been forgotten, almost as the man who has been wounded feels an ache in the hand he has lost."[29] Thomas Carlyle echoed Burke, took a dim view of the French Revolution, and lamented the loss of a laden heritage, rashly washed away in blood. Alexis de Tocqueville, writing of France and America, stressed above all the habits of mind and political customs in a nation's history. On France he said, "Though the men of '89 had overthrown the ancient edifice, its foundations had been laid immutably in the minds of all Frenchmen, even its destroyers; thus there was little trouble in re-establishing it not only rapidly but in a more stable, shockproof form." And about America he concluded it was the origins of the people, their race and background, and the customs the colonists carried, that destined the nation to be democratic.[30]

There was then this weighty record of historical interpretation, compiled by writers separated by centuries and a host of doctrines but united by this: that the ruling conditions in history are the heritage and ways of the people, that change comes only as the people themselves change, and that laws and government rise out of their customs—and not the other way around. This view has fallen under some disrepute in the twentieth century, as the writing of history took on the qualities of a science; the study of class, ideology, economics, and statistics displaced the study of human nature and manners. But recently a modified historicism has crept into our thoughts, and today its earlier repudiation seems a bit precipitate, the science a bit too pallid. Two and a half centuries after Vico, Gunnar Myrdal concluded, after an exhaustive study of poverty and government in Asia, that it was fallacy to assume that the principles of Western democracy were suited to the customs of Asian peoples.[31] And our own experience in Southeast Asia and Latin America should remind us that Vico had a point.

It was to this point that Southerners returned. They did so in the 1950s, desperately, under pressure, for *Brown* had shocked them.[32] The Court was unequivocal and also unanimous, but more than that it raised in many Southern minds the spectre of miscegenation. The Southern myth was invoked, and old fears sprang to life. In a pamphlet titled *Black Monday: Segregation or Amalgamation . . . America Has Its Choice,* Judge Tom Brady—the segregationists' philosophe, the "old fire-eatin judge," according to one fellow-Mississippian—cut to the heart of the matter:[33] "Whenever and wherever his blood has been infused with the blood of the negro, the whiteman, his intellect and his culture have died." He was more explicit: "You cannot place little white and negro children together in classrooms and not have integration. They will sing together, dance together. . . . Constantly the negro will be endeavoring to usurp every right and privilege which will lead to intermarriage. This is the way it has worked in the North." Why did the South resist, what was there to protect? It was this: "The loveliest and purest of God's creatures, the nearest thing to an angelic being that treads this terrestrial ball"—"a well-bred cultural Southern white woman, or her blue-eyed, gold-haired, little girl."[34]

Brady then turned to history, echoing Sumner: "A law is never paramount to mores. Habits and customs produce folkways which in turn evolve into mores. . . . Laws like bullets cannot kill a sacred custom." Race was the driving force in history, for it was his understanding—and here the pallor of a little science would not have hurt him—that the Anglos, the Britons, the Slavs, the Teutons, and the Huns "developed a well regulated, efficient form of government," but

> the negroid man, like the modern lizard, evolved not. While the two other species of man [the "Great White Race" and "Mongolians"] were in the violent throes of change and growth, the negro remained in a primitive status. Although both the other races of mankind had for some time tabooed it, cannibalism was an expected risk in the life of the negro of this period. Why was it that the negro was unable and failed to evolve and develop? It is obvious that many rationalizations and explanations will be offered by minority group leaders and educators, but the fact remains that he did not evolve simply because of his inherent limitations. Water does not rise above its source, and the negro could not by his inherent qualities rise above his environment as had the other races. His inheritance was wanting. The potential did not exist. This is neither right nor wrong; it is simply a stubborn biological fact.[35]

For ninety pages he went on, attacking communism, the welfare state, Washington, blacks, the NAACP, integration, and defending

Christianity, the white woman, and the power of a people to choose their ways. *Brown* had put the Southern mind in an uproar. It was frenzied as it had not been since the days of populism, challenged on the vital issues of sex and caste. The South began to resist.

Its political leaders, all of them Democrats, summoned the people to the cause. On May 18, 1954, the day after the Supreme Court acted, Richard Russell denounced the decision on the Senate floor. On May 27, James Eastland did the same, defended segregation, and told the Senate that it was the law of nature that every race have the right and duty to perpetuate itself. More to the point, he said: "I know that Southern people, by and large, will neither recognize, abide by, nor comply with this decision. I know that in the foreseeable future, they will not permit their schools to be racially integrated. I know that there will be no compromise."[36] Herman Talmadge, the bright and soft-spoken, courtly governor (now senator) of Georgia, shared a dais with Judge Tom Brady, the intellectual father of the resistance, and listened while the judge explained that the Court could not shrink the skull of a black man, "which is one eighth of an inch thicker than a white man's." Governor Timmerman of South Carolina and Governor Folsom of Alabama, both moderates on racial questions, joined the resistance and declared themselves against integration.[37]

All this bluster led to the rebirth of interposition, a doctrine made famous by John Calhoun, now revived by Harry Byrd and James Eastland. Interposition, like nullification, meant that states had the right and duty to nullify federal law, interposing themselves between the federal government and the people it was tyrannizing. Senator Harry Byrd, as late as 1956, said that interposition was "a perfectly legal means of appeal from the Supreme Court's order." Herman Talmadge saw things differently: the problem of interposition, tantamount to secession, "was pretty-well settled by the Civil War."[38] Eastland knew this, too, but had no choice. "*Brown* shocked everybody," a friend explained. "That caused the breach. We had to do something, and without interposition we had nothing. Harry Byrd and Jimmy [Eastland] were the daddies of it. And it gave us time. Jimmy spoke to the legislature and put the proposition of interposition to them and they adopted it. Politicians needed time, an exit. We was just buying time."[39] These leaders, like Calhoun before them, found they had to keep abreast of the growing hysteria, which they, invoking the Southern myth, had helped induce. It was a dangerous business, this appeal to the people's fear and blood.

They outdid each other in defying the law. The Alabama legislature passed resolutions denouncing desegregation, the Supreme Court, and the NAACP, then declared the Court decision "null, void and of no effect." Georgia and South Carolina forbade the expenditure of state funds on desegregated schools, then joined Mississippi and Alabama in repealing the constitutional requirement that the state maintain a school system. Eugene Cook, attorney general of Georgia, urged enactment of a law that would impose the death penalty on anyone helping federal authorities enforce the *Brown* decision. Alabama, Louisiana, and Texas outlawed the NAACP, whose purpose was, according to one state senator, to "open the bedroom doors of our white women to the Negro man." Citizens' councils elected slates of delegates to the Democratic National Convention. Council leaders criticized Alabama congressmen not vocal in segregationist politics. By July 1956 all nine of the state's congressmen and Senators Lister Hill and John Sparkman—Adlai Stevenson's running mate in 1952— had publicly declared their interest in speaking at council rallies.[40] The pressure was awesome.

There were other tactics. In 1955 John Barr of Louisiana set up the Federation for Constitutional Government, a states' rights group committed to fight liberals and desegregation. Eastland became a leader of it, and in 1956 he called for a national organization to "fight the Court, to fight the CIO, to fight the NAACP and to fight all the conscienceless pressure groups who are attempting our destruction." On the federation's advisory council sat, after Eastland, Talmadge, Governor Griffin of Georgia, former Governor Fielding Wright and Congressman John Bell Williams of Mississippi, former Governor Coke Stevenson of Texas, and Senator Strom Thurmond of South Carolina. This was not an isolated minority. This was the leadership of the South, and in the U.S. House of Representatives they mustered enough votes to pass bills restricting the Court's power and in the Senate came within eight votes of nullifying Court decisions—a questionable constitutional action.[41] Nor did they desist as the campaign year came on. During the opening of the presidential primaries, on February 11, 1956, Democratic leaders and citizens' councils convened in Montgomery, Alabama, where they sponsored the biggest segregationist rally ever held. Ten to fifteen thousand people came to hear council leaders and James Eastland exhort their followers (or leaders) never to compromise on the caste system. Leaflets were passed out, as the band played "Dixie"; one read: "We hold these truths to be self-evident, that all whites are created equal with certain rights; among these are life, liberty, and the pursuit of dead niggers." Eastland made a triumphal arrival, rushed there in a highway patrol car, alighting to declare, "Thank God the state of Alabama has started the offense; from this day, the direction is forward."[42]

There were still other ways to defend white supremacy. There was violence—more than there had been for several years. From 1955 to 1958, 530 cases of racial violence and intimidation were reported. There was also disfranchisement. Registration of blacks in the South jumped from approximately 80,000 before the 1944 Court decision, which outlawed the white primary, to 595,000 in 1947, then jumped again during Truman's administration to over one million in 1952. From then until 1956 the increase continued but was smaller, only 200,000, and from 1956 to 1958 registration stayed stable, with enormous drops in many counties, especially those where black population was highest and hence racial tension the worst. Throughout the South 25 percent of eligible blacks registered to vote; 60 percent of the whites did. From 1955 to 1959 less than 1 percent of the eligible blacks registered in half of Mississippi's eighty-two counties. Much of this imbalance stemmed from old patterns, but much also came from the purging of voting lists by the citizens' councils. Registrars, at the behest of the councils or on their own, barred the registration of blacks, alleging they could not pass the literacy test, did not reside in the county or parish, could not recite or interpret the state constitution, or had omitted their initial in signing their name. In a period of several months during 1956 and 1957, eleven thousand blacks were stricken from the voting lists in twelve parishes in Louisiana. State Senator William Rainach, chairman of the Joint Legislative Committee on Segregation, and head of Louisiana's Association of Citizens' Councils, announced his intention in 1959 to purge another 100,000 of his state's 130,000 black voters. His intention was, as he put it, to "solve our segregation problem."[43]

The resistance was in full swing, touting purity and the immovable folkways of the South, when on May 31, 1955, the Supreme Court issued its implementation decree. It was a compromise. It took into account the arguments of the attorneys for the Summerton, South Carolina, school board: the South was not all the same, they argued, and the Court's decision should be implemented with local facts borne in mind. One fact, for instance, was that the parents of 295 white Summerton students would never send their children to school with 2,799 black students.[44] The lawyers had a point: the South was not all of a piece. Blacks fared worst in blackbelt regions where they outnumbered the whites, somewhat better in such coastal counties as Beaufort, South Carolina, and perhaps best of all in Southern cities, which contributed most of the South's black votes. The Court duly took account and decreed, "Because of their proximity to local conditions and the possible need for further hearings, the courts which originally heard these cases can best perform this judicial appraisal." The justices instructed the lower courts to require a "prompt and reasonable start toward full compliance with our May 17, 1954, ruling. Once such a start has been made, the courts may find that additional time is necessary to carry out the ruling in an effective manner. The burden rests upon the defendant to establish that such time is necessary to the public interest." The district courts must enter such orders and decrees that are "necessary and proper to admit to public schools on a racially non-discriminatory basis with all deliberate speed the parties to the cases."[45] "All deliberate speed"—Rauh found it regressive, and the South sighed in relief. One lieutenant governor said, "A 'reasonable' time can be construed as one year or two hundred. . . . Thank God we've got good federal judges." Resistance, far from relaxing, stiffened. By the end of 1955, the citizens' councils claimed over 200,000 members in 568 local councils spread across the South. The Summerton attorney was pleased—and defiant: "Nothing happened. Nothing's happened *yet*. And nothing's *going* to happen."[46]

The implementation decree compounded the Democrats' political problem. It left the timetable and means of integration open to interpretation and thus brought the matter into the political campaigns of 1956. The decree also deepened the Democrats' division. It encouraged the South, swelled its confidence and made resistance spread. Southerners grew more isolated; defiance bedimmed their vision. In six states they passed bills of interposition. They discerned a Northern conspiracy, led by labor and civil rights groups, dedicated to the overthrow of "our Government" by means of integration. They imagined Northern blacks, instigated by liberals, working to undermine the Southern way of life: "These new deal, square deal, liberated, black qualified electors," said Brady, "are determined to indoctrinate the Southern negro with this ideal, and arouse him to follow them in their social program

for amalgamation of the two races."[47] Rumor and propaganda
deepened divisions.

The nation may be thankful that the Democratic party happened to contain these divisions. The Court had decided for the
long term the fate of the caste system and also of the Southern
mind, but it created a severe political crisis, especially in its implementation decree, and it was the Democratic party, a party
encompassing both sides, that bore the brunt of this tension.
The party had reached a hiatus in its ideological struggle, a moment
when the papered compromise of 1952 was crumbling in shreds,
and at that moment, the Court put the Democrats on the spot.
For ten years they had given their views on the equality of opportunity and the freedom of man. Now the Court refined the questions—how long should integration take and by what means should
it come about, what was the machinery and what the timetable
to meet the goals one professed to champion? It was a hard test.
It brought the contest of ideology into sharp focus. It was an
inescapable and cruel issue, especially for thoughtful men, like
Adlai Stevenson.

EIGHT

THE 1956 CAMPAIGN

Lyndon Johnson turned to Richard Russell and explained, "I had Stevenson in a room up against the wall, my knife in his stomach. He might have given in when I felt a knife in my ribs, and I turned around—it was Finnegan."

The story was this. In 1956 Adlai Stevenson needed either the liberals or the South to win the nomination in Chicago. He wanted several large delegations—Michigan, New York, Texas—but the first two considered him a moderate, and they were liberal. So Jim Finnegan, the Philadelphia leader and Stevenson's campaign manager, went after Texas and arranged a meeting with Johnson, who wanted the nomination or at least to control it; Finnegan went along, and so did Jim Rowe, advising Johnson. The meeting began. Johnson said to Stevenson he would do better with the Southern delegations if he let up on civil rights. Stevenson said nothing. There was a pause. From behind Lyndon Johnson came the word, "No." "What?" he asked, and wheeled around. And Finnegan told him: "We can't budge on civil rights." The meeting ended.[1]

Civil rights, the center of controversy at the 1956 convention, again raised its head to govern the politics of the Democratic party. Stevenson tried to slide, but Finnegan held him, and so did Kefauver, his opponent in the spring primaries, who along with Harriman strongly supported the Court's decision and forced Stevenson left, behind integration. This was crucial. But they did even more. For by moving so far left they not only dragged Stevenson with them but also kept him in the center, a center which was shifting: Stevenson might be strong on civil rights now, but he was always more moderate than Kefauver; and by staying in the middle of the leftward moving screen, he held the South for himself and also for the party. He still seemed the appeaser, as in 1952, still the compromise choice of North and South, but so much had happened

since—*Brown,* the Southern resistance, and the spring primaries—
that the party was more liberal and the South more confined. So
when Finnegan said "No"—a "no" which four years before had
been a "yes"—the meeting ended, Johnson went back to his hotel
room, and the South went back to Stevenson.

The Primaries

Estes Kefauver announced his candidacy on December 16,
1955, and campaigned in California and Minnesota in February
and March. He was a success. On February 4, 1956, he spoke to
a convention of the Democratic Clubs of California in Fresno and
gave a hard-hitting liberal speech, interrupted forty-three times by
applause.[2] That weekend he met with black leaders and satisfied
them with promises he never revealed. Then the controversial
Powell amendment surfaced—an amendment to a school construction bill that would bar federal funds from schools that defied
the Court's desegregation order—and Kefauver said, on February
10, that if the president did not himself bar funds from such
schools, he, Kevauver, might be compelled to vote for the amendment. No other major politician, save Averell Harriman, who
endorsed the amendment outright, had come so close to supporting Powell's proposal. But Kefauver sensed a rising Northern tide
of reaction against the South and was aiming to ride its crest. For
next he strengthened his position on the Court decisions: "The
Supreme Court is the final authority on constitutional matters.
When it rendered its school decision that decision was and is the
law of the land. . . . I think the President ought to exert his own
influence and good offices." He also promised to end discrimination in the Federal Government, spoke of his support for abolition
of the poll tax and filibuster, and urged that people of all races
get together to plan to implement the Court's decision.[3] These
positions on civil rights appealed to California's large minority
population. They also—along with Kefauver's vigorous handshaking and tireless campaigning—scared the Stevenson people. Kefauver again had found the right issue.

National primaries require a special campaign. Heated issues,
some small, others not, crop up every few days in a variety of
states; and the candidate succeeds who can answer quickly and to
the point, almost any point, so long as he gets it across—standing
in a shopping mall or on the back of a pickup truck, then on to
a new street corner in a different state and a new local issue. Adlai

Stevenson never before had campaigned in national primaries, and at first he floundered. His uplifting speeches ignored the local issues. He lectured the audience, tried to educate it. He repeated the Evansville and Harlem episodes of 1952 and told his listeners what they did not want to hear, as if to reprove them, or perhaps himself, for doing what he thought he should disdain.

On February 4 he too spoke to the Democratic Clubs convention in Fresno. His was a long, eloquent oration on democratic ideals and integrity, which bored his listeners, who thought he was dodging the issues.[4] It was a Kefauver triumph and a Stevenson disaster, the sort that hurts at the campaign's start. Three days later Stevenson spoke to a group of blacks in Los Angeles. He said he would not as president cut off federal funds from segregated schools, nor use troops to enforce the Court order—"It can't be done by troops, or bayonets. We must proceed gradually, not upsetting habits or traditions that are older than the Republic." The crowd murmured. He said he did not understand "interposition"—the crowd grew angry—that the North and South had to live together, that he could not imagine a "balkanized America," that, finally, a target date for integration might be January 1, 1963, the 100th anniversary of the Emancipation Proclamation. The crowd groaned. The *New York Times* carried the headline on its first page, "Stevenson Backs 'Gradual' Moves For Integration," and Stevenson was pegged a "gradualist," outflanked on the left by Kefauver.[5] It was a lousy beginning.

This first California trip established Stevenson's reputation as a moderate on racial matters—or even a man who cared little about the condition of black Americans. Members of his staff, most of them liberal intellectuals, were dismayed. A rumor spread that Stevenson's campaign train in 1952 had been segregated; a woman reporter alleged that while on the train in Georgia she had been obliged to eat in a separate dining car, an unlikely story—Stevenson had no campaign train in Georgia in 1952. The story hurt nonetheless. One advisor thought that their candidate's stand on interposition, gradualism, and the Powell amendment gave people the impression that Stevenson lacked a "deep and genuine sense of concern." Some thought this unfair, for Stevenson honestly believed, according to one staff aide, that "these things were not going to be done that quickly. . . . He thought the solution was long-term education." Another said he was not indifferent to civil rights only tired of talking about it; he complained about the persistence of the issue and threatened to quit discussing desegregation altogether.[6] Stevenson never liked to be pressured.

Trouble deepened for Stevenson when on March 24 Kefauver defeated him in the Minnesota primary. He had campaigned hard there with the support of Hubert Humphrey's powerful Democratic Farmer-Labor party. But Kefauver's folksiness, his smile and a handshake—and also the Republican crossover into the Democratic primary—were enough to beat Stevenson. This came after Kefauver's New Hampshire victory, and now he looked good for Florida and California. Suddenly another problem: the Southern manifesto appeared. Senator George of Georgia introduced this "Declaration of Constitutional Principles" to the Senate on March 12, a statement signed by ninety-six congressmen (representing eleven states), among them Senators Russell, Stennis, Thurmond, Byrd, McClellan, Hill, Eastland, Smathers, Fulbright, Sparkman, and Ervin—every Southern senator but Johnson, Kefauver, and Gore. They undertook to justify the Southern resistance of the last two years. Segregation was "a part of the life of the people of many of the States and [it] confirmed their habits, customs, traditions, and way of life," they said, echoing Sumner and the historicists. "It is founded on elemental humanity and common sense." In outlawing segregation the Court had abused its power and upset the system of checks and balances; the congressmen called upon the states to assert their authority, commending those "which have declared the intention to resist forced integration by any lawful means." They called upon the people to reverse the Court's decision.[7]

The Southern resistance had festered for two years, seeped out of the South into Washington, and produced the manifesto. Now it entered national politics. It hardened the ideological positions in the party and divided the sides as with an axe. It could only help Kefauver. He refused to sign the manifesto and, as a Southerner, led the liberal reaction to it. In a press conference on March 22 he said that the Southern states would not be able to resist successfully the Court's decision, that he opposed interposition, and that the Court's decisions were the law of the land. He walked through the streets of San Francisco and said he had not signed the manifesto—as a Southerner, all he need have said. The crowds cheered.[8] Stevenson was in trouble.

The campaign got tougher. Not only Stevenson but also Kefauver was bedeviled. For they ran not only in California, where the Democratic voters were strongly pro–civil rights, but at the same time in Florida, where such up-country districts as the Panhandle were filled with violently segregationist voters. It was hard to say the same thing in both California and Florida—and if one did not, the national press would notice. On February 15, Kefauver had told a campus audience in Florida that local conditions should be taken into account before setting a date for integration, emphasizing of course what he chose not to emphasize in California. He also said he would "oppose any effort to bar proposed Federal school construction funds to states which have segregated schools"—the opposite of his position in California five days earlier. Then he changed his strategy. Since California was the important primary, and since he would lose Florida anyway—the South hated him so—Kefauver decided in early April to come out strongly for civil rights. And he would do it in Florida. He would get credit for his courage, and that might give him California. On a television program in Orlando, Kefauver proclaimed it was "ridiculous to say that a Supreme Court decision is unconstitutional," hardly a radical position, but in Florida unpopular.[9] It was a shrewd maneuver, and now, after this, the Minnesota primary, and the Southern manifesto, Stevenson's campaign was sinking. A voter survey in Illinois showed that blacks were leaving him.[10] It was April already. Stevenson had to act.

He moved left. It was not an easy move for him. For two years he had solicited advice from his Southern friends and concurred in their opinion that conciliation was the best policy. Even in early April he told his campaign staff, during a meeting at his home in Libertyville, "how [in the words of one of those present] his role was that of the conciliator, that this was a role requiring far more courage than pro-civil rights demagoguery, and that making remarks which provoked the South would only delay the eventual achievement of the objective." He said he might call for a one-year moratorium on all civil rights actions, and when Schlesinger asked if this meant he thought the Democratic platform could avoid endorsing the Court decision, he "said he didn't know about that, hoped the question could be avoided, and wanted to talk to his southern friends about it." Schlesinger and others left the meeting disappointed, with the sense that their candidate did "not feel any strong moral issue in the civil rights fight; that he identifies instinctively with the problems of the southern white rather than with the sufferings of the southern negro."[11] On civil rights, on which all his tendencies—his upbringing, his conception of politics as an educational forum, and the image he held of himself as the conciliator of warring factions—

militated against his taking a strong position.

But he had little choice, as his staff saw the matter, and on the road, little by little, they pushed him left in April. They got him to quit saying he did not understand interposition and to declare himself against it.[12] They got him to stop using the word "bayonet" when saying he opposed sending troops to enforce the Court's decree in the South—Eastland had made the word popular, and blacks resented it. Of most importance, he quit saying the word "gradual." Though he would not specify a means for implementing the Court's decision, Stevenson said in California that were he president, "I would work ceaselessly and with a sense of crucial urgency—with public officials, private groups, and educators—to meet this challenge in our life as a nation."[13] He might be tired of civil rights, but he did not show it, and what he did show forced Kefauver to take even more liberal positions. He made more promises and supported measures he had opposed two months before. On May 10—two days after Stevenson avowed his sense of crucial urgency—Kefauver reversed his position of former years and said that segregation could not be justified— earlier he had merely affirmed the Court's authority. On May 19 Kefauver spoke out again on the Powell amendment, for the third time and with a third position: he implied that any school defying the Court's desegregation order should be barred from receiving federal funds.[14]

The campaign intensified. Kefauver called Stevenson a racist, but this hurt himself more than Stevenson. It also kept civil rights in center stage and Stevenson moving leftward.

On May 22 former Governor Millard Caldwell, a segregationist, introduced Adlai Stevenson to a rally on the steps of the State Capitol in Tallahassee, Florida. Caldwell read from an editorial in the *Richmond News Leader,* which maligned Kefauver for not having signed the Southern manifesto and described him as "a far-left liberal and a sycophant for the Negro and union vote." Caldwell, who led Stevenson's Florida slate of delegates in the primary, went on to say that Stevenson was the "most moderate man the South can elect," then implied Stevenson favored white supremacy. There was a pause as Caldwell moved from the microphone. Stevenson stood up and, apparently not having listened to the introduction, calmly acknowledged Caldwell's praise and began his speech. His aides were horrified and later told him of the remarks. Stevenson called a press conference to disavow Caldwell's views and the editorial, but the damage was done. Kefauver accused Stevenson of duplicity—of using Caldwell and Congressman Sikes, who signed the manifesto, in Florida and Eleanor Roosevelt in California.[15] Of course this was true.

On May 29 Stevenson won in Florida by a narrow margin. He won overwhelmingly in only one district—Congressman Sikes' Third District in the Panhandle, a "bigoted, woolhatted, backward section, the one place where we really shouldn't win."[16] He had said little about civil rights in the last weeks, hoping to squeak by as the lesser evil in a segregationist state. It worked.

But it hurt in California. After the Florida defeat, Kefauver's campaign manager, Jiggs Donohue, charged that "Stevenson's White Supremacy supporters functioned on a low level with the knowledge of the former Governor of Illinois. . . . A vote for Stevenson is a vote for Eastland, Talmadge, Ellender, and the other White Supremacy boys."[17] In the last week of the campaign Kefauver grew desperate and shrill. Five days before the California election, he said Stevenson was the captive of Sikes, Caldwell, and the segregationist South, that he had refused to repudiate Caldwell's remarks, and that he had no record on civil rights. He was bitter and it showed: he lost California in a landslide. He was, as throughout his career, trapped; blacks voted five to one for Stevenson, because Kefauver was Southern; and whites were afraid he was reckless or too liberal.[18]

But it took a little recklessness to be bold on civil rights. For two years neither the Democratic leadership nor the Republican administration had challenged the massive Southern resistance, much of it illegal. Then in California Kefauver spoke out, and around the nation others did, too—G. Mennen Williams in Michigan, Averell Harriman in New York, and Adlai Stevenson in California. The ball was rolling; civil rights got its biggest push since 1948; Southern defiance was now an issue. Kefauver's role was crucial. All he did, it seemed, was announce his support for the law of the land and accuse Stevenson of harboring affection for white supremacy. But for a Southerner this was a dramatic move—and the only ploy he had for winning the nomination— yet he did not benefit from it, for once again he permitted Stevenson to emerge as the unity candidate, only now a unity candidate of a different sort.

The Convention

Adlai Stevenson had won the 1952 nomination without staking out an ideological position—he was drafted, after a liberal speech and a pro-Southern switch in the Illinois credentials vote—

but now in 1956 he did not have the advantage of the reluctant, unknown, and called-upon leader. He was known, and he sought the nomination. To win it he had to commit himself to a line, gather votes, and lay claims to blocs of states. He had to become, in short, more political, especially since a party wounded by the Court decisions, Southern resistance, and primary fights would be hard to coalesce. But Stevenson supporters were good politicians; Arvey's mastering of the credentials vote was political practice at its keenest. Again they would work hard in Chicago.

The first problem was the South: it supported him too much. Senator Stennis of Mississippi said that Southern Democrats saw Stevenson as "their candidate" because of his "moderate" views on segregation. Ellender of Louisiana on "Face the Nation" said that Stevenson realized progress on civil rights "will take time," that if Kefauver or Harriman were nominated "there may be a move for a third party in the South," that the Southern position was to press the Supreme Court to reverse its decision. On May 14, the *New York Times* ran a page-one headline—"Talmadge For Stevenson"—and next day it read: "Kefauver Scorns Talmadge's Snub: Asserts He Will Not Change Stand on Rights to Gain Georgian's Support."[19] Stevenson looked conservative.

And it was not only the conservatives' doing. For as the national convention approached, liberals took strong civil rights positions to isolate Stevenson. In June, Kefauver announced he would support an antilynching bill, a constitutional amendment to abolish the poll tax, and a right-to-vote bill. G. Mennen Williams called for a platform plank requiring immediate implementation of the Court decision, abolition of the filibuster, and reform of the seniority system that gave an inordinate number of congressional committee chairmanships to Southerners.[20] The AFL-CIO lamented the formation of citizens' councils and supported the desegregation decisions. Stevenson faced a liberal strategy similar to that of 1952: split the convention, drive Stevenson into a conservative corner, and nominate a liberal. Schlesinger warned Stevenson of Harriman's intentions: "I should emphasize the fact that Harriman . . . and the others have (I think) sincerely persuaded themselves that you really are basically pro-southern and pro-conservative; that the Democratic party can win only as a liberal party; and that they are therefore rescuing the party from a fate worse than death. They are genuine in this conviction."[21]

Stevenson realized in June that he had to stake a claim to the New Deal–Fair Deal heritage. Did he like the liberal program? In

1957, he would write to a close friend, defending his moderation in civil rights and attacking "our intolerant northern liberals that irritate me so much." And the next year he would write again to this friend to tell her how happy he was that she thought as he did that "gradualism" was the best solution to the race problem. But in June 1956, seeking nomination with a liberal tide running, Stevenson needed to change his image. He sought the help of his friends. When Adolf Berle congratulated him, on June 7, for the success of his "moderation" in the primaries, Stevenson replied that he was tired of the "incessant talk about moderation manufactured by the Republican press" and hoped Berle would write an article explaining Stevenson's liberal record on civil rights. On June 8, Stevenson complained to Eleanor Roosevelt that "the Republican press will make an effort to portray Averell as the only authentic successor to the New Deal–Fair Deal. . . . dismissing me meanwhile as a pale imitation of Eisenhower." The same day he sent Schlesinger an almost identical letter, forgetting it was Schlesinger who had written Stevenson four years before (in April 1952), saying Harriman seemed the proper heir to the New Deal–Fair Deal policies.[22]

Stevenson worked so hard to shed his conservative image that former Democratic National Committee Chairman Stephen Mitchell thought he might lose his Southern support in the few weeks before the convention.[23] But he did not; the South could not afford to abandon him, even as he took a more liberal position on civil rights, for the alternative was Kefauver. Having trapped himself in a liberal corner, Kefauver recognized the futility of his position. He made a dramatic, though risky move. On July 31 he withdrew and, seeking the vice-presidential nomination, threw his support to Stevenson.

Kefauver's support helped Stevenson's standing with the liberals. So did Eleanor Roosevelt's backing, though not so much as expected, for she too favored moderation and was helping Paul Butler write a civil rights plank that would keep the South happy. School desegregation, she told Stevenson, must be gradual. On August 12 she went before a press conference to defend Stevenson and the policies of "moderation" and "gradualism."[24] The widow of the first New Dealer, she once had been the foremost white champion of civil rights, but she was not now. As ideology evolved with events, the post–New Deal claimants to liberalism composed the liberal vanguard in the 1950s. Time had moved. Truman had advanced and altered the liberal emphasis; the Court had set the sides afire; and Kefauver had forced the issue. Eleanor Roosevelt was no more the liberal spokesman than was Adlai Stevenson. That lot had fallen to Truman, Harriman, Kefauver, Williams, Humphrey, Lehman, Douglas, Reuther, the ADA, and the NAACP, which in California had opposed Stevenson in favor of Kefauver. There were several liberal spokesmen. So even with Kefauver out, Stevenson was not yet in.

There was still Averell Harriman. As the delegates gathered in Chicago, Harry Truman took the force out of Eleanor Roosevelt's endorsement of Stevenson by endorsing Harriman. Always a fighter, even at seventy-two, he went even further. He called a second press conference and condemned Stevenson's moderation, said Stevenson was born conservative, and said:

> His counsel of moderation seems in reality a counsel of hesitation, and was, in fact, a surrender of the basic principles of the Demo-cratic Party. . . . The destruction of this [New Deal–Fair Deal] social philosophy is the aim of the conservatives and reactionaries in both Parties. What the Democratic Party needs is a dynamic and fighting candidate who will not compromise on fundamental issues. Governor Stevenson is not that type of candidate. . . . He lacks the kind of fighting spirit that we need to win and keep the Party from falling into the hands of a minority group—a conservative minority group.[25]

This pressure both helped and hurt Stevenson. He went to Johnson for Southern votes, which he was sure of getting now, but in nego-tiating he was confined. He could not yield on civil rights. But Harriman was in the same situation, both hurt and helped. Back in 1952 Harriman had opposed the seating of Dixiecrat delega-tions and pushed civil rights and tried hard to split the convention. But he had failed, and now he thought the matter over. He went to see Johnson. He wanted Southern states; he asked for Johnson's help. Johnson was surprised: Harriman was a renowned liberal; how would he get Southern backing? Harriman said he would go soft on civil rights. Johnson was aghast—"You goddamn liberals!" he later said to a friend—and the meeting ended.[26]

On August 6, hearings on the platform began in the Conrad Hilton Hotel in Chicago. For several reasons, the civil rights fight focused on the platform this year and not on credentials. After 1952 the Democratic National Committee had set up a committee, chaired by former Virginia Governor John S. Battle and Senator Humphrey, to formulate rules regarding delegates' credentials. Their report, adopted by the 1956 convention, called for "an understanding" that when each state Democratic party certified its delegates to the national convention, it was also assuring that voters from the state would get a chance to vote for the convention's nominees. So long as the Southern delegates put the nominee on Southern ballots, they would not be subject to a loyalty oath and could work for any candidate they chose.[27] With no loyalty controversy, attention centered on the platform, which in some fashion would have to address the *Brown* decision.

On August 9, Harry Truman testified. He told the platform committee that if it read *To Secure These Rights,* "You would find out then that all these proceedings which have taken place, including the decision of the Supreme Court, about which there is so much controversy, was an enforcement of the law which has been a part of the fundamental and basic law of this United States since the late 1860s."[28] On the next day labor leaders testified. After attacking the white citizens' councils, George Meany said that because of the illegal segregationist resistance, the convention should adopt a strong position in support of the Court's decision. Reuther and Woodcock of the Auto Workers and spokesmen for local labor organizations around the country also spoke, and they linked civil rights action to demands for a higher minimum wage, increased Social Security, housing, medical care aid, and unemployment compensation. Reuther attacked the Democratic and Republican conservative bloc in Congress for keeping liberal legislation from ever reaching a vote, and said that in view of the failure of the Republicans, especially Eisenhower, to commit themselves to uphold the law, it fell to the Democratic party to provide leadership and support the Court's decision. The chairman of the Democratic National Advisory Committee on Labor counted the FEPC among his demands for labor. James B. Carey, president of the International Union of Electrical, Radio and Machine Workers, endorsed the statements of Meany and others and said, "Now we need a Fair Deal, and these recommendations being made I think point the way."[29]

On August 10, other liberal groups testified, most of them concerned with a strong civil rights plank. Roy Wilkins, speaking for the NAACP and the Leadership Conference, said that if the convention supported federal enforcement of the Court's decisions, an end to the filibuster, and a guarantee of the right to vote, the Democratic party would once again "represent the plain people of America." A. Philip Randolph was more direct. "Moderation," he said, "presupposes the continued existence of segrega-

tion, of course, in moderation. . . . Moderate segregation is just as
unacceptable, unsound and inconceivable as moderate pregnancy,
moderate crime, moderate disease, a moderate lie or moderate
poverty." He then attacked Eisenhower, condemned Southern
discrimination, and said the 1956 plank had to be bolder than the
weak, vague civil rights plank of 1952. Senator Herbert Lehman
of New York stressed that a strong civil rights plank would give
direction to the party (just as a white supremacist plank would).
He said, "I believe that the successful fight that was waged in
1948 at the Democratic Convention for a more adequate civil
rights plank gained for the Democratic Party a new maturity.
By resolving openly and above-board the differences that were
in the Party at that time, the Democratic Party demonstrated its
courage and honesty." The American Civil Liberties Union joined
the ranks, too, submitted a statement endorsing the Wilkins speech,
and advocated labor and civil rights measures to protect human
rights.[30]

But it was Joseph Rauh and the ADA that most clearly expressed the liberals' position. The party had reached a crossroads,
its ideology uncertain, and the civil rights fight, Rauh believed,
would determine the future. The moment was upon them: the
Democrats would become the

> Party of unsegregated federal aid or it will no longer be the Party of
> federal aid. The Democratic Party's claims in this area now depend
> on its becoming the all-out spokesman for civil rights. Thus civil
> rights is no longer a single or a separate issue for the Democratic
> Party; the good faith of its proposals for welfare legislation is tied
> to its support of the Supreme Court's school decisions. Just because
> so much of the liberal base of the Democratic Party's program is at
> stake, the 1956 platform on civil rights must be unequivocal. Once
> and for all, the Democratic Party must set to rest the notion that the
> geographical division of the Party requires compromise; once and for
> all the Party must surmount this geographical division and put itself
> wholeheartedly on the side of civil rights.[31]

He recited the party's liberal tradition, spoke of Wilson, Roosevelt,
and Truman, then concluded his testimony:

> In other words, the Supreme Court has pointed the way for the
> future . . . and therefore if this Party, as I would hope, is going to
> remain the Party of welfare legislation, of Federal aid to education,
> housing, and health, it is going to have to face up to the civil rights

problem, and therefore, we ask you on behalf of the A.D.A. for a foursquare plank stating that the Supreme Court's decisions on segregation are moral and must be implemented by the Executive and Legislative Branches of the Government.[32]

Joe Rauh had a driving mind. When he caught hold of an idea, he would not let go. His interest was always labor rights and civil rights, and he served as general counsel for the UAW and for the Leadership Conference on Civil Rights, as chairman of the ADA, and as board member of the NAACP. (Out of law school, he had clerked for Cardozo and Frankfurter on the Supreme Court.) He was persistent—whether in leading the fight for the minority plank in 1948, or in picketing a Safeway Market in support of migrant workers on a Saturday in February 1976. This year, in 1956, he grasped and stated the significance of the civil rights issue. The issue had divided the Democrats since Truman's presidency, though its meaning never had been fully explained. It was coming into the open now. Civil rights was crucial in itself, but crucial also for what it meant to the South and meant to liberals, who had found in the federal government an answer to social injustice. For itself and for what it evoked, civil rights was to both sides the last stand and the first issue in the ideological conflict. This was what Rauh made clear.

And so did the South. South Carolina's Governor George Bell Timmerman spoke the same day as Rauh. "We in the South," he said, "know from generations of experience that segregation is best for both the Negro and the white. For this Party to approve the desegregation decision would be to ask us to support what we know is wrong." He listed the acts of defiance, taken by Southern Democratic parties and legislatures, and said the South would never change. Then he gave his interpretation of the party's purpose, antithetical to Rauh's: "The Democratic Party has been the champion of the rights of the States and the rights of the people"— not of minority people, nor of federal power. But on one matter he agreed with Rauh, saying the issue before the Convention was not just civil rights but also what it stood for, what it threatened to change; at stake was the very survival of "this great Democratic Party of individual freedom and states' rights." To him as well as to Rauh, more than race relations stood in the balance. And Timmerman was not alone. A Louisianan attacked the "professional liberal organizations," Sam Ervin lamented the Court's "usurpation of power," and George Wallace attacked Truman and predicted the disruption of Democratic unity. Both sides felt the tension. The South was defensive, not exuberant; it sensed defeat. The day Wallace testified, the platform committee opened its session with a morning prayer by the Reverend Martin Luther King, Jr., who the year before had led the bus boycott in Montgomery, Alabama.[33]

The platform committee adopted a plank endorsing civil rights and repudiating the Southern resistance, saying, with regard to the school desegregation cases,

> We reject all proposals for the use of force to interfere with the orderly determination of these matters by the courts. The Democratic Party emphatically reaffirms its support of the historic principle that ours is a government of laws and not of men; it recognizes the Supreme Court of the United States as one of three Constitutional and coordinate branches of the Federal Government, superior to and separate from any political party, the decisions of which are part of the law of the land.[34]

Rauh, Lehman, and Williams were outraged. They called for outright endorsement of implementation and regarded the "use of force" clause as potentially a segregationist defense—in the event that troops should be required to integrate schools. But others sought to placate them. Dever of Massachusetts emphasized the liberal slant of the platform, mentioning in the committee's executive session that it had won the endorsement of Harry Truman. Chairman of the platform committee John McCormack insisted the platform was not a compromise and said it "would probably be fair to assume that all members of the Committee from the Southern states . . . have voted against the adoption of the Civil Rights Plank." He said the South had conceded much to a plank that was "affirmative far beyond the 1952 plank."[35] When McCormack presented the platform to the convention, Lehman and Williams backed a more explicit civil rights plank that called for implementation of the segregation decisions. McCormack defended the majority plank and pointed out its advances beyond the 1952 plank:

> The 1952 plank refers to the arguing of civil rights cases in courts. In this plank, Supreme Court decisions on civil rights are recognized as part of the law of the land. . . . the 1952 plank refers to the rights of property, employment and higher education only as being litigated. The plank before us proposes the full rights of voting,

of occupation, of personal security, and education in all publicly
supported institutions. . . . no segregation was mentioned in 1952.
Segregation is specifically mentioned in 1956. . . . What did we say
in 1952 on [education]? "Every American child, irrespective of
color, national origin, economic status or place of residence, should
have every educational opportunity to develop his potentialities."
What have we . . . in this platform tonight; "Every American child,
irrespective of race or national origin, economic status or place of
residence" . . . not "should have" as in 1952, but "has full right" . . .
"under law."[36]

McCormack had a point: the platform was substantially stronger
on civil rights than in 1952.

But a handful wanted it even stronger. Averell Harriman, his
overtures to Johnson having failed, pushed for a stronger plank
now. And so did Lehman of New York, Williams of Michigan,
Douglas of Illinois, the ADA, AFL-CIO, and the NAACP—fourteen votes in the platform committee. The minority caucus knew
it would lose in the committee and decided to take its fight to
the floor, where it knew it would lose again if Rayburn refused to
call the roll. If Rayburn called only a voice vote, the liberals knew
he would declare their plank lost; so meeting in the Pick Congress
Hotel they planned to demand a roll call and hoped that the three
big states they controlled—Michigan, Minnesota, New York—
would persuade Rayburn to comply. The floor fight came, and
McCormack spoke for the majority plank and Douglas, Lehman,
and Williams for the minority. Rayburn ruled as expected that the
strong plank lost by voice vote, but suddenly the demand for a
roll call collapsed. Michigan and Minnesota fell silent, and of the
big states only New York, led by Lehman, pressed for the vote.
The bandwagon stopped and the majority plank stayed.[37]

What stopped the ADA movement, it seems, was Walter
Reuther. When the time came for Michigan to demand the roll
call, Reuther told Williams to be silent, not to go ahead with the
fight—"We've got all we can get so let's stop." And the roll call
ended.[38] Reuther's motives are not clear. Perhaps he saw a repeat
of 1948, when a small group roused the convention to force a
platform issue and drive the South out. Perhaps he thought the
liberals had won the main battle with the plank as it was. Perhaps
he wanted Stevenson for the nominee and feared a split convention would hurt his chances. Perhaps—we do not know—this was
his thinking. If it was, he was right.

For the South was already humiliated. Not only was the civil rights plank offensive, but Harry Truman had praised it from the floor, saying "I have had a hand in going over this platform and it is the best one this Convention has ever had put before it. . . . John McCormack and the Committee that wrote up this platform have just as liberal views as I ever had in my life." There was no Southern plank, no floor fight, no bolt. One observer found the Southern mood one of "apathy."[39] Perhaps the South feared that if it fought for a plank of its own, the convention, provoked, would adopt the Lehman plank. Perhaps it simply knew the fight was useless. It also knew that its hope lay in Stevenson, and a fight or split would hurt his chances.

Those chances were entangled, as usual, in the platform. Harriman's early strategy had been to split the convention with a strong civil rights plank and put Stevenson on the Southern and losing side. The Stevenson forces, realizing this, rewrote the plank that Paul Butler and Eleanor Roosevelt had designed to appease the South, adding to it approval of the Supreme Court decision. But still the Stevenson people feared a Harriman surge, so on August 6 Stevenson moved left again. On the day the platform committee opened its hearings a reporter asked Stevenson on the sidewalk if he still believed in "moderation." He said that he did not know, that "no one has ever defined it for me," and that, "I've had a very strong feeling that the platform should express unequivocal approval of the Court's decision."[40] The Southerners went into an uproar, their candidate was betraying them; Butler and Stevenson aides tried to calm them. Three days later Truman made his appearance before the platform committee and pointedly omitted a call for "implementation" of the Court decision, a stand that would have helped Harriman. Two days later, August 11, Truman endorsed Harriman, but by then Harriman's strategy of outflanking Stevenson on the left was pointless—Stevenson had repudiated moderation, gone to the left of Eleanor Roosevelt on desegregation, and picked up the fighting civil rights crusader, Estes Kefauver. Harriman was left attacking a moderate that no longer existed.

Yet Stevenson did not lose the South. There was, as in 1952, no place for the South to go. Stevenson was less shrill than Kefauver and less liberal than Harriman—despite Harriman's proffer to Johnson, which Johnson chose not to consider serious. In addition, Stevenson had a backlog of moderation and appeasement; he seemed to be the Southerners' only Northern friend. The South could also be pleased that Stevenson and his partisans stayed clear of the platform hearings, an evasion that annoyed Rauh and others.[41] Yet, still, the final civil rights plank was similar to the one Stevenson had supported on August 6 and privately agreed upon with his staff. It was also similar to the one Harriman and Kefauver had been advocating since the primaries, and it differed only from the ADA version, which called for immediate integration. As it turned out, then, Stevenson's platform position was hardly better than Harriman's for Southerners, but in temperament and style he was their only choice. The liberals, too, were content with Stevenson. Rauh, who deplored the civil rights plank, called it an "outrage, one of our lowest points, a terrible clause," also said that liberals "could live with it"—because of Stevenson.[42] So Stevenson was nominated.

He threw open the vice-presidential nomination. Kennedy fought Kefauver for it, and when Kefauver won, it was something of a defeat for Southerners, who long since had come to despise him—the last in a series of defeats Southerners received at this convention.

But their defeat was not absolute. Implementation of the Court's decision had been the searing issue—the South by its defiance had made it so—yet the platform conspicuously avoided any mention of it. The men with influence—Johnson, Truman, Stevenson, Reuther, Rayburn—would not have it. Perhaps they had made a deal on this point, an understanding by which the Southerners agreed to abide by the convention proceedings if the platform did not call for outright implementation. Though there is no evidence of a deal, the strangeness of events suggested one. It had been an odd ten days in Chicago. When Harriman offered to eschew civil rights, Johnson ignored him; yet when Stevenson refused to temporize on civil rights, Johnson backed him—perhaps with the understanding that Stevenson would not—as he did not—call for implementation. When Truman announced for Harriman he did not also call for implementation, even though he knew that the party's endorsement of implementation was Harriman's only way of getting the nomination; always a party man, Truman backed Harriman, but not so far as he could have, not so far as to split the party. When the ADA mounted the effort to include implementation in the platform, the effort suddenly and mysteriously collapsed, perhaps because Reuther was told that it would hopelessly split the party. When Truman and McCormack defended the civil rights plank they took pains to persuade the liberals of its forthrightness, but made no equivalent effort to appease the

Southerners, who perhaps they knew would accept it anyway. And the Southerners did accept it, accepted the platform so fully that they offered no minority plank—the first time they had not since 1944. Of all the recent conventions it should have been at this one, after the *Brown* decision, that the South would try to influence the party—yet it did not, perhaps assured that if it made no protest, neither would the convention endorse the dreaded implementation. Perhaps in 1956 this compromise controlled the convention's strange proceedings.

All this is speculation, having no better grounding than the very confusion it seeks to explain; but arranged or not there was a compromise, and Adlai Stevenson was again its beneficiary. It was, however, unlike the compromise of 1952. The Court decision, the Southern defiance, and the primaries all had pushed the candidates left, and though Stevenson was still the unity candidate— the only bridge from North to South—he was more liberal than in 1952, presiding over a more liberal party. An observer described the Southerners as apathetic, which was no surprise. They had to choose between candidates, all of whom repudiated "moderation"; they had to accept Kefauver as the vice-presidential nominee, the most ardent supporter of civil rights; they had to pray with Martin Luther King, Jr. And they had to run on a platform which was, as McCormack said, more vehement on civil rights than all previous platforms. The compromise thus included enormous civil rights gains, and though the liberals were disappointed when they lost the implementation fight—and indeed it was a loss—perhaps they missed the peculiar quality of this compromise, which gave the party the appearance of unchanging moderation and also a moderate nominee—when in fact the party was changing and so was Adlai Stevenson.

Harry Truman bore witness to that change. He long had had mixed feelings about Stevenson and unqualified dislike for Kefauver, but by the close of the convention he was happy with its results. He left Chicago and returned to Kansas City, whence he wrote Stevenson a confidential longhand letter. In it he explained why he was happy: Stevenson, he thought, had changed. "Dear Governor," he wrote,

> I hope that the next time I send you a letter of congratulation I can say Dear Mr. President. I do sincerely congratulate you on your great victory in the Convention.
>
> Something had to be done to wake up the Party and I undertook

to do it. I was in deadly earnest, as a Democratic Politician, to put some life and leadership into the Party. It was my purpose in 1952 to do just that for you. I am sure that you did not understand that.

The Democratic Party and the United States of America never needed a leader as badly as it does at this time. You have all the qualifications for that position if you will just let them come to the top. In California and Florida primaries it began to come out—but complete satisfaction did not come to me until the Convention fight and your victory there.

I was not putting on a show at that Convention. The principle of the Democratic Party and the welfare of the nation and the world, I felt, were at stake. The Party cannot exist as a 'me too party.' It must exist as a Party for all the people, rich and poor, priviledged and underpriviledged [sic]. It must be ever ready to see justice done to those who cannot hire expensive representatives to look after their welfare in Washington. Only the President can do that. He must be a fighter and one whose heart is in the General Welfare.

I have never had a desire to be a party boss or to be the No. 1 Democrat. I tried to abdicate in 1952. The happenings at Chicago gave you the leadership *on your own.* Now I am ready to do whatever I can to help the Party and its Leader to win.

It is up to you to decide what that will be. I do hope you will have a central headquarters and someone in charge who understands leadership politics.

I wouldn't blame you if you'd never speak to me again—but let's win this campaign and think of that afterwards if it is ever necessary to be thought about.

Sincerely

Harry S Truman[43]

NINE

THE LIBERAL TRIUMPH

Since the end of the 1930s the Southern conservatives had controlled roughly half the Democratic Senate votes, and when they joined with Republicans to vote on labor and civil rights issues, as often they did, the liberals always lost. Relations in the Senate were poor. But they improved when Lyndon Johnson became majority leader, for he saw little purpose to the Democrats' fratricide. And he saw other purposes—a strong party and himself president. He worked in the Congress, much as Stevenson worked in the party, to mediate between the two sides and compose their differences, so that by the end of the 1950s Congress passed bills which, though not the dreams of liberals, were not the dreams of conservatives, either. The Democrats in Congress were moving with the national party, by half steps, holding their ranks together but always sidling left; and for this the liberals had to thank Johnson's ambition. If he was to be president, he had to face civil rights.

Kennedy, when he decided to run for president, also had to face the civil rights issue, and in manipulating it to his advantage he helped the liberals even more than Johnson did. In the spring of 1960, the liberals made it known that to get their support a candidate must pledge himself to a strong civil rights program, including implementation of the *Brown* decision. Kennedy had not been a leader on civil rights, but he recognized the liberals' growing power, and he came out for civil rights and made the 1960 platform, which his supporters controlled, a proclamation of civil rights. When he won the nomination, the liberals won their postwar struggle for mastery of the party.

In the Kennedy administration, and more fully in Johnson's, the liberals won control of not just the party but also the nation— of policy making in the federal government, which now they used to advance civil rights. Political exigencies prohibited Kennedy from presenting his civil rights program until 1963; then he was killed. When Johnson succeeded him, he sought immediately to assure the nation of his liberal leanings, and did so by committing himself to civil rights; then he went on to do more for civil rights than Kennedy had proposed or anyone had thought was possible. But the civil rights issue was not the only liberal concern of these administrations. It pointed, in fact, to other and newer issues—residential segregation, endemic unemployment, and, newest of all, poverty. Laws did not endow a man with equal conditions, the liberals found; so they went beyond them and assailed the social origins of inequality. This, a rather new strategy for the liberals, they did not arrive at until they had come to power; but it did not represent a departure from the logic of the civil rights quest. It was wholly in keeping with that quest. For once the liberals adopted civil rights as their central concern, they jumped the hurdle of racism, which before World War II always had limited their social analysis, and were destined, whenever they came to power, not just to grant the black man his rights, but to examine as well the society that had denied them.

Change in the Congress

Johnson was a big man. He was tall, had enormous features and a habit of pushing his bulk up against his listener and forcing his point with his body. He loved size and talked of it—of Texas and power, of his control of subordinates and mastery of the Senate. He was bright and a little afraid, also practical and vengeful. He espoused no ideology but nonetheless resented the liberals who imagined him a riverboat gambler and an ugly Texan. He got back at them by presenting himself on occasion as vulgar and ugly, what they expected of him and hated him for. He was an appealing man, brighter than all the characters he played—all except the ambitious man. For Johnson was ambitious above all; he altered his ways to suit the times to fulfill his ambition.

The times, it is clear, were rife with ideological discord. The Democrats in Congress were as divided as those in the conventions. For Johnson to succeed, he had to take account of this division—respond to it and work with it. Unable to heal the division, he could keep it from destroying the party and himself, and in this he was much like Stevenson. He played both sides of the street. As the party in Congress moved on, he moved with it but kept also links with those left behind. He reconciled opponents and infiltrated camps: he was a magician. And when he pulled his own success out of the hat, out with it came a tenuous party unity.

When Johnson arrived in the House of Representatives in 1937, Roosevelt was president and the South was leading the revolt against the court-packing plan. Johnson stuck by the president. In Texas he was a Populist but in Washington he was a New Dealer, making friends with other New Dealers, like Jim Rowe and Abe Fortas, who would advise him for thirty years. But then the conservative resurgence, which began in 1939 and reached a peak after the war ended, engulfed Lyndon Johnson. He voted for the Taft-Hartley Labor Act; he opposed Truman's civil rights program. Even so, his opponent for the Senate in 1948, Coke Stevenson, was so firm a racist and conservative that Harry Truman and Joseph Rauh found themselves helping Johnson. He won and went to the Senate, where he found his choices sharply limited. Truman long since had lost control of Congress, and majority leaders Scott Lucas and later Ernest McFarland, passive men at any rate, never could manage the divided Senate. The center of largest power—split between Republican conservatives and Westerners and Democratic Southerners and liberals—was Richard Russell, a Southerner like Johnson. Russell was a member of the conservative coalition, which, united by a simple principle, dominated Congress: Northern Republicans voted against civil rights in exchange for Southern votes against labor and economic legislation (though the value of the exchange is overrated: both were happy to vote this way). It was hard for Johnson to succeed in this group and also in the national party, which was growing more liberal—yet succeed he did.[1]

Johnson succeeded as Stevenson did. He was cautious. He refused to join the Southern caucus, the gathering of Southern Democrats held apart from the Democratic caucus. He made friends with a few liberals, notably Hubert Humphrey, and with many moderates, notably John Kennedy. Yet he also listened to Richard Russell and won committee assignments with his help. In 1950, Scott Lucas and Frank Myers lost their elections and vacated the offices of majority leader and whip—Lucas saying his two years as leader were the most unhappy in his life—and Russell made McFarland leader and Johnson whip. These were not strong positions, had not been since Joe Robinson died in 1937 and could not be on account of the party's division, but when McFarland left in 1952 and Johnson became leader of the Democrats, he resolved to change that.

For close to twenty years the office of leader had been the helpless victim of warring ideological powers. Johnson, minority leader until 1954 when the Democrats won a majority, sought now to make it the arbiter of those powers. He strove to make the business of legislation more a matter of politics, of trading and cajoling, and less a matter of ideology. He gave committee seats to younger men, breaking the seniority system, in exchange for a bit of loyalty. He opposed dogma and declarations, killing Kefauver's liberal agenda in 1954, refusing to sign the Southern manifesto in 1956. Allied with the liberals in 1955 he supported—and passed—a raise in the minimum wage (to one dollar), but allied with Eisenhower and Russell he opposed—and killed—its extension to retail and service trades. He opposed Paul Douglas in his campaign for civil rights laws, yet got Southerners to vote for 800,000 housing units when Eisenhower was dismantling the housing program. Douglas came to Johnson's celebration after the vote, and Johnson said to him, "Well, Paul, you got what you wanted, didn't you?" "I didn't think you could do it," said Douglas. "And I will never know how you did it, but you did it, and I'm grateful." This was his success: he did things, for everyone. In 1956 the liberals proposed an amendment to the Social Security law. The 1935 law had erected a simple retirement plan; in 1939 it grew to cover widows and orphans; and now some wanted to extend it to cover disabled workers—an adventurous step that would bring the federal government into the health insurance business. It was a touchstone to liberals, anathema to Republicans, the South, and the AMA. Johnson said nothing. But quietly he lined up the votes, promised favors to Republicans, mortgaged future liberal votes, and passed the amendment 47 to 45. It was a premonition of things to come.

One of the things was civil rights laws. Congress had not passed a civil rights law since Reconstruction when, in 1956, one began to make its way through the House of Representatives. Eisenhower, urged by his attorney general, Herbert Brownell, proposed a bill calling for a larger civil rights division in the Justice Department, a Commission on Civil Rights, and enforcement of the Court decision and voting rights. This was a portion of Truman's program, offered by the administration to embarrass the Democrats who, it assumed, never would pass such a bill. The House passed a version and sent it to the Senate where on July 23,

before the Democratic convention, Johnson cooperated with Eastland in sending it to the latter's Judiciary Committee, where it
died. Lehman and Douglas tried to discharge it. Humphrey helped
delay the discharging, himself afraid of the bill's effects on his
chances in the convention. In 1957 Eisenhower returned the bill
to Congress. No one knew what Johnson would do—he was silent—
but one could have suspected.

For in the meantime the Democrats had had their convention
and had written a strong platform and nominated a more liberal
Stevenson and the audacious Kefauver. They also had waged a
liberal campaign, in which Stevenson carried the party's message
to North and South alike. He had gone to Little Rock, Arkansas,
on September 25 and said to that Southern audience, "The
Supreme Court of the United States has determined unanimously
that the Constitution does not permit segregation in the schools.
. . . I believe that decision to be right. . . . But what is important
is that . . . we accept that decision as law-abiding citizens. . . . The
office of the Presidency should be used to bring together those of
opposing views in this matter—to the end of creating a climate for
peaceful acceptance of this decision."[2] Then he went to Harlem,
said the same thing, recited his own record and the Democratic
achievements in civil rights, supported the decision, and attacked
the president's inaction. He avowed to the crowd as he seldom
did that progress in civil rights mattered not because of foreign
policy but because it was right: "The profound questions of our
time remain questions of conscience and of will. And the answers
will come, at the last 'not by might, nor by power but by this
spirit.' For ours is a time like that of which the prophet Amos
wrote, 'let justice roll down as waters, and righteousness as a
mighty stream.' "[3] Far changed from the man who fumbled his
speech in Harlem four years before, Stevenson—and the Democratic party—had moved on civil rights, so much in fact that he
again gave up the four Deep South states and added another,
Louisiana, to Eisenhower's victory. After the election a black
publisher wrote to the Democratic loser, "The nation and the
Democratic Party need your leadership no less than prior to yesterday. Millions of Americans are still anxiously awaiting a definition of a political philosophy which interprets their real convictions. . . . It is a job that an unshackled Democratic Party can do.
Congratulations on bringing that definition substantially nearer
to realization."[4]

It was at this time, when the party was shedding its shackles, that Johnson felt prepared to pass a civil rights bill and call the president's bluff. On June 18 the House overwhelmingly passed it and sent it to the Senate. Russell tried to send it to Judiciary and kill it. Johnson voted for committal but did not lead the effort, which without the leader's support failed. A filibuster was in the offing now. Johnson wanted to head it off, knew some bill was necessary, but wanted to keep the Southerners from tying up the Senate and maligning their fellow Democrats. He searched for a compromise. And he found it in two clauses, one he would add to the bill, the other he would cut. He thought to add a provision for jury trials in contempt of court cases arising from violations of the act. This meant a man could not be jailed or fined without a jury conviction; it also meant few men would be jailed or fined for civil rights violations in the South, where juries resented civil rights laws. And he thought to delete Part III, a section that gave the attorney general power to file suits to protect the right to vote and other rights, including the right to desegregate school facilities. This was Johnson's plan to avert a filibuster. But Russell, too, had doubts about the filibuster. He feared that if he attempted one and failed, the North would retaliate with still stronger civil rights legislation. So he was amenable to Johnson's compromise, and Johnson began trading favors. He got Russell to help the liberals pass the Hell's Canyon bill, a public power project which in other circumstances Southerners would detest. But now they liked it, for liberals would repay the kindness by accepting the civil rights compromise. By the end of July 1957, Part III was eliminated from the bill. The Democrats were coming together.

Still outstanding was the jury trial amendment. And here Johnson clouded the issue of civil rights with legal history and Magna Carta and labor rights; and ideology got lost in the haze. Aided by Dean Acheson and Benjamin Cohen, Johnson argued that the distinction between civil and criminal contempt of court was crucial, that in the former a jury trial might be waived but that in the latter, where the verdict was punitive as well as remedial, the weight of Anglo-American legal history bore heavily on the shoulders of the Senate: here a man deserved a jury. This distinction, he thought, would make the bill acceptable to both sides, and he pressed it upon his colleagues. Kefauver and Church backed the idea, and so did liberals sensitive to labor pressure, for labor always had abhorred court injunctions. John Lewis backed the new clause, then Green and Pastore of Rhode Island,

and Kennedy of Massachusetts. The jury trial provision carried, and by August the civil rights bill belonged to Johnson and the Democrats; they had wrenched it from the administration and turned it to their advantage. Only Strom Thurmond, who perhaps saw the future better than Russell, staged a filibuster, his own, the longest for one man, lasting twenty-four hours and eighteen minutes. Johnson, on the other hand, spoke of reasonable men working on reasonable bills, confronting extremists from both sides. "I tell you," he said before the vote,

> out of whatever experience I have, that there is no political capital in this issue. Nothing lasting, nothing enduring has ever been born from hatred and prejudice—except more hatred and prejudice. Political ambition which feeds off hatred of the North or hatred of the South is doomed to frustration. There is a compelling need for a solution that will enable all Americans to live in dignity and in unity. This bill is the greatest step toward that objective that has ever been made.

As a bridge to ideologies, he was Stevensonian in his genius.

As legislation, the bill was somewhat meager. Joseph Rauh complained the Southerners could go home and say that the Senate, by cutting Part III, had repudiated the Supreme Court's desegregation decisions.[5] The voting rights provision was paltry: the commission had no enforcement power, and the attorney general could seek injunctions only against individuals, not against states. The jury trial provision made enforcement hard: The citizens' councils went ahead undaunted, disfranchising thousands of black voters, and Senator Rainach sanguinely predicted "it is not going to be easy to get Louisiana people to indict Louisiana people."[6] Blacks were dissatisfied. In 1957 Martin Luther King, Jr., and other leaders began the Southern Christian Leadership Conference to win the ballot for blacks. Yet the bill had its one success: it passed. After three quarters of a century, in this tentative but necessary first step, the federal government once again took up the task of legislating civil rights. And it was Johnson's doing.[7]

The year following, in 1958, several Southerners and conservative Republicans proposed laws curbing the powers of the Supreme Court, including one which would make state law superior to federal law when the two conflicted. Johnson delayed action on these by keeping them in the Democratic policy committee (which was neither democratic nor in the habit of making policy), but the Southerners prevailed in discharging the bills at the end of session. Johnson arrayed his forces in sufficient strength to kill all but the one subverting the federal system, which had passed the House easily. Johnson was worried. He asked that the liberals not offer counter amendments, for fear the Senate would become provoked enough to pass the bill. All obeyed, except Paul Douglas, as intransigent in his liberalism as Thurmond in his conservatism, who proposed an amendment by which Congress would declare its "full support and approval of the recent, historic decisions of the Supreme Court of the United States holding racial segregation unlawful in public education and transportation." The Senate was miffed. Twice it passed the states' rights bill. Johnson, weary and furious, said to Humphrey, "Well, Hubert, that's your liberals for you," and only with difficulty connived to recommit and bury the bill at last. Such was Johnson's style.

Yet there were many who loathed this style. After the 1956 election, Paul Butler and the Democratic National Committee formed the Democratic Advisory Committee (later called the Democratic Advisory Council), a group whose purpose it was, as it had been that of the Finletter group, to shape an "aggressive, forward-looking program" for the party and provide the liberal direction the Congress had not. Johnson saw it as a rival to himself, a move by the Northern liberals to establish control of party policy.[8] Stevenson, ever wary of ideological fighting and hence not a party to the committee's formation, hailed it as the proper body to "advance Democratic programs and principles."[9] Others challenged Johnson. Joseph Rauh said that under Johnson, "the Congressional Democrats have become indistinguishable from the party they allegedly oppose." Blacks, too, found the administration and the Democratic leadership indistinguishable and fell back, as they had in the past but now in greater numbers, on their own resources. In December 1955, blacks refused to ride the segregated Montgomery buses, so they walked to work, for a year, with little political support, until they won in court. At the same time the University of Alabama expelled Autherine Lucy, though the Supreme Court had ordered her admitted. In 1957, Governor Orval Faubus called out the National Guard to prevent nine black students from entering Central High School in Little Rock, Arkansas, but then called it back when a court injunction made him. The students entered, and a riot broke out. On September 24, Eisenhower sent soldiers to Little Rock; the next day the students entered school; and soon after the school closed down and stayed closed until 1958. For the first time since 1954 the President supported the *Brown* decision. Adlai Stevenson appeared on "Face the Nation" and denounced Southern intransigence.[10] Again the South responded to the past, unmindful of the future.

This had happened before, it would happen again. It was in fact an established process: blacks acted and the South reacted, then Democrats and labor, indignant or embarrassed, came to the blacks' defense. The line of battle moved a step forward. Johnson, the most powerful man in Congress, caught in the crossfire, was ally to none of the groups—the Advisory Council, Stevenson, blacks, the Southern old guard, or Eisenhower—but conspirator with them all. He had drinks with Eisenhower, and Butler fumed; he mangled the civil rights bill, and Douglas fumed; he passed the civil rights bill, and Thurmond harangued the Senate for twenty-four hours. He did all these things to pass bills and also to keep the Senate Democrats together and himself abreast of the party's changing mood. He considered himself a "moderate," trying to "resolve issues rather than create them," to "unify, rather than divide, our people." In the year of the civil rights act he said, "I want to run this Senate. I want to pass the bills that need to be passed. I want my party to do right. But all I ever hear from the liberals is Nigra, Nigra, Nigra."

By 1960 his power was waning. In 1958 the people had sent new men to Congress. The Democrats outnumbered Republicans in the House 283 to 153, in the Senate 65 to 35. New liberals like Muskie, Proxmire, and Eugene McCarthy were beginning their Senate careers, and older ones like Joseph Clark were joining Douglas in his intransigence. Johnson saw trouble ahead. Douglas' perennial effort to reform the cloture rule, which required two-thirds of the Senate to cut off debate, had greater support in the 1959 session than ever before, and Johnson sought a compromise. He persuaded both liberals and Southerners to avert a filibuster and agree that instead of the present rule and instead of the simple majority the liberals wanted, the Senate should adopt a new rule, one that would require two-thirds of the Senators present, sitting and voting, to cut off debate. It was a momentous change, destined to loosen the Southern strangling grasp on civil rights legislation.

But the grasp was not loose yet. In 1959 and 1960, the Congress faced a new civil rights bill, inspired by the continued denial of voting rights. Emmanuel Celler, Paul Douglas, and other liberals hoped to pass a bill that would allow the president to appoint federal registrars when local ones refused to register blacks; establish an equal employment commission; extend the Civil Rights Commission; and include Part III, excluded from the 1957 Act. Southerners bristled. Herman Talmadge likened the registration plan to Hitler's subversion of Germany's democratic process. James Eastland, opposing a resolution in support of the *Brown* decision, averred he did not want "this Record cluttered by such crap as the court writes." Sam Ervin badgered those who came to testify in behalf of the legislation. And Howard W. Smith, venerable chairman of the House Rules Committee, made himself scarce to delay the bill's reaching the floor, as he had in 1957. (Then he had announced upon his return that he had left because his barn had burned down. Rayburn said he knew Smith was against civil rights but had not expected him to resort to arson.) But a bill was needed; the liberals were adamant, and the lunch counter sit-ins had begun. The Senate split wide open. A filibuster tied up business for six weeks, and Lyndon Johnson fairly lost control of his party.[11]

Richard Russell, Johnson's erstwhile mentor, parted with Johnson here and addressed the Senate:

> Mr. President, in all of this controversy and discussion we have heard a great deal about minorities. The only minority in the Senate that is considered not to have any rights at all is the group of Southern Democrats that has been undertaking to protect its people and the rights of its States. . . . It has become popular in this country—and certain groups favor it—to lump together as "civil rights" all kind of legislation to invade the schoolhouse of the Southern States, to take over the voting privileges of the people of the Southern States, to bring all kinds of harassment against the 40 million people who happen to live in the South—all on the ground that this is "civil rights."

Russell was adamant. In the early spring of 1960 he staged a filibuster; the liberals tried to invoke cloture—against Johnson's advice—and failed even to muster a majority. Only then did Johnson's mediation succeed. Congress passed an ineffectual bill extending the Civil Rights Commission and empowering the courts to appoint voting referees where they found patterns of voting discrimination. Eisenhower signed it May 6. Harry Byrd called it a victory for the South, in which "so few at such great odds have done so much for so many." Joseph Clark called it a "sham," wrought by the "defenders of the way of life of the Old South," assisted by Eisenhower, Dirksen, and Johnson.[12]

But it was in fact a bill that no one liked.

This bill brought to a close the period of Johnson's hegemony. It was an unfortunate ending. Johnson had controlled the Senate for six years, the Democrats for eight, and now, in 1960, he lost his touch. As the liberals grew stronger and the South more defiant, civil rights issues grew more demanding and intractable; the Senate would not be managed. Johnson, like Stevenson, had performed a service, but compromise, even a compromise that inclined to the left, would no longer do. He would again perform a service, one of a different sort, as controversial as his rule over the Senate. But for the time being, his usefulness was at an end.

Kennedy

By the spring of 1960, the civil rights issue was snowballing. Congress had passed two civil rights acts in three years, and none in the eighty-two years before. Blacks, too, were acting. The sit-in movement began in February, when four black students sat down at a lunch counter in Greensboro, North Carolina, and refused to leave until they were served. And, as ever, the liberals acted. They were determined, said Rauh, that the Democratic convention support the Supreme Court and that the candidates in 1960 be men committed to civil rights.[13] Stevenson and Johnson were not so committed, but they had held their party together while it fought and found its path. Then suddenly the decade of the fifties, of search and struggle, gave way to a new era, born of that struggle but released from its bindings, when Democrats dropped the debate in their party, chose a president, then another, and engraved their decisions upon the nation.

John Kennedy was not by nature a fighting ideologue, and in the House and Senate he did not distinguish himself by voting liberal. In 1957 he helped Johnson weaken the civil rights bill and investigated labor racketeers, in a celebrated series of hearings that went far, though not deliberately, to discredit organized labor. Yet he was by no means a conservative. While investigating the Kohler strike he found the company far more culpable than the workers. He sought to reform labor practices, not revoke the rights of labor, and to that end he fought Eisenhower and Senator McClellan and other Southerners, who in 1959 twisted a labor reform bill into an antilabor act. (The Landrum-Griffin bill, among other things, strengthened the Taft-Hartley Act by severely restricting secondary boycotts and picketing.) So by 1960, Kennedy's ideological bearings were not fixed. He was rich and thus like Roosevelt not beholden to corporate interests. He was pragmatic and so, learning from his 1956 defeat, interested in wooing the liberals.[14] And above all he was young, quick, and endowed with the ability to grow.

But on January 2, 1960, when he announced his candidacy, he was no one's favorite. Southerners wanted Johnson and so did others—James Rowe and Dean Acheson—because he could win and unify the nation as he had tried the Senate. But Johnson feared losing and delayed his decision. Acheson went to Symington, as did Truman—who complained of Kennedy, "It's not the Pope, it's the Pop"—and Rowe went to Humphrey. ADA men like Rauh and Loeb and Marvin Rosenberg also settled on Humphrey, Rauh becoming his speech coordinator. But on May 10, the air cleared when West Virginia voted and Kennedy won and Humphrey lost. Humphrey withdrew and the liberals lost their candidate. Kennedy became the leading contender now, but his path was not unobstructed. Johnson was having second thoughts, and Stevenson did nothing to stop a draft, though neither entered the primaries. Kennedy's supporters grew nervous. They saw momentum building for Stevenson as the old liberal warrior; they feared he might divide the liberal vote enough to open the door to Johnson. The Johnson people were happy with the Stevenson commotion, as was Eugene McCarthy, who hoped to become Johnson's running-mate and who for that reason supported Adlai Stevenson.

Kennedy decided that he must strengthen his standing among liberals. His defeat at Kefauver's hands four years before had impressed upon him his party's growing liberal resolve. Now a surge of liberal nostalgia, with Stevenson its object but Johnson perhaps its result, threatened his nomination. And there were other pressures—Little Rock, the civil rights acts, the sit-ins, and also the national committee, which emerged from the 1956 convention more liberal, more dogmatic than ever before. In 1959 Paul Butler predicted that the Dixiecrats would fall into line at the 1960 convention.[15] Then he and the committee chose Chester Bowles to preside over the platform committee, an old liberal of Truman's administration. Kennedy after West Virginia, then, had to join the movement, in fact he had to lead it. He sent the liberals a signal; he promised them he would fully support the Supreme Court's desegregation decision. With this promise in hand, Joseph Rauh and other liberals wrote a public letter avowing their support of

Kennedy. It appeared on June 17, written by Rauh and Henry Steele Commager (and also signed by John Kenneth Galbraith, Arthur Goldberg, Arthur Schlesinger, Jr., James MacGregor Burns, Edith Green, and others). It read: "The purpose of this letter is to urge, now that Senator Humphrey has withdrawn from the race and Mr. Stevenson continues to stand aside, that the liberals of America turn to Senator Kennedy for President"; and then drew particular attention to civil rights: "He has assured us that he favors pledging the Democratic Party to Congressional and Executive action in support of the Supreme Court's desegregation decisions and to whatever measures may be necessary to make voting a reality for all citizens."[16]

Less than a month later, on July 11, the convention convened in Los Angeles. The platform committee, controlled by Kennedy supporters, had deliberated and written the strongest civil rights plank in the party's history—"every demand put forth by the civil rights movement," as Rauh later said.[17] It called for an end to segregated lunch counters and proposed legislation to eliminate literacy tests and poll taxes, to require segregated school districts to submit plans for desegregation by 1963, to give technical and financial assistance to desegregating schools, to authorize the attorney general to file suits seeking court injunctions against deprivation of any civil rights, to establish a federal Fair Employment Practices Commission (FEPC), and to strengthen and make permanent the Civil Rights Commission. It also pledged the Democratic administration to end segregation in federal activities and end discrimination in federal housing programs. It was a long list, bringing to conclusion the party's civil rights struggle. And unlike the 1948 plank, this, in 1960, was the majority plank. "The Kennedys," said Rauh, had "made their commitment and they stuck to it."[18]

On Monday morning, the day the convention opened, twenty-five Kennedy workers gathered in their headquarters in the Biltmore Hotel to hear Robert Kennedy's instructions:

> I want to say a few words about civil rights. We have the best civil rights plank the Democratic Party has ever had. I want you fellows to make it clear to your delegations that the Kennedy forces are unequivocally in favor of this plank and that we want it passed in the convention. Those of you who are dealing with southern delegations make it absolutely clear how we stand on civil rights. Don't fuzz it up. Tell the southern states that we hope they will see other reasons why we are united as Democrats and why they should sup-

port Kennedy, but don't let there be doubt anywhere as to how the
Kennedy people stand on this.[19]

On Tuesday the convention adopted the majority plank by voice
vote and quickly rejected a Southern minority report. Kennedy's
support foreclosed the matter, and the liberals knew it.[20]

The meshing of ambition and ideology worked its queer results again. For in 1960, as in the past, the platform's expression
of the party's beliefs directly affected the choosing of a candidate.
In 1952, the party torn, Richard Russell commanded the veto
power, and the Illinois delegation conciliated the South, in the
platform and the credentials, so Stevenson could win. In 1956,
Johnson held the power to tip the balance for Stevenson, Harriman, or Kefauver. Now, in 1960, as Arthur Schlesinger, Jr., has
said,[21] Stevenson held the cards, able almost to stop the Kennedy
sweep—Kennedy did not win until the roll reached Wyoming—yet
equally able to have assured his victory. (Stevenson helped Kennedy not at all; it was Humphrey who declared for Kennedy on
Wednesday, the morning of the balloting, and clinched the nomination.) The balance of power had shifted during these eight unsettled
years from a Southerner of the old guard to a Southerner of ambiguous ideology and finally to the liberals. Kennedy jumped fast,
and caught the crest of the flowing tide.

Soon he was swimming ahead of it. After the convention he
and twenty-three other Democratic senators condemned the
Republican record on civil rights and called for action to implement the Democratic platform's civil rights goals. That fall,
Kennedy described the situation of the American black: "The
Negro baby has one-half, regardless of his talents, statistically has
one-half as much chance of finishing high school as the white
baby, one-third as much chance of finishing college, one-fourth
as much chance of being a professional man or woman, four times
as much chance of being out of work." He mentioned repeatedly
what the president could do in the absence of congressional action—
eliminate discrimination in federal housing programs and also
"provide the leadership and the direction . . . to eliminate racial
and religious discrimination from American society." On October
24, Martin Luther King, Jr., went to jail in Georgia. Kennedy,
against the counsel of some of his advisors, called King's wife, who
was pregnant, and later his brother Robert called the Georgia
judge and requested bail for King. It was this sort of campaigning,
inspired perhaps by political considerations (though it seems not),

that brought civil rights constantly before the nation, made it a respectable issue, and spurred the Republicans. (Two weeks after the Democratic convention, Richard Nixon had prevailed upon the Republicans to adopt the strongest civil rights plank his party had ever written, though it fell somewhat short of the Democrats' plank.)[22] When the nation voted on November 8, 1960, blacks and labor came out for Kennedy as they had not for a Democratic candidate since Franklin Roosevelt. It seemed a special though narrow mandate.

•   •   •

No one has written a history of the Kennedy administration, nor is this the place for it, for what concerns us here is the course of liberalism during the years of Kennedy's government.[23] Kennedy did as much as he could, considering his troubles with Congress, to promote civil rights, but perhaps it was more important that he spoke out and drew the public's attention to inequities between the races, committing the presidency, for only the second time in history, to the cause of civil rights. He communicated a new sense of concern. And when he could not act on civil rights, he acted on poverty—and this too was new, both for the nation and for liberals.

Kennedy surrounded himself with liberals, many of them from Stevenson's retinue—Schlesinger, Galbraith, Martin, Minow, Blair, Rivkin, Wirtz, and Ball. Kennedy's close advisor and liaison to Capitol Hill, Larry O'Brien, was a longtime member of the ADA. Liberals like Rauh and Humphrey and Douglas worked closely with the White House, meeting with the president to discuss proposed legislation. They and black leaders trusted Kennedy though sometimes thought him too cautious, but neither group could afford to break with Kennedy. They regarded him not as one of themselves but as the first sign of hope after years of despair.

It was Kennedy himself, young and critical, who generated the sense of expectation and hope that the New Frontier imparted. He was not sanguine about America's prospects—this by itself was fresh—and spoke of the "seven peaceful revolutions of our time." He recognized change and thought America should become its purveyor. The population explosion had "not been matched in public plans and programs. Fifteen million American families live in substandard housing . . . nearly five million of our urban homes still lack plumbing of any kind—nearly seven million urban homes need to be totally replaced—and still our crowded cities grow." He complained that the benefits of progress fell not with an even hand. Amid American prosperity, "millions of workers have no Federal protection against substandard wages, particularly women in our retail stores and service establishments. . . . Increasing and extending our minimum wage laws—so that all Americans can share this revolutionary standard of living—is an essential program." And in foreign affairs America had erred:

> Too often it is a struggle between a white minority and a colored majority, with dangerous implications for our future. This requires that we in this nation make completely clear our strong, unequivocal stand on civil rights—not only to help us abroad but to strengthen us here at home. We cannot doubt that these peoples eventually will, and ought to be, free and equal. . . . This nation, the home of the Declaration of Independence, should have led this nationalist revolution instead of helping to throttle it.[24]

This was in Seattle, 1959.

In the White House, in 1961, Kennedy was no less critical. He was concerned, Schlesinger has said, less with economic growth "than with the quality of life in a society which, in the main, had achieved abundance." In February he sent to Congress messages on health and hospital care, education, and natural resources; in March, housing and community development. He passed a comprehensive housing act and tried but failed, in 1961 and again in 1962, to get Congress to authorize a Department of Urban Affairs; some in Congress worried that he would appoint to the new post his Housing Administrator, Robert Weaver, a black. Kennedy worried about youth unemployment and disaffection. His brother Robert worked to create the National Service Corps, which later became VISTA (Volunteers in Service to America), and the President twice tried and failed to pass education bills granting federal funds to local schools and higher education. The Area Redevelopment Act, twice vetoed by Eisenhower, passed the Congress in 1961. It sought to relieve economic depression in specially hard-hit areas, such as Appalachia; so did the Accelerated Public Works Act of 1962. The Executive Committee on Juvenile Delinquency also aimed at poverty. Under Robert Kennedy it coordinated federal, state, local, and private aid to help the urban young; more importantly, from this effort came the idea of community action, the participation of the poor in the assault on poverty. Kennedy passed a Manpower Development and Training

Act, proposed a youth conservation corps, which lost in the House, and by the last month of his life, had decided to launch a full-scale war on poverty. In 1964, it would be his central request of Congress. He suspected that the middle class would feel threatened by such a program but he would go ahead anyway.[25]

With this identification of poverty as a structural problem, Kennedy was striking out in a new direction. He and his advisors approached the problem of indigence as one afflicting not just the unlucky but also, and mainly, those who, by their color or their youth or their age or their geographical location, could not partake of the nation's abundance. Such analysis implied an appraisal of society, not of men, and though it was not carried to great lengths in Kennedy's time, it did begin. It was a break with the past.

So was his handling of civil rights. In April 1961, Kennedy issued Executive Order 10925, which guaranteed equality of opportunity in federal employment and authorized a committee, under Vice-President Johnson, to review the behavior of agencies and contractors and to enforce their compliance.[26] Kennedy also appointed blacks to high office—Weaver to the Housing Administration and Marshall to the Second Circuit Court. (Marshall had argued *Brown* before the Supreme Court in 1952-54.) Robert Kennedy at the Justice Department appointed the first black U.S. attorneys and, in two and a half years, brought four times the number of suits Eisenhower did to contest voting disfranchisement. In 1961, when the freedom riders went through the South protesting bus terminal segregation and ran into trouble in Alabama, Robert Kennedy sent 600 federal marshals to protect the endangered riders. That fall the Interstate Commerce Commission issued regulations (on his request) desegregating all bus terminals servicing interstate travel. The president backed him fully.[27]

In 1961, James Meredith applied to the University of Mississippi and was rejected because he was black. After a year of litigation a federal court decided for Meredith, and Hugo Black of the Supreme Court upheld the decision. Ross Barnett, governor of Mississippi, versed in the language of the Southern resistance, declared, "We will not surrender to the evil and illegal forces of tyranny." Robert Kennedy called Barnett and suggested he reconsider defying a federal court order, but when Meredith arrived on the campus of Ole Miss in Oxford, Mississippi, Barnett was firm. Fortified by the popular sentiment, the legislature, and the newspapers, he rejected Meredith himself. Robert Kennedy had three officers of the University cited for contempt of court, but Barnett remained firm: "I consider," he told Kennedy, "the Mississippi courts as high as any other court and a lot more capable. . . . I am going to obey the laws of Mississippi." When Meredith again tried to register, this time with a restraining order from the circuit court enjoining Barnett to desist, Barnett physically stopped him. A mob gathered; that night Barnett told Kennedy, "It's best for him [Meredith] not to go to Ole Miss," and Kennedy said, "But he likes Ole Miss."[28]

Negotiations dragged on for two days, the Kennedys anxious to avoid violence, Barnett to avoid embarrassment. The Southern pride was prodded: People flocked to Oxford from surrounding areas, some with guns, prepared to fight communism, mongrelism, and Washington. Barnett was trapped. It had happened before—to Calhoun and Eastland—and it happened to Barnett, who, once committed, could not escape the charm of his rhetoric except with a fight. He was not hostile to the Kennedys; at one point on the phone he thanked the president for his "help on the poultry problem." But he needed a way out. He told Robert Kennedy that if the government could muster enough marshals and have them draw their guns, then he might back down. But the Kennedys were not eager to stage a confrontation; they declined. A court found Barnett guilty of contempt, and the president federalized the Mississippi National Guard and ordered army troops to Memphis. Barnett gave in. Meredith arrived on the campus surrounded by marshals, a mob gathered, and Kennedy went on national television. "If this country," he told the nation, "should ever reach the point where any man or group of men by force or threat of force could long defy the commands of our court and our Constitution, then no law would stand free from doubt, no judge would be sure of his writ, and no citizen would be safe from his neighbors." He called upon the students to uphold the honor of their university and their state.[29]

Meanwhile, the crowd at Ole Miss grew to 2500. They shouted racial epithets and denounced Kennedy and hurled bottles and bricks at the marshals, wounding a third of them. The marshals responded with tear gas. Two men died. Army troops arrived from Memphis. Kennedy stayed up till dawn, and Meredith stayed in school, protected by marshals for months. For the deaths, Mississippians blamed Washington and the marshals—"They were untrained," said an aide to Eastland. "They were political appointees. They shot tear-gas into the crowd, not above it, like they was supposed to. The marshals caused it. They probably shot that Paris correspondent, too." Washington of course blamed Barnett's belligerent attitude, but in any event, the crisis marked a watershed in Kennedy's administration. Kennedy learned that integration in some instances could not be achieved without a show of force (Mississippians thought without violence); if he was to make good on his promises, he would have to be bold, bolder perhaps than at Oxford. For their part Southerners learned what to expect from the Kennedys. Senator Eastland had become close to Robert Kennedy; he was head of the Judiciary Committee and worked often with the attorney general. But after Ole Miss the Kennedys became "anathema to the South," and this hostility only deepened when, not two months later, on November 20, 1962, the President issued an executive order forbidding discrimination in federally funded housing.[30]

The next spring the South bristled again, and Kennedy got a mandate for further action. In April and May of 1963 Martin Luther King, Jr., led the blacks of Birmingham in a campaign of demonstrations to end discrimination in restaurants and jobs. Police Commissioner Connor set upon the blacks with dogs and fire hoses and arrested most of them, but not before white rioters had showered them with bricks and bombed several homes. Kennedy sent federal troops. The problem deepened when, on May 21, a federal district judge ordered the University of Alabama to admit two blacks, and Governor George Wallace said, "I am the embodiment of the sovereignty of this state, and I will be present to bar the entrance of any Negro who attempts to enroll."[31] Kennedy acted quickly. On June 12, he told Wallace not to interfere with the blacks' enrollment, and when Wallace blocked their entry, Kennedy federalized part of the Alabama National Guard and sent it to the campus. Wallace backed down. In the midst of all this, on the night of June 11, Kennedy spoke to the nation on civil rights. He said that the rights of all were diminished when the rights of one were challenged, that it should be possible for Americans of any color to attend any public institution, to receive equal service in hotels, restaurants, theaters, and stores, and to register to vote. "In short, every American ought to have the right to be treated as he would wish to be treated, as one would wish his children to be treated. But this is not the case." "Who among us," he asked, "would be content to have the color of his skin changed and stand in his place? Who among us would then be content with the counsels of patience and delay?" Do we mean "that we have no second-class citizens except Negroes; that we have no class or caste system, no ghettos, no master race except with respect to Negroes?" He called this a "moral issue," one that would be settled in the streets if Congress did not act.[32] It was the most powerful case for civil rights a president had ever made.

That night a white man murdered Medgar Evers, a friend of James Meredith and a civil rights leader in Mississippi. Kennedy invited Evers's family to the White House, and Robert went to his funeral. The momentum to act increased. The president held meetings in the White House on civil rights legislation, and on June 19 he sent his bill to Congress. He called for desegregation of public facilities, power for the attorney general to sue for school desegregation, support for fair employment (the Hill added the FEPC), and the withholding of funds for programs which discriminated by race. On June 22 Kennedy and the vice-president met with civil rights leaders to discuss the bill and a proposed march on Washington. Kennedy counselled against the march—it would jeopardize the bill—but A. Philip Randolph argued that blacks already were in the streets, that nothing civil rights leaders might do could get them off, and that if the leaders did not lead them, their people would follow others, perhaps men less committed to nonviolence. Kennedy agreed that demonstrations had brought results but feared violence. Johnson explained the votes in Congress. Then James Farmer of CORE stated more clearly what Randolph had suggested: "We understand your political problem in getting the legislation through, and we want to help in that as best we can. But the civil rights forces have their problems too. We would be in a difficult if not untenable position if we called the street demonstrations off and then were defeated in the legislative battle. The result would be that frustration would grow into violence and would demand new leadership."[33] It was the problem of Ross Barnett and James Eastland, made doubly difficult for the blacks; for theirs was a revolution, a snapping of the bonds of thought and self-regard, where the Southern task was one of resistance, to shore up defenses. The impulse to revolt was spinning more freely and less exactly than the Southern momentum to restore.

In the summer of 1963, however, the civil rights leaders still led the blacks. Kennedy had vowed his good faith to them and insisted they "keep in touch"; and they for their part worked to make the march large and peaceful. It turned out to be both. On

August 28, almost one quarter of a million people came to Washington, black and white, and gathered before the Lincoln Memorial. The crowd listened to speeches, the best by Martin Luther King, Jr., and sang "We shall overcome," then departed peacefully into the night. Kennedy congratulated the leaders and said the nation could take pride in the march and its meaning. That fall he worked with the Hill to produce a civil rights bill.

Some have accused Kennedy of delaying on civil rights, notwithstanding his vigorous response in Ole Miss and Birmingham. And delay he did. He waited until November 1962 to issue his housing order and until the following February to send a civil rights message to Congress, a weak one at that, followed by the strong one in June, only after Evers's death and Bull Connor's dogs. Kennedy waited. For he had political problems. In 1960 he had won less than half the votes cast, and of this fact he was keenly aware; and, partly because of this fact, he had little control over Congress. In 1961 King and Rauh and others pressured Kennedy to issue the housing order and send to Congress a bill embodying the platform's demands. Kennedy refused. He wanted to pass bills providing manpower training, aid to education, and an increase in the minimum wage; and he knew if he forced the civil rights legislation he might lose these bills. (The education bill failed anyway.) Pressure kept up through 1961. The Civil Rights Commission and King argued for the housing order, but Kennedy had a new bill, more important, he thought: He was asking Congress for authorization of a new department, the Department of Urban Affairs, with Robert Weaver as secretary. That Congress rebuffed him, in 1961 and 1962, indicated that he and Johnson and O'Brien had not misjudged its continued ambivalence on civil rights; nor were they surprised when, in the spring of 1962, Richard Russell and his confederates staged a successful filibuster against a bill outlawing literacy tests (used to disqualify Southern blacks). The liberals had not strength enough to muster even a majority for cloture. In the Congress Kennedy delayed because he had little choice.

But in the nation, he had an option and he exercised it. His speeches and troop movements during the Ole Miss and Birmingham crises helped prepare the nation for the revolution in rights it had tried to ignore. When the opportunity came, in the summer of 1963, Kennedy jumped. He strengthened his civil rights bill and lectured the people. In October, he worked out a compromise bill that kept the FEPC, gave the attorney general broad powers to initiate suits, helped desegregate schools, and cut funds off from ones still segregated. Robert Kennedy called it a "better bill than the administration's." It went to the House floor two days before Kennedy was shot.[34]

Kennedy, one aide said, "was not an irrational fellow."[35] He had served in the House and Senate for fourteen years and knew the limits to presidential power. Howard Smith, chairman of the House Rules Committee, could go home and tend to his barns to delay consideration of civil rights bills. Eastland in the Senate, chairman of the Judiciary Committee, could likewise slowly strangle bills. Kennedy had to wait until the mood was right, acting in the meantime with executive orders and the Justice Department. When, in 1963, Medgar Evers was shot in the back; the house of King's brother was bombed; four black girls died in another bombing; and Southern police arrested 14,000 civil rights demonstrators— then the mood was right. Then he spoke to the people on television, told them what they must do, then started on Congress. It was a start; then he was dead.

Johnson

When John Kennedy died, Johnson was afraid. He was afraid of the presidency, as anyone should be. He was afraid of the dark, and asked an aide to sit near his bed one night while he lay awake and Lady Bird slept. When the aide thought Johnson had fallen asleep he crept toward the door but stopped when Johnson called out in the dark that he was still awake.[36] And, always sensible to what people thought of him, Johnson was afraid the nation was afraid of him, afraid he was unqualified, a redneck, a man unequal to Kennedy's bold tasks. Those first few days were hard. The nation needed assurance, and so did Johnson.

Five days after the assassination, before a joint session of Congress, he made his first address to the country and tried to allay its doubts. First of all, he spoke on civil rights. "Today, in this moment of new resolve, I would say to all my fellow Americans, let us continue"—Kennedy had said, "Let us begin."

> First, no memorial oration or eulogy could more eloquently honor President Kennedy's memory than the earliest possible passage of the civil rights bill for which he fought so long. We have talked long enough about equal rights in this country. We have talked for one hundred years or more. It is time now to write the next chapter and to write it in the books of law. I urge you again, as I did in 1957

and again in 1960, to enact a civil rights law so that we can move
forward to eliminate from this nation every trace of discrimination
and oppression that is based on race or color.[37]

Johnson, ever adroit in the use of symbols, used civil rights to
place himself in the vanguard of liberalism. He sent the nation a
signal (and demonstrated by it the continuing and special meaning
of the civil rights issue). Soon he began framing bills, and then it
became clear that where Kennedy had changed attitudes, had emphasized the morality of civil rights, where by his posture and his
death he had adorned the mythology of the liberals, Johnson was
creating a mounting structure of power. In a few furious years he
made into law the liberal words. He began with civil rights.

One day late in 1963 Richard Daley, mayor of Chicago and
leader of its machine, told a visitor that Johnson would have
trouble with his wheat and cotton bill if he dallied on civil rights:
the labor and city congressmen would keep the new president in
line.[38] But Johnson needed no pushing. He was, according to a
friend of thirty years, "completely without bias—it was not in
his character. He used bias with politicians. And he was cautious
because of the South. But he had no racial prejudice." Another
adviser, one who was later to criticize Johnson, asserted that the
legal equality of blacks was "an article of faith for Johnson"; he
was fully committed to it. But even if his friend and critic were
wrong and Daley not so powerful, there was the one irrepressible
force, impelling Johnson on civil rights: he was Texan. And as a
Texan bent on proving his liberalism he had to do the most un-
Southern of things, act on civil rights. Fellow Southerners knew
and feared this. One recalled with a smile a day when Kennedy
was president: "A bunch of Catholic prelates came in to see
Jimmy [Eastland]. They complained to him that Kennedy wouldn't
appoint an ambassador to the Pope though Truman, a Baptist,
did. They wanted to know why Kennedy wouldn't do it. Well,
we explained it to them. And the same thing happened to us.
Johnson turned on us. The last thing we want is another Southern
president."[39]

Early in the winter of 1964 Johnson called to the White House
civil rights and congressional leaders. He made clear he would
trade nothing, not the FEPC nor the Part III; he wanted the whole
bill. He let it be known that he backed the bill fully, and it passed
the House on February 10. (After passage, a poll of congressional
leaders indicated that even had Kennedy lived, the bill would have

passed. Its time had come, said Everett Dirksen.) Then he urged Joseph Rauh to get working on the Senate and called in Humphrey and Mansfield, telling them he was prepared to tie up the Senate for months, if necessary, to beat the impending filibuster.[40] And it was necessary: For fifty-seven days, the longest filibuster ever, the debate dragged on. On June 10, the Democratic and Republican leadership held a vote on cloture, and for the first time in history, by a vote of 71 to 29, the Senate cut off debate on a civil rights measure. Without compromise or equanimity or amity, the Southerners were thoroughly vanquished, not as before in the party councils, but in the Congress and in law. Russell was old, the Southerners were tired; but more than that, Johnson was president and behind the bill.

The 1964 Civil Rights Act, signed July 2, prohibited the unequal application of voting registration requirements and made a sixth grade education the standard of literacy. It barred discrimination in most public accommodations. It authorized federal aid to desegregating schools and empowered the attorney general to file suit for school desegregation. It barred discrimination in any program receiving federal assistance and authorized the government to cut off assistance where discrimination was found. It outlawed discrimination and segregation in most employment and erected an Equal Employment Opportunity Commission to enforce compliance. It was a broad act, attempting to "close the springs of racial poison," as Johnson said when he signed it. One Atlanta Democrat, Charles Weltner, changed his vote and said, "I would urge that we at home now move on to the unfinished task of building a new South. We must not remain forever bound to another lost cause." Twenty-seven in the Senate and 126 in the House voted for the lost cause.[41]

They could console themselves with the continued discrimination in voting, for the 1964 act did little to enforce equal registration. This became clear in Selma, Alabama. Martin Luther King, Jr., and other civil rights leaders chose this town to besiege; they wanted to register blacks but more importantly to illustrate the difficulties entailed in registration. There they showed that a prospective voter routinely had to fill in fifty blanks, write from dictation a part of the Constitution, answer four questions on the governmental process, read four passages from the Constitution and answer four questions concerning them, and sign an oath of loyalty to the United States and to the State of Alabama. Only 335 blacks of 15,115 eligible were registered. There were those who wanted to keep it that way. When the civil rights sympathizers began a march from Selma to Montgomery, on March 7, 1965, state police broke it up with tear gas, night sticks, and whips. Two nights later, a group of white men beat a white Unitarian minister, James Reeb, of Boston. He died on March 11. Two weeks before, a black man from Selma, Jimmie Lee Jackson, who said he was beaten and shot by state police, died. All this was in the press, some of it on television. Johnson federalized the Alabama National Guard, the march resumed on March 21 and was completed four days later, and that night Klan members killed Mrs. Viola Liuzzo of Detroit, on the road from Selma to Montgomery.[42]

The Southern resistance was uncontrollable and, as usual, ill-advised. Johnson ordered the Justice Department to draft legislation providing federal registrars in counties which discriminated against blacks, a provision he had fought as majority leader in 1960. At the height of the Selma crisis, he went to the Hill and said before the nation, "Their cause must be our cause too. Because it is not just Negroes but really it is all of us who must overcome the crippling legacy of bigotry and injustice. And we shall overcome."[43]

With a phrase, borrowed from the early civil rights movement and Pete Seeger, Johnson put himself in the camp of the outsiders, among those seeking a revolution in race relations. He knew where to touch the right chord, when to preempt a position; and the reaction was as he desired. Ten years later a spokesman for the old guard, still astonished, would despise him for it: "Do you remember Johnson said, 'We shall overcome'? Do you remember that!"[44] And two days later, when the president submitted his legislation, Congress was bound to enact it. On April 22, the Senate began its debate and little more than a month later voted to invoke cloture, ending it; on August 6, Johnson signed the law. The next day the Justice Department filed a suit to strike down the Mississippi poll tax, and three days later it filed against Alabama, Texas, and Virginia. The department suspended literacy tests in nine Southern states. On August 9, Attorney General Katzenbach chose counties in Alabama, Louisiana, and Mississippi where federal examiners would process black voter applicants. At the end of August, Johnson announced federal registrars had registered 27,385 blacks in the first nineteen days of the Voting Rights Act. The liberals' success was easy to measure.[45]

And so was their failure. For two years the liberals failed to pass another civil rights measure. But then in 1968, Congress enacted the open housing law. There was little hope the bill

could be passed; for two years it had come before the Senate but
the Senate had taken no action. The Republicans, led by Dirksen,
had not collaborated with Northern Democrats and so cloture had
failed. Senator Ervin had offered a crippling amendment to the
bill, and there was no reason to suppose he and the Southerners
could not again muster Republican strength enough to defeat the
open housing law. But when Walter Mondale offered to widen
the exemptions in the open housing law, Dirksen agreed to seek
a compromise. At the end of February, they drafted a bill that
covered roughly 80 percent of the nation's housing. A cloture
motion passed on March 4, and after six weeks of debate, the
Senate passed the bill. It went to the House, where it stalled in
the Rules Committee, which on March 19 refused to clear it for
action. But when the committee met again, on April 9, things
had changed: Martin Luther King, Jr., had been shot at dusk in
Memphis on April 4, and 100 cities, including Washington, had
burst into rioting. The committee cleared the bill, the House
passed it April 10, and Johnson signed it the 11th. A combination
of Clarence Mitchell, liberal Republicans, Dirksen's turnabout,
an ill-timed real estate campaign, and King's death made possible,
to everyone's surprise, this last of Johnson's civil rights acts.[46]

But Johnson also had the power of the executive order, and
he used it with effect. On September 24, 1965, he signed Order
11246, prohibiting racial discrimination in employment by federal
contractors, later amended to add discrimination by sex as a proscribed action. This order, elaborating Kennedy's order of 1961,
established what became known as the affirmative action policy.
(The 1964 Civil Rights Act was not the basis of affirmative action.
Its Title VI referred only to participation and benefits in programs
receiving federal assistance and not to employment. And Title VII,
referring to employment, did not specify affirmative action.) HEW
and the Department of Labor proceeded to issue a series of guidelines to enforce the order, instructing institutions of higher education, for example, "to do more than ensure employment neutrality
with regard to race, color, religion, sex, and national origin. As
the phrase implies, affirmative action requires the employer to
make additional efforts to recruit, employ and promote qualified
members of groups formerly excluded, even if that exclusion
cannot be traced to particular discriminatory actions on the part
of the employer." The order also compelled large contractors to
submit to the government affirmative action plans and goals—how
many minority people they would hire and how long it would

take. Quotas, said the government, were not its aim, though this policy implied them.[47]

Guidelines were also issued to enforce the sections of the 1964 Civil Rights Act, and perhaps none were so important as those enforcing the desegregation of public schools.[48] In March 1968, acting under authority of Title VI (cutting off federal assistance to discriminatory programs), HEW set forth its policy. It proscribed discrimination in the assignment of students to schools and classrooms; in athletics and extracurricular activities; in the crowding of classrooms and the assignment of teachers; in the offering of books and counselling; and in the disbursement of money—discrimination, in short, in the smallest and largest of school activities. HEW required each school to submit written assurance of compliance. It made periodic reviews, and if a school was found at fault HEW could cut off its funds (a serious loss after the 1965 education appropriations) or ask the Justice Department to file suit against the district. In return, HEW offered its technical assistance to the schools and also a sample letter schools might write to parents, explaining the process of desegregation. HEW expected schools integrated by 1968-69—"or, at the latest, 1969-70."[49]

Such was the bustle and the hope of Lyndon Johnson's civil rights program.

•   •   •

Four years before, in 1964, the war on poverty had begun. Kennedy was to have begun it in the same year, but he died, and instead Johnson did. "The Administration," said Johnson on January 8, 1964, "here and now, declares unconditional war on poverty in America." Within a month he had appointed Sargent Shriver head of the Office of Economic Opportunity, and by August Congress had passed a package of poverty programs. The first year $800 million was appropriated, the second $1.5 billion, the third $1.6 billion, and by 1968 almost $2 billion. It was a wide range of programs and agencies, some run by cities and states, some by the federal government—a set of experiments, testing how best to help people and areas that seemed perpetually excluded from the operation of the economy.

There were Jobs Corps to train and keep busy unemployed young people; community action programs to offer a variety of neighborhood services and to involve the poor in solving the problems of poverty; legal services to help the poor deal with the law; Head Start to educate preschool children; Upward Bound to prepare students for college. In 1966 Congress gave these programs legislative authority and money, and in the next two years added Follow Through, an extension of Head Start to early school years; Emergency Food and Medical Care; Family Planning; and Senior Opportunities and Service. Still others were designed to employ or train city slumdwellers—Neighborhood Youth Corps; Operation Mainstream; New Careers; and Impact. There were VISTA, rural and migrant family programs, the 1966 Emergency Family Loan Program, and the 1967 Day Care program. And there were others.

Most of these programs fell under the Office of Economic Opportunity (OEO). Some, like the Neighborhood Youth Corps, went to the Department of Labor, and others, like Work-Training, might have joined it. The education programs, such as Head Start, Follow Through, and Work-Study, might have gone to the Education division of HEW, and the slum rehabilitation program might have gone to HUD. But they did not. New agencies and departments did not eliminate old ones but took their place alongside them, much in the fashion that the English bureaucracy, over centuries, grew and elaborated itself into a curious blend of archaic and active offices. But this was as Johnson and his aides wanted it: Their aim was to establish one bureau, the OEO, to dramatize the plight of the poor and also to be flexible, so that programs could be launched and tried and if successful continued, if not abandoned. The process of experimentation, they thought, would take at least five years—a freewheeling assault, partly federal programs, partly grants to state and local programs. The time had come, it was thought, to try every way to help the poor—a grand experiment.[50]

Johnson's domestic program did not end with the civil rights and poverty programs, though they were perhaps his boldest efforts. After the large Democratic victory in 1964 he got more—all he could from a cooperative Congress—Medicare for old people, Medicaid for poor people, the first general aid to elementary and secondary education, and aid to higher education. These programs involved considerable expense. Medicaid, administered by the states and paid for by both states and the federal government, cost in the first year $2 billion, of which the government paid $975 million. Ten years later the total cost was $15 billion. In 1967-68, the government spent $2.6 billion on public schools, which amounted to more than 7 percent of all public school expenses; ten years

before the government had paid for only .7 percent of those expenses. Housing was also expensive. By 1968, guided by the
administration, Congress had doubled the production of public
housing units, increased the annual rate of housing production
for the poor by six times over the rate of the 1950s, and authorized
$5.3 billion for the construction of 1.7 million units within three
years. The Johnson people planned big.

But it was not size alone that distinguished the Great Society
programs. It was also their focus—the poor. All money for the
poverty programs, and most of the money spent in the education
and medical and housing programs, was intended to help the poor.
This was new. And so was the objective the planners had in mind,
which can be plainly seen in the housing program. For some time
the Federal Housing Administration had insured mortgages on
homes, and since 1949 the FHA had ruled that its benefits should
go to all, regardless of color. But in 1965 the government's housing bill went beyond mortgage insurance and housing units; it
authorized rent supplements to help poor persons pay rent in
standard, not slum or poor, housing. This was a dramatic departure
from the past. No longer would income difference stand in the
way of integration. Blacks and whites of different classes would
live together, because government would make up the difference
between rent and income. (Supplements met formidable opposition, but passed.) Then the 1968 housing act helped the poor buy
their own homes, helped them to get, in other words, what all
Americans always had wanted. The housing program thus entailed
more than shelters alone. It implied a rather daring vision, in
which the government bore the duty and had the ability not just
to end discrimination and legal segregation, and not just to build
housing, even housing for the poor, but to raise the standard of
living of poor people and to integrate the races.[51]

This vision was implied as well by the Great Society's program
for the cities. It was natural that Johnson turned to the cities, that
he was the first president to send a message to Congress on them,
for once liberal analysis had moved from race problems to economic problems, it was but a small step to consider the special
problems of the cities. They were a separate and troubled part
of America, a physical and economic and racial entity by itself,
both a cause and a result of poverty and racial discord. In 1964,
Johnson appointed a task force on urban problems and named as
its head Robert C. Wood, a political scientist from Harvard. Wood
and his group, with some dissension, advocated the rent supple-

ments program adopted by Congress the following year. In 1965, a new task force, also under Wood, reported in December to the president, recommending a federal program that would pool local and federal money, the participation of professional and government experts and of the poor, in an effort to arrest the physical decay of the slums and the mounting disaffection of their dwellers. Johnson liked the idea, made Wood under secretary of HUD, and sent his message to Congress in January 1966. The Model Cities program emerged. Enacted in the fall of 1966 after protracted debate, it provided one year planning grants to seventy-five cities, which after the first year would implement a number of programs, drawing from federal categorical grants, state monies, and supplemental Model Cities appropriations, all intended to improve the quality of life in the worst slums of cities—renovate buildings, make the poor responsible for service programs and planning, finance housing, encourage new business, provide clothing for children, open addiction and mental health facilities, expand legal aid, open cultural centers, plant trees, buy land, raise literacy. It was a "demonstrations" act. There was no certainty the program would work; like the OEO programs, it was designed as an experiment, in which the cities had one year to plan their projects and five years to make them work. The concept was not to build more apartments, though more were needed and built, but to "restructure the total environment," not just to tear down buildings, displace tenants, put up new structures, but to make neighborhoods livable and lively, give them commerce and cultural opportunity, and to give the poor a measure of control over their own lives.[52]

These were the principal programs. We need at present only to form an idea of their purpose—not to study and assess each one—though even this is a difficult task. For though the programs seem to have had a common purpose, it was variously interpreted by the Great Society officials.

Some believed that the poverty programs did not exemplify the Great Society's purpose, for they affected only the standard of living—a concern of the New Deal, which the Great Society went beyond. Its concern was more ethereal, expressing a concept, the quality of life. Where former programs appropriated money to build schools, the Great Society asked what went on inside them; where urban renewal tore buildings down, it built a livable environment, developed neighborhoods, and struck down the barriers of race; where once the government built public housing, the rent supplements program put old and poor and black people into middle class housing. For above all, according to this view, the Great Society was an assault on attitudes. This was the message of Johnson's speech in May 1964, when the phrase "Great Society" first appeared.[53] The Great Society was a place that knew no poverty and racial hatred, but also that accommodated "the desire for beauty and the hunger for community," that gave leisure for thought and honored nature and creativity—a place "where men are more concerned with the quality of their goals than the quantity of their goods." For some, such as Richard Goodwin, Johnson's gifted speechwriter (and the author of this speech), this was the meaning of the Great Society.

For others the distinguishing feature of the Great Society was its political innovation. The New Deal exemplified the politics of distribution, by which government shifted around fixed resources to the majority of the population; but the Great Society was an exercise in innovative politics, drawing from expanding resources, giving thought and money to new concerns and groups. Urban renewal and Social Security and unemployment compensation fell under distributive politics. But rent supplements were innovative: they took new money and gave it to new people, a minority of the population, for a new and special reason.[54]

There was still a third view of Johnson's work. The New Deal and the early 1960s gave legal sanction to the rights of labor and blacks, leaving unfinished the economic and social battle. The Great Society, in its poverty programs, housing bills, executive orders, and Medicaid, tried to make good on society's promise, to fulfill the expectations all Americans had of enjoying a decent life. Laws are papers, but equality is a condition.[55]

But to Lyndon Johnson, the maker of it all, the Great Society had a special purpose. Johnson had lived in government for close to four decades, and through those years his hero was the first of four presidents he worked with, Franklin Roosevelt. He had watched Roosevelt at work much as Roosevelt had watched Wilson. He wanted to be a Roosevelt, even outdo him, according to one friend, and after the 1964 landslide he got the chance. His Great Society would do everything the New Deal had done and more. He worked tirelessly, knowing he had not much time; perhaps his task moved him, certainly he seemed committed.[56] When he signed a bill, the moment sometimes overwhelmed him, and he spoke of the greatness of America. Long before, his ambition had led him to move away from Texas and toward the growing liberal wing of his party and now, as president, it led him to surpass all previous presidents. And surpass them he did.

There is another way to look at the Great Society, however, and that is as the culmination of postwar liberalism. First the Great Society granted what liberals had demanded since 1948—equal protection of the rights of blacks. Then it went beyond civil rights and identified defects in society—poverty, residential segregation—and resolved that the government bore the duty of removing these. This was postwar liberalism at its height. Before the New Frontier, of course, the liberals had not outlined the full range of this activity, had directed their attention, logically enough, to removing the legal impediments to equal opportunity. But once in power they found that their goal of equality required an analysis of society and of the economy, and it was in this sense that the civil rights issue liberated liberalism. It permitted the liberals, almost compelled them by Johnson's time to explore society and expose its flaws, to declare blacks equal at last, and then to ask why they were not equal yet. This critical thinking had little in common with prewar liberalism. It justified a government that strived not to make business competitive or workers secure, nor even to benefit the majority of citizens, but instead to reverse social patterns and help the few that were deprived. This was the distinction—and the climax—of postwar liberal endeavor.

PART THREE

CIVIL RIGHTS
AND THE LIBERAL FAILURE

TEN

―――❦―――

BEYOND LIBERALISM

Liberalism had reached its height, and then, in the midst of its prodigious accomplishment, it was deserted. For twenty-five years the liberals had struggled in the party and the nation to carry out their ideas, but by the end of the Great Society, and for several years after, few men even dared to identify themselves as liberals. And when they did it was with embarrassment and bewilderment, as if defending an idea acquired a long time ago which suddenly, and owing to no mistake of their own, had gone out of fashion. Why?

There were many reasons for the liberals' failure, first among them perhaps being their success. They enacted the civil rights legislation and improved medical care for the poor and old—goals since the 1940s, which, once realized, could no longer serve as the focus and unifying purpose of the liberal movement. This was their first problem. Then, having fulfilled their original mission, the liberals confronted new problems—poverty, urban blight, endemic unemployment and segregation—which were the logical successors to the old ones, but harder to solve, larger and more complicated. Over the years the geographical distribution of income and races, by design and default, had created inequality. This inequality was impervious, unaffected by the economy's cycles, and irremediable short of drastic action—the redistribution of income; the large-scale integration of the races, not just in school districts but across district, even metropolitan lines, and not just in schools but in communities as well. These solutions, the liberals found, were beyond their reach: neither Congress, nor the Supreme Court, nor many people would sanction them. Thus the liberals met their second failure by exposing a problem they could not solve. They did just enough to reveal the enormity of the problem and, by their minor attempts to appease it, to arouse the wrath of those who wanted the problem left alone. And here they ran into their third failure: Many of their programs few people liked. Programs had technical troubles, many were accounted failures, but, more important, resistance grew in reaction to the government's attempt to integrate the races, to rebuild the cities, to give blacks an edge in the job market. Compared with what was needed, if one was to integrate society and rid it of a permanently impoverished class, the programs were meager; yet they were opposed. The nation was not behind them.

At the same time others wanted more—wanted the liberals to make good on their promise of equal opportunity for all people. The Democratic party, from 1964 on, increasingly responded to this demand by minority peoples, not just for programs but for control of the party, until it gave them that control in 1972. And outside the party, the Black Power movement overtook the civil rights movement and called for drastic action. These Democrats and blacks, who had not taken part in the liberal struggle and civil rights movement of the 1940s, 1950s, and 1960s, replaced the liberals as the vanguard of reform. They thought the liberals timid and trembling, members of the power structure, and despised them as much as the rest of the nation did. Thus the liberals were, on the one hand, in the eyes of the radicals, hardly distinguishable from the rest of the reactionary nation, and on the other, in the eyes of the nation, hardly distinguishable from the radicals themselves. In fact, the liberals were neither. They were isolated, in the middle, assaulted by both sides at once.

There was, however, a deeper source to the liberal failure, one that made it more than coincidence that liberals were assaulted from the right and the left at once. Liberalism in its triumph entailed the exercise of federal power to secure rights and benefits for the disadvantaged, the poor and old and black. It emphasized the virtues of power and the problem of race—power to integrate schools and bus children, power to impose quotas and starve a school of funds, power to reorganize cities, tax heavily, and pay the poor's rent. In these programs, liberalism reached its point of tensile strength, its purpose realized, its power certain—and then it snapped. This startling use of power, always promised in the liberal ideology, pricked the nation's memory and called to mind an older liberalism, reminded men that it first had meant the liberty of people and the dangers of power. And when power was exercised to alter race relations, especially the more complex ones of the North, resistance swelled. Washington and busing became odious symbols, the code words of reaction against the liberals' use of power. At the same time, the radicals underwent a similar reaction. The machines, loan institutions, businesses, and unions, even the federal government, the Southern-dominated Congress—these symbols of power long had been arrayed against blacks in America. What blacks wanted now, when liberals brought attention to their problems, was power for themselves. When the liberals gave them some—in community action programs and the Democratic party—the minorities used it to denounce the government and protest the liberals' paternalism. They had no use for liberals, loathed their use of power as much as conservatives did, and, sounding remarkably like the conservatives, asserted the people's right to govern their own affairs. (Though blacks shared with conservative whites this loathing of the liberals' power, they of course differed in their reasons, which, when given expression, brought an even greater outcry from the right, from those who never had liked liberalism and now were able to say, as one senator did, that liberals gave money and power to Black Panthers. This escalating exchange of charges also hurt the liberals.) For both sides, the complaint was against the liberals' use of power.

This was a hard and sad irony for those to understand who had fought for twenty-five years. When finally the liberals put into practice what they had preached, they were denounced. They had tampered with race relations and used extraordinary power, and by so doing had given new life to old sentiments—racism and the American dread of power—which, far from surmounting, the liberals succumbed to, as had so many reformers in the past.

The Slums

When John Kennedy took office, he followed a liberal idea that led him to the heart of Appalachia. When Johnson came, he followed the same idea, and it led him into Harlem and Roxbury. Both of them acted on the liberal precept that all had rights and that the government should protect them. One of the rights was that to a decent life. Both of them identified poverty as the problem and spent billions of dollars, yet poverty persisted. Both of them failed.

The problem they pointed to but could not solve was enormous. It was the persistence of poverty among certain people in certain places, conspicuously black people: isolated geographically in the centers of big cities; isolated economically, for they had no jobs and few skills; isolated culturally, for the values of the society were not theirs. Food stamps and welfare reduced by half the number of those people living below the poverty level in the 1960s; and busing brought a few blacks and whites together in schools. But neither these nor any other Great Society program, except perhaps rent supplements, retarded the process by which the black and poor were segregated from the rich and white. They could not—the process had begun long before.

At the time of the First World War, when blacks began their migration North, they were not received with open arms. Poor, ignorant, hopeful, they streamed North from the hot slow South-land to such cities as Chicago—lively industrial center, glittering on the shores of Lake Michigan. They went to the South Side, most of them to an area between Thirty-First and Thirty-Ninth Streets, from State Street to the lake—the "Black Belt." When blacks tried to move out, to the west side, whites resisted; home-owners organized—some threw bombs—and not just homeowners, for most large real estate firms and loan institutions (even those where blacks deposited their savings) refused to deal in property owned by blacks. Only three downtown banks made no restrictions on loans to blacks. Rigorously, intentionally, the races were segregated, and it was because they mingled a little on a Sunday in July 1919 that a race riot punished the city for three days, leaving 38 people dead and 537 injured.[1]

Again, during World War II, blacks came North, 2,000 a day some days, and again they were segregated. They came by rail and got off the train at the Illinois Central Station, by the corner of Michigan and Roosevelt. Then they looked for a home. For a house near the Loop, banks made money scarce—20 to 40 percent down payment, five to ten year mortgages—so blacks went else-where, but not to the South Side, where established blacks had made their home and prices were high, instead to the West Side, where they filled what became the nation's largest slum. The far-ther west they moved (in the city limits) the easier the terms; so they went, down Roosevelt Road. And if by chance the mortgage practices and high costs did not push them west, restrictive cove-nants did: at one time 80 percent of Chicago's land was legally restricted to whites. In later years the Court might prohibit re-strictive covenants (1948) and school segregation (1954), and the Congress might end discrimination (1964) and disfranchisement (1965), but neither the Court nor the Congress ended the slums; they continued. In fact, they grew worse. In 1910, 73 percent of America's blacks lived in rural areas; in 1960, 73 percent lived in cities. And in the 1960s the slums grew larger, not just in Chicago but in every major city.[2]

As they grew larger, so did their problems. Taxes rose and industries left the cities, and some of those that remained automated their production. Unemployment became endemic. During the mid-1970s, 4.4 million of the nation's 71.4 million families bought food stamps every year (one in every five black families, one in every twenty-five white); 11 million people received welfare benefits under Aid to Families with Dependent Children (in New York alone over 1 million); and federal and state governments spent almost $18 billion on unemployment compensation for 5 million workers. The size of this relief was awesome (and not all of it connected with the slums), but more awesome yet was the inability of economic prosperity to reduce it in the inner cities. In fact welfare rolls increased during the 1960s, despite great economic growth. And despite the general improvement in the income of blacks, both income and employment in the cities declined. At the height of the Great Society, the nation's poor black slums thus remained impervious to change, becoming poorer and blacker. In the postwar years, Western Europe eradicated its worst slums; in America they grew worse.[3]

This persistence of poverty has led some to believe that a "culture of poverty" sustains the conditions of the slums, and others to study the history of the black family, and others to question the moral fiber of black people. "You build public housing and in two months it's a slum. Abraham Lincoln was raised in what today would be a slum—with a dirt floor—yet he," says Herman Talmadge, whose Georgia was laid waste by Lincoln's troops, "yet he was a moral man."[4] This moral failure, some say, is apparent in the violent life of the slums; and indeed slums are congenial to violence. In Watts, before the riot, one in every two men had some sort of police record, and, in 1964, police recorded 17,000 offenses there. Yet these statistics are not surprising, when one considers others. Watts was nearly completely segregated—90 percent black. One out of every three adults was unemployed. As national income rose in the early 1960s, income in Watts dropped by 8 percent. Public transportation was meager, the distance to Los Angeles great; and only 14 percent of the residents had cars, so most could not seek a job or get to it if they found one. They stayed in the slum. In 1965, the slum erupted in a riot lasting four days. Former President Eisenhower blamed the civil rights movement for the lawlessness, but the truth was that the civil rights movement neither caused the riot nor could have prevented it.[5] The goals of integration and suffrage bore little relations to the ills of Watts. The problem was—and always has been—one of income.

The income was denied for several reasons: first perhaps because the people were black; later because they lived in slums; had no skills, were far from job centers; and finally because, denied so long the benefits of American society, they had no reason to believe that by adopting a spirit of industry and frugality the fruits of society would be theirs. One may attribute the conditions of slumlife to a culture of poverty, to a history of weak families, to moral turpitude; but it seems more reasonable to describe these as results and to assign the cause to the fact of the slum itself. And the origins of the slum are no mystery.

The Remedy and the Reaction

As we have seen, many programs dealt with the slum, none of which, however, reduced its size. Some did not try; others tried but were too small for such a big problem; and still others were outlawed by the Supreme Court. The liberals hence failed and were disdained for having done so. But perhaps they were more disdained for having tried to succeed, for having exercised unprecedented power and bringing unprecedented attention to the problem of race. It was on account of this ideological problem, more than on account of technical failures—of which most citizens were anyhow ignorant—that the liberals earned the people's hatred.

Few Great Society programs had as their aim the elimination of the slum. Most, as we have seen, provided services—legal aid and day care centers—or they provided food stamps, temporary employment, and public housing. These did not break down the pattern of segregation and poverty. Other programs had little effect of any sort; job training programs often trained people for jobs that no longer existed. And some had a way of keeping people in the slums. The 1968 Housing Act sought to help poor people buy their own homes. In that year the average house cost $35,000, yet the Act, which subsidized mortgages for the poor, restricted most subsidies to houses costing $12- to $15,000. Such federal help, novel as it was, did not help people buy standard housing; instead it made certain that the beneficiary dwelled in the slum. Inflation also kept the poor in the slum. The price of land and housing boomed, and a negative correlation grew between the plight of the poor and the cost of standard housing. Between 1956 and 1966, while the wholesale price index rose annually 1 percent, the increase in land value was 6.9 percent. And suburban land rose fastest of all: land values outside Philadelphia showed an increase of 1,460 percent in twenty years.[6] It was no surprise that the poor stayed in the slums, nor that, eight years after the Housing Act, only 42 percent of black families, as against 65 percent of white, owned their own homes. Today the average house costs $50,000.[7] In rural slums, an answer has been found—mobile homes—but in the city there is no room to park them.

Several programs, however, were relevant to the problem. They tried to break down the isolation of the slum, the segregation that kept blacks together in their poverty, beyond the reach of social and economic influence. Yet these programs failed. Rent supplements failed for a simple reason—money. It was a program, as we have seen, designed to pay the rent of poor people, so they could live in middle-class housing, outside the slum. But in 1967 Congress appropriated only $10 million for the program, and however one estimated the number of poor minority people, living in substandard housing, this amount allotted an average of several cents per family per month. It was a bold idea, a meager effort.

Two other bold ideas—Model Cities and school busing—also failed, but their failure was more complex, and for that more interesting. They failed because the problem they attacked was bigger than anyone had imagined, but also because—and this was unexpected—no one liked the power the liberals exercised.

In the Model Cities program, the administration had several aims. One was to give the poor services: food, day care centers, education, transportation, legal aid. Another was to concentrate the talent of federal, state, and municipal government on the problem of slums. And a third was to resurrect Robert Kennedy's idea of making the poor themselves partakers in the renovation and rule of the cities. This last, to consider the "identity, security, status, or political power" of the poor, was the boldest.[8] It sought to fill the political vacuum caused by the disintegration of city machines and also to relieve the sense of powerlessness, one of the debilitating effects of poverty. But this aim clashed sometimes with one or both of the other two, and all three ran afoul of the sheer amount of poverty and the corrosion it made. These problems came to light in the city of Denver.[9]

Denver was a beautiful city. It was a large city, one-half million when it applied for the Model Cities grant (twice that in the metropolitan area), but not so large as to be unmanageable. The air was clean; there was no other large city within 500 miles; the Rocky Mountains were next door. It had industry, packing plants, insurance companies, and national defense work; its average growth

rate was one-fourth higher than the national rate. It was an educated city. Colorado was one of eleven states where more than
2 percent of the population engaged in scientific and engineering
work; only the District of Columbia had a higher percentage of
college degrees. Most citizens of Denver liked the city in the mid-
1960s; few considered race relations a problem. The slums were
not enormous, and the minority population, most of it Mexican
and black, comprised only 16 percent of the city. It did not seem
a troubled city.

The Denver city government nonetheless applied for a Model
Cities grant to arrest the decay of its center city, where a slum had
grown up near the business district. Denver won the grant and
spent a year, 1967/68, planning how it intended to combine
federal, state, and local efforts to rebuild the slum. Trouble started
immediately. The Department of Housing and Urban Development, controlling Model Cities, insisted that the process of decision
making was as important as the rehabilitation, and required cities
to include the poor in planning and managing Model Cities. City
machines in America had all but vanished, precinct captains were
gone. Blacks did not vote. The city government had little idea how
to reach the poor. In 1967, Congress further complicated the
matter by passing the Green Amendment, which said that OEO
could bypass local groups and administer its programs directly if
cooperation with the poor was not feasible. The Denver OEO
organization, Denver Opportunity, had already fallen into disfavor
with the poor; now it was thoroughly distrusted. Model Cities had
to find the spokesmen of the poor.

At length, it found them. A city worker found two black jazz
musicians who seemed to have contacts with residents of the slums,
and they were chosen to bring blacks and Mexicans to planning
meetings. But HUD was skeptical still; it wanted more poor. Then
a solution offered itself. The most outspoken members of the slum
community came forward and attended meetings of the planning
committees, met with city hall and private professionals and even
federal government authorities. Soon they dominated the Denver
Model Cities.

In January 1967, the Black Panthers opened a chapter in
Denver. By 1968, they and other militants (Black Nationalists,
Crusade for Justice, and others) represented the participation of
the Denver poor in Model Cities. They did not come regularly to
the meetings of their steering committee and neglected to keep
records, regarding records as a "White middle class habit." Though

they made up only 10 to 15 percent of the residents' planning committees, they made their views felt and, in this time of assassination and riots, spoke for the poor. Relations between city hall and these residents were shaky. The Denver police ran a check on the planners and found that 40 percent of them had felony arrest records. The residents accused city hall of "domestic colonialism." They made city officials come to a club—"Au Natural"—a headquarters of the Black Panthers, to argue over "Whitey's" role in the impending program. One day when the city government met with a Labor Department official to sign a contract for a grant, Frank Bailey, a young black leader, arrived at city hall in the company of Sir Stanley, a militant brought from Des Moines under the auspices of the Black Panthers. They complained to the Labor official of the city's indifference to local participation. The Labor official delayed the grant until the city could compose its troubles with the poor. What seems to have saved the grant and perhaps the Denver Model Cities program was the 1968 march of the poor on Washington: most of the poor's representatives went along and stayed out of Denver for several weeks.

But trouble continued throughout the year. In the summer of 1968, a crowd gathered one night at the Holly Shopping Center, and when the police arrived, they saw a young man, injured and dazed. They came upon him, saw his gun, told him to put his hands up. He fired, hitting one policeman. They fired back, four shots, and he fell. They drove away. Rioting followed for several days. The resident Model Cities committees took a hand in quieting it, organizing a vigilante group, manned by Black Panthers and others, to patrol the streets and prevent violence. One night at the shopping center the police responded to a call and found a crowd, several looters, and sixteen armed Panthers, there to control the crowd. The Panthers and the police confronted one another, neither eager for a shoot-out, until after nervous consultation the Panthers "allowed" the police to arrest a woman who had stolen a turkey, then the two armed forces departed. After this, the Police Department came to regard the Model Cities as a haven for dangerous militants. The police were not alone, however, for soon others were fretting over the participation of the poor. The city auditor, while approving checks for the Model Cities, noticed the name of Loren Watson, who he knew was the local chief of the Black Panthers. He called the district attorney, who likewise took a dim view of this expenditure, and soon Senators Dominick and McClellan began an investigation. They wanted to know whether federal money purchased guns for Black Panthers. By January 1969, Richard Nixon was president and Denver was just beginning its first projects. In the two and a half years since the enactment, Model Cities in Denver had not begun; and yet it was stumbling badly already.

The participating poor caused it to stumble in technical ways, too. HUD had expected that in the first year of the program the cities would make comprehensive studies of slum problems. They were to analyze problems, relate them to other problems, and find the root cause: how transportation affected employment, employment affected crime, crime affected business, etc. Then the planners were to set five-year goals, directly related to the analysis of connected problems, and in 1969 the first projects were to begin. In Denver the resident committees dominated this planning process. They knew what was wrong in their community and condemned the deficiencies in existing programs; they also disputed the intentions of city hall and fought among themselves. But they did not link the various causes of urban blight and gave scant attention to long-term goals. For the first year of execution, their plan, entailing 75 projects and costing $30 million, emphasized additional services for the poor, not structural economic change. The residents wanted more money for legal aid services and convenient sites for food stamp distribution. In education, rather than altering the curriculum or the school system, the residents called for better food services, a clothing allowance, and "sensitivity training programs for professionals." Model Cities became just another agency, foregoing the task of comprehensive analysis and planning and assault, a task the government had ordered but one which its emphasis on the poor participation had also made impossible.

But the role of the poor was not the only problem, for the role of the government was equally uncertain. Poverty programs were divided among several departments and agencies, often clashing with one another.[10] Sometimes the constituents of programs fought with constituents of other programs; in Denver the poor in OEO programs, largely Mexican, struggled for leadership with the poor in Model Cities committees, largely black. This chaos also hindered the delivery of services and money. There were 450 federal assistance programs, scattered among 11 departments and agencies, most of which channeled their money through state agencies. When Model Cities identified a problem and asked for funds appropriated in the 1966 authorization, it went to several state agencies and requested the money. Often a state agency stalled; often the state government and city hall were in the hands of different political parties; often one agency released the funds and another would not, jeopardizing coordination; often a federal department froze funds for any one of several reasons. The main goal of Model Cities—to coordinate the myriad agencies and grant programs and change the slums—failed. The delivery of services and grants was slow, and the increasingly complex federal inventory was not made simple; the federal system proved as much the problem as the slums. Perhaps, thought one Model Cities expert, instead of pitting the city hall against the poor, both against the state, and all three against Washington, the federal government might better have served the needs of the poor by giving them direct payments—simple hard cash.[11]

Such were the failures of Johnson's most innovative program. Model Cities put into action what liberals had demanded—power and money for the poor and black—and then, long before Nixon came into office and the funds dried up, it ran into trouble. It looked bad. Money to Black Panthers, power to ungrateful poor people, a cumbersome and bumbling bureaucracy—all these brought liberal verities into question. And Model Cities functioned poorly. By splitting power among several groups, including the poor, the program paralyzed itself and became a public brawl. And yet the poor would not have accepted a less important role for themselves; as it was, they protested. They complained of a hostile police power, paternalistic whites, and a callous and ineffectual bureaucracy. Everyone, therefore, protested and suspected the liberals and criticized their use of power. The program tapped deep hatreds, and perhaps created new ones. The visceral issue of race took on new life. Suddenly the slum was not the issue; the means of fixing it was.

Busing had a similar effect. No program was less popular or more damaging to liberalism than the forcible integration of school children. Race, power, force, and miscegenation—with busing the liberals evoked several hatreds at once and, when one considers what little relation busing bore to the problem of the slums, seemed to be squandering what influence they had.

In 1954, as we have seen, the Supreme Court ruled that public school segregation was unconstitutional, and the next year it ordered schools desegregated with all deliberate speed, leaving to the lower courts the task of accepting or rejecting local plans for integration. In 1964, when only 1.2 percent of the South's nearly 3 million blacks went to school with whites, the Court said, "The time for mere 'deliberate speed' has run out," and in 1968 and 1969 it said "free choice" plans for parents would not work and more forcible means were needed. In 1971, it found that busing was an acceptable means, and in 1973 it found that even where no law had segregated students but where instead official policy had done so, lower courts must order desegregation. In 1974, in Boston, Judge W. Arthur Garrity found that the construction of schools, the busing of blacks, the drawing of district lines, and the assignment of pupils and teachers all tended to segregate the school system. He ordered the system desegregated by busing. When the school committee stalled he put the system into federal receivership. And Boston became a symbol, as it had so often before—as the home of the Puritans and later of revolutionaries and later still of abolitionists—only now as the home of the Southern spirit in a Northern city, of people fighting against power.[12]

In the late 1960s, a short, dark-haired woman went every year to the Massachusetts statehouse to urge repeal of a state law prohibiting racial imbalance in schools. Elvira ("Pixie") Palladino, married to a city housing inspector, always had participated in local activities—the hockey team, girl scouts—and now she joined a segregationist movement. She met other parents, who came to testify before the assembly, and several years later, when Garrity ordered busing, they formed ROAR (Restore Our Alienated Rights), not an organization but a "fellowship." ROAR tried to stop busing—with boycotts and marches—and violence hit Boston's schools, "the spontaneous rising of the people," she later said.[13]

Most of her arguments were Southern. The federal government had "seriously encroached upon states' rights and usurped the rights of the legislative branch of states." She found no need to integrate schools, jobs, or society at large and believed *Brown* was misinterpreted, for it had held that to "deny a student a seat in school because of his color is wrong"; yet the court made her son travel to an overcrowded school, without cafeteria or gymnasium, and barred him from a nearer school, newly built. She spoke in the tradition of Sumner and Brady. "Integrated schools should come about by natural means," said Palladino, "and if it doesn't come about, that's all right with me."[14]

But she had a new argument, too, one with a Northern slant: "Cities are increasingly inhabited by minorities, and so we're being penalized for living with our brothers."[15] Others agreed. The working class men of South Boston formed a vigilante group, the

Marshals Corps, to patrol the streets with citizen band radios; they had no use for liberals. Once they had showered their warmth on John Kennedy, but in the busing melee they said of Ted Kennedy they would "dance on his grave." Many, like Palladino, quit the Democratic party. Her parents, immigrants from Italy, always had voted Democratic, but in the early 1970s she and others changed allegiance, if not to the Republicans, to a different sort of Democrats, to those who respected the integrity of their neighborhoods. In the 1976 Democratic primary George Wallace carried Boston over Henry Jackson and Morris Udall, bettering his vote of four years before by almost three times—busing had intervened. In the same year Palladino was elected to Boston's School Committee, where she continued her fight against busing, contributing, in the eyes of the U.S. Commission on Civil Rights, to violence and noncompliance. "When does sin wash away," she asked, "if there ever was any? When are we absolved of sin, which we never touched? The government can afford to experiment so it experiments with civil rights. We need a taxpayers revolt"—she said two years before the revolt began—"Suppress me with my own money!"[16]

If Boston's whites had shifted their arguments, so too had its blacks. Melvin King, a large black man with beard and moustache and round shaved head, held that the Democratic party was "not instrumental in the civil rights movement. The civil rights movement was carried by itself and mainly by the blacks in it. The federal government also has been hostile to blacks. It began by saying I was 3/5 of a man"—a reference to the weight assigned to blacks in the Constitution's apportionment of taxation. King, who Palladino said was not representative of Boston's blacks, though he often ran unopposed for his seat in the state assembly, represented the South End, one of America's worst slums; he, like Palladino, was sure of his purpose. "If by integration," he said, "you mean, 'Can you and I be friends,' then integration doesn't matter. If you mean, on the other hand, 'Can you continue to exercise power over me and deny my rights as you have always done,' then integration matters. Power is the issue in integration." He saw that quest for power as largely the work of blacks—God helps those who help themselves—but invited alliance with others. Only, "there is a point of self-love and togetherness before you ally with others. As with a marriage, each must first be self-dependent and in love with oneself." ROAR, he thought, was the "tool and pawn of real estate speculators. They have brutalized people, used the weapons of fear and ostracism. They have oppressed others and themselves." It is difficult to imagine two peoples, those of South Boston and those of the South End, more hostile to one another, sharing only their suspicion of liberal promises and the government's power, and sharing, too, the unbounded trust each puts in the endeavor of its own people.[17]

Boston was not alone. Summerton, South Carolina, one of the original defendants in the 1954 Supreme Court case, was still segregated in 1965, a year when 97 percent of all black children in the Deep South went to black schools. In Louisville, Kentucky, where a court ordered busing in 1975, citizens intimidated businessmen who refused to help the antibusing movement, threatening to burn one store down. Little Rock, Arkansas, where federal troops protected nine black students in their effort to attend the white high school in 1957, stalled for close to twenty years, until in 1975 desegregation began. Bogalusa, Louisiana, remains intransigent; once a year it holds two proms, one for blacks and one for whites. And the Topeka, Kansas, school district, which in 1954 was the principal defendant, resisted desegregation for twenty-two years and in 1976 prevailed upon the federal government not to terminate its funding, as the 1964 Civil Rights Act stipulated. Resistance goes on.[18]

Yet resistance is not always necessary—flight will do. In 1964, white parents in New York City boycotted schools on account of busing, but then the situation changed: From 1960 to 1975, New York City's population shifted from 78 percent white and 22 percent minority to 62 percent white and 38 percent minority. From 1970 to 1975 alone New York City lost 600,000 whites (and the Bronx became more black and Puerto Rican than white). The city's 1978 public school enrollment was 71 percent minority and 29 percent white. Integration under such circumstances became meaningless, for as one school official put it, there were not enough whites to go around. Andrew Jackson High School in Queens had one white student, 2,529 minority. When a federal court ordered the Board of Education to desegregate the school, the Board explained that to do so would cause integration in the rest of Queens to collapse; the other schools would lose the few whites they had. "We're regressing, all right," said Kenneth B. Clark, who helped prepare the blacks' brief in *Brown.* [19]

New York is not alone. Between 1960 and 1966 blacks in America's central cities increased by 2 million; the number of whites decreased by 1 million. And over ten million whites went to the suburbs—an act which Theodore Lowi has called "a failure of citizenship."[20] Dallas civil rights advocates pointed with pride to the successful busing of 18,000 students in 1976; yet in the five years before, Dallas lost 30,000 white students. Garrity's plan was law in Boston, backed up by scores of police, but in three years 20,000 whites left Boston's schools, and for the first time blacks composed a majority of Boston's students (though but 17 percent of the population). In the South, 3,500 private academies appeared in twenty years, enrolling one out of every ten white children. But the South is no longer the main issue; the city, North and South, has become the problem. In school districts with more than 100,000 students, three out of every five black students in the North (and two out of every five in the South) attend schools with enrollment more than half minority. In Northern cities, 30 percent of the black students attend schools with an enrollment almost 100 percent minority. Whether by law or by practice, in North and South, segregation goes on, and so does resistance, passive and active, to integration.[21]

The circumstances—though not the central issue—changed, and the liberals were confounded. They began their struggle against an avowedly racist caste system in the South and they got the Supreme Court to outlaw the segregationist gerrymandering of school districts. But while they looked to the South, they missed what happened in the cities, and when they saw, it was too late. Housing patterns, economic differences, and demographic shifts had segregated blacks and whites as if law had decreed it. The cities, with their slums, were more segregated than the rural South ever had been, and to integrate schools there required not just moving white and black children to different schools but to different neighborhoods. It also required the assignment of children by race—a practice, the resistors were quick to point out, prohibited by *Brown*. Moreover the whites were too few fully to integrate the schools; so the school boards sprinkled the few remaining whites around the city's schools, as if by their daily presence for several hours the whites would emit some superior quality to rub off on the blacks—a notion imbued with racist belief. Blacks and whites alike had little patience for such a remedy—so ill-suited to the needs of each—and little patience, therefore, for liberals.[22]

Affirmative action had a similar effect on liberalism. Beginning in 1961, elaborated in 1965, this program aroused little opposition—until the 1970s. Only then, after the Model Cities program, the riots, and the busing controversy, did affirmative action anger whites. Then they attacked, using the arguments they used against busing. They said it was coercive and that it violated the principle

of a color-blind Constitution. They challenged it in court, alleging
it was a violation of the Fourteenth Amendment and the 1964
Civil Rights Act, laws created to help the blacks. In 1977, the
Equal Opportunity Commission, established to enforce the 1964
Civil Rights Act, took up for the first time the case of a white
male. A Gallup poll in the same year found that 83 percent of
Americans opposed preferential treatment for minorities (and
64 percent of the minority people polled agreed). This reaction
was damaging to liberals, not just because they had created affirmative action, but because, like busing, the issue of affirmative action
obscured the larger issue, that of slums and endemic poverty and
segregation, drowned it in a noisy debate as to whether or not
sixteen places should be reserved for minorities at a University
of California medical school. This debate at best could have a
marginal effect on the life of a slumdweller. To him affirmative
action was largely irrelevant; indeed it had little effect on the rise
of black wages in general. It and busing nonetheless became the
central civil rights debates, as the spirited quest for equal rights
ended in a nasty dispute about coercion.[23]

Thus the liberal failure was a double one, for the programs
not only aroused the animosity of the people, black and white,
but also left the deeper problems untouched. Social services, food
stamps, rent supplements, Model Cities, school busing, affirmative
action—all these were bitterly debated but none of them came
close to breaking down the concentration of poor and black people
in the slums. On the rare occasions that the liberals touched this
deeper problem, the courts stopped them cold. In 1973, the poorer
of two school districts in San Antonio, Texas, argued before the
Supreme Court that it should receive more money from the state
than the richer one, across town, where the property tax was high
and revenue therefore plentiful. The Court upheld the local property tax as the source of school revenue, regardless of the unequal
support it led to. The following year the Court strengthened again
the line separating rich from poor and white from black districts.
It struck down Detroit's integration plan, which had proposed to
integrate inner city blacks with suburban whites. The Court held
that the suburbs were not responsible for, nor had they contributed to, the concentration of blacks in Detroit. Finally, the
Court upheld a local zoning ordinance that prohibited construction of multiple-family—therefore low-income—housing. These
cases were significant. They cut to the heart of the segregation
crisis; and in each one the Court held that one people bore no

responsibility for the isolation and indigence of another; nor could the resources and people of adjacent towns be pooled to alleviate the conditions of the slum. But even had the Court not outlawed these efforts, their chances of success were slim, for resistance to integration, contrary to popular belief, rises in accord with increasing socio-economic status and increasing homogeneity of the neighborhood. Suburbs fight integration in housing and schools more doggedly than do the cities. The people who went there went for a reason.[24]

Barring these radical steps—and others even more radical—it remains unclear how slums can be eliminated, or, since for a variety of reasons slums propagate poverty, how that can be eliminated either. In the meantime, conditions have imposed their own solutions: Crime to titillate and excite and keep up one's flagging powers of rebellion; narcotics to dull and blunt one's mind to squalor; television and film, which have learned the rhythm of ghetto talk and return a pacifying racist image; and black political leaders, who rule over ruined cities.

These are current solutions. They function in the place of more humane ones. For the liberal programs did not provide solutions so readily as they stirred up resistance to all quarters. There was a lesson in this resistance, hidden in the 1976 report of the Civil Rights Commission, which stressed the successes in school integration—in Kalamazoo and Tampa and Corpus Christi and Minneapolis (though not in Chicago or Detroit or New York or Los Angeles—left out of the report). But it could not overlook the lingering problems. The primary obstacle to peaceful integration, the commission found, was the recalcitrant attitude of local leaders, the School Committee and Mayor White in Boston, businesses and clergy and Judge Hollenbach in Louisville. In Hillsborough County, Florida, the commission found that community approval was the key to peaceful integration. In Denver plans for integration progressed until, in 1969, the people elected a segregationist school committee.[25] The commission extolled the helpful citizens and, at the same time, condemned the obstruction of others. It did not consider (nor was it obliged to) that if the people determined the outcome of the school battle then perhaps it mattered little whether they were good or bad, cooperative or recalcitrant; perhaps it mattered only that they were the final arbiters.

The people—the liberals had left them out of their equation. Now the programs, the reaction they induced, brought them back in. For behind the programs the people saw a structure of menacing power—and indeed government grew in Johnson's time—and they ranked this power high among political evils. But it was not power of any sort; it was the power that undertook to alter race relations which probably provoked the people. Though there is no proof of this point, there is the preceding evidence, and also a survey, which shows that although the population had been evenly split between conservatives and liberals (as defined by their position on welfare and civil rights) in 1956 and 1960, it was more conservative than liberal in 1968 and 1972; and that the only group to grow more liberal from the 1950s to the 1970s was the blacks.[26] (Though even blacks, as we have seen, placed little trust in the liberals' government.) In trying to narrow the extraordinary gap between the races, the liberals used extraordinary power, and thereby brought power and civil rights—the means and ends of the liberal program—into disrepute. The liberals departed; the gap remained.

The Democratic Party, 1964-1976

In these years, when the Great Society incited a reaction against federal power and civil rights, the Democrats by their unrepentant behavior made the reaction even worse. They carried liberalism to its logical conclusion, exaggerating the very things that had induced the conservative reaction. If community action programs had given minority people a measure of power, the Democrats, by 1972, gave them control of their convention; if affirmative action had implied the use of quotas, the Democrats made the use explicit; and if busing had relied upon the coercive authority of the federal government, the Democratic platforms called for more coercion. In short, the Democrats, once committed to liberalism, found themselves powerless to check its snowballing effect, even when that effect was politically reckless.

Their blind adherence to liberal ideas, however, led not just to unpopularity but also to illiberal results. As the liberals gave minorities increasing attention and control in party councils, they themselves—the machine leaders, labor leaders, and liberal spokesmen—became superfluous. Their clients took their place in the liberal vanguard—blacks and poor people, and later young people, women, Indians, homosexuals, and others—people who no longer needed liberal spokesmen and wanted instead to speak for themselves. Liberals, who had pushed a theory, found themselves confronted with its result; they no longer controlled the party. It should have been their vindication—this empowering of outcast people—but it was instead their nemesis. They could only stand aside and watch their coalition dissolve. Fractured into small competing groups, the liberal coalition fell apart; without that coalition—the alliance of labor and bosses and liberals that had captured the party for liberalism—liberal ideas lacked a constituency. Moreover, when the various minorities fought each other and the liberals, they fought over issues important to themselves but extraneous to liberalism—the Vietnam War, gay rights, abortion—and obscured the larger issues of poverty and the slums. This was perhaps the worst blow to liberalism, affecting it as the Great Society did when the storm over programs all but obliterated the deeper issues. In the Democratic party the blow was felt worst in 1972, but also in 1968, when Ralph Abernathy brought the poor people to Chicago and their voice was lost in the noise—then and since—caused by people with things other than poverty on their minds.

Several things thus happened at once in the Democratic party. Not only did the party—and therefore liberalism—lose national support by its reforms, but also it destroyed the liberal alliance and lost sight of liberal issues. These events all were part of the same process, one by which liberalism undermined itself. For the logic of liberal thought led to the granting of power to minorities and hence to both backlash and political fragmentation, just as it led, in the Great Society programs, to an unpopular emphasis on race and power. The process was more damaging in the party, however, for it was there that postwar liberalism had emerged, sustained by a coalition and nurtured by bold ideas—things the party now lost.

One may see this process beginning, if not in 1948—for it would seem that the rise and fall of liberalism were of a piece— then in the 1964 Democratic convention, when the liberals first lost control of their forces.[27] Several civil rights organizations, ranging from the NAACP to SNCC (Student Nonviolent Coordinating Committee) founded the Mississippi Freedom Democratic Party (MFDP) to wrest political control from the traditional and segregated state Democratic party. The MFDP chose a slate of delegates and alternates, sixty-four blacks and four whites, which it sent to the Democratic convention in Atlantic City, hoping to unseat the white delegation. Lyndon Johnson, always striving for unanimity, wanted to avoid a civil rights credentials fight. He got Hubert Humphrey and Walter Reuther to badger Joe Rauh, lawyer for the MFDP, to get him not to press for a minority report, which required eleven votes in the credentials committee, or for a roll call on the floor, which required the votes of eight state delegates. Rauh was adamant; the MFDP should be seated. On Saturday, August 22, two days before the convention opened, he and the MFDP presented their case to the committee while national television watched. They described discrimination in Mississippi. When they were through, seventeen members of the committee backed the seating of the challenging delegation, and Johnson could no longer quiet the civil rights fight. He needed a solution fast. To get one he sent out his emissaries, Clark Clifford, Hubert Humphrey, Walter Reuther, and relied on the chairman of the credentials committee, David Lawrence, the Pittsburgh leader instrumental in the civil rights fight of 1948.

On Sunday, solution was no nearer. The administration forces in the credentials committee were willing to declare the MFDP delegation guests of the convention and to seat two of its members but refused to unseat the regulars. The MFDP wanted more. Then Walter Mondale, speaking for Humphrey, urged Rauh to seek not a floor fight but instead a compromise in committee. Rauh agreed, and acting with the MFDP's approval he proposed that the convention seat both delegations. Now Johnson refused. He knew even the Southern moderates might assent to ousting the regulars but would never allow the MFDP, nearly all black, to be seated. Texas Governor Connally, reportedly told him, "If those buggers walk onto the convention floor, we walk out." So on Monday, when the convention opened, trouble was certain. The credentials committee was to meet at 2 p.m. and report its decision to the floor that night. Humphrey was desperate. At noon he met in his hotel suite with Aaron Henry and Bob Moses, leaders of the MFDP, and Congresswoman Edith Green, Joe Rauh, and several others. He argued that the president and convention would only go so far, that it behooved the challengers to compromise. The MFDP said they would have to go further. Rauh went to Lawrence and got him to postpone the credentials report to the following day. That night both sides were intransigent, and Humphrey was worried. He wanted the vice-presidency, which was Johnson's to give, so he sought a compromise to placate Johnson; but he sympathized with the civil rights challenge. He grew morose, fatalistic, said he did not want to be vice-president after all. Johnson had a way of using people.

Tuesday morning Rauh met with the MFDP in their headquarters, a church. He explained that Johnson was putting considerable pressure on labor and liberals to seat the regulars—or at least not to seat the challengers; that in one instance Johnson had threatened not to appoint a certain judge, who was expecting appointment, if the judge's wife, a credentials committee member, voted for the MFDP. They had achieved a victory in dramatizing the issue of racial discrimination in Southern politics; they would get no more. Rauh sat down. One of the MFDP staff rose and denounced Rauh, said he had sold out to the party regulars. Rauh answered briefly, then left to attend the credentials committee meeting, starting at noon. He went to the convention hall where Charles Diggs, a black congressman from Detroit, stopped him and instructed him to call a certain number. Rauh hesitated. He thought it was a scheme to keep him out of the committee while the decision on seating was made. Lawrence assured him it was not; the committee would wait. Rauh went to a phone and called. It was Reuther. He told Rauh a formula had been found: the regular Mississippi delegation would be ousted; two MFDP delegates (Aaron Henry and Ed King) would be seated; and the party would vow never to seat a discriminatory delegation again. Reuther was insistent—he seldom was—and it was powerful pressure. As president of the UAW (for which Rauh was counsel), Reuther had worked for years to further civil rights. He instructed Rauh to accept the plan. "The convention," he said, "has made its decision."

Rauh said he had promised never to accept a decision without first consulting the MFDP. He went to the credentials committee to request a postponement until he could talk with his clients. Lawrence had kept his word not to start without him, but now Johnson's people insisted on a vote. Mondale gave a report, one which included the compromise as Reuther had outlined it, then the committee members called for a vote. Rauh got up and asked for a delay, but shouts of "Vote, vote," silenced him. In the oral vote that followed the report won overwhelmingly, only Rauh and six others favoring the seating of the MFDP, four short of the number needed to file a minority report and bring the matter to the convention floor. Rauh returned to the church. There he learned that during the credentials committee meeting several civil rights and MFDP leaders had met with Johnson emissaries. Martin Luther King, Jr., Bayard Rustin, Ralph Abernathy, Aaron Henry, Bob Moses, Ed King, and Walter Reuther were conferring when they heard a television newsman announce (erroneously) that the credentials committee had unanimously accepted the

Mondale compromise. Bob Moses left the meeting, enraged and, he thought, betrayed.

In the church there was bitterness and discord. The MFDP barred Martin Luther King, Jr., from addressing it; he was for accepting the compromise. Rauh spoke and said there was no way to take the fight to the convention floor. Then Bob Moses spoke. He resented the compromise, said it was imposed upon them, and did not like the party to tell the MFDP which two delegates it would seat. He swayed the gathering, which voted to reject the compromise. Later Moses staged an illegal "walk-in" at the convention and appropriated the vacant seats of the regular Mississippi delegation, which already had left the city. The next night, when Johnson was nominated, convention aides filled the empty chairs, but the MFDP delegates came again and sat on the floor. Southerners were outraged, one Mississippian saying the MFDP represented no one and, "The older niggers in our area like us. They like the Old Guard."[28] Liberals, too, thought the MFDP behavior extreme. Rauh, the liberal most faithful to the cause of the challengers, later refused to serve as their counsel in another matter.

The civil rights episode in Atlantic City represented a turning point for civil rights and its place in Democratic party politics. The next two conventions would develop more fully a trend that began here, a trend that both fulfilled the aims of liberalism and badly undercut them. For in 1964 the Mississippi blacks sought to redeem liberal promises, not only to demand equal opportunity but also to make the Southern delegations represent blacks. In 1964, too, the blacks spoke for themselves and refused to delegate their powers to white intermediaries. But these same achievements, wrought as they were in an atmosphere of vehemence, alienated most whites, including liberals, who thought that in 1964, especially, civil rights was winning. Those who had fought for civil rights—labor leaders like Reuther, city leaders like Lawrence, senators like Humphrey—and who, in 1964, had also passed the Civil Rights Act, resented the black militance, thought Moses was unreasonable, and knew he was fomenting a backlash of white hatred. Joseph Rauh was alone among the major liberal figures in supporting the MFDP, and even he saw reason for disappointment. Prominent civil rights leaders of the 1950s, like Martin Luther King, Jr., also parted with their intransigent comrades. The liberal alliance, long before Vietnam and the problems it raised, was fragmenting in a most natural and unsettling way.

The 1968 convention was a morass. The issues were confused—

Vietnam and civil rights, young people and policemen—and one had difficulty, threading his way through Grant Park and hotel suites, in finding his ideological bearings. Had Robert Kennedy lived it is possible that this search would have been easier, that civil rights and the peace movement, blacks and labor and young people, would all have been arrayed in a liberal phalanx against the mythical villain, Lyndon Johnson. But Kennedy was killed. And with him the chance of coalition and clarity died. Humphrey arrived in Chicago the hero of labor, party regulars, and most liberals. Vietnam to this group was bothersome. It seemed a portentous issue but they were uncertain of its meaning. There were, they thought, other marks of the liberal man. But to the students and to Eugene McCarthy, who had sought the vice-presidency twice, both times as Johnson's running mate, Vietnam was the transcendent issue. They linked peace with civil rights, and though losing to the liberals they thoroughly confounded them. They addled the liberal mind.

Since Humphrey was in the lead, his purpose in Chicago was not to offend anyone. But McCarthy's tactic was to disrupt. He backed an insurgent group in the Democratic party of Georgia, hoping to split the convention along sectional lines, as Kefauver and Harriman had tried in the 1950s. In doing this, McCarthy clashed with liberal labor leaders, first of all, Al Kehrer, an Atlanta AFL-CIO staff member, head of the insurgent group. When the McCarthy forces captured the reform group, Kehrer resigned and Julian Bond took over. It was a McCarthy victory, for he came to the convention fighting for the integrated Georgia delegation and portraying Humphrey as a backslider on civil rights.

But McCarthy succeeded not so much with the race issue as with the peace issue in making himself the leader of reform. He in fact lost his battles in Chicago—the nomination, most credentials fights, the streets brawls, and the peace issue—but in the process became the beneficiary of a wave of disenchantment. He allied himself with those, mainly students, who opposed the war, and with them began to redefine the ideological conflict. No more would it be a conflict between civil rights and segregation, big government and states' rights, but rather between doves and hawks, the people and the bosses. This conflict, the peace movement itself, was not a social matter and so was not, strictly speaking, a liberal matter. But as so often in the past, images and emotions and not strict thinking shaped political mythology; and McCarthy, as the leader of the insurgents against the power structure, became known as "liberal." Thus Humphrey was a villain—the lackey of the bosses and vice-president of the war-maker—despite his liberal record. And when Daley beat up the students, he became the arch villain—the symbol of corrupt and backroom politics—despite the record of the Chicago political machine (and despite the parade permit he granted to Ralph Abernathy's Poor People's Campaign). For in the new conflict taking shape—which later we shall look more closely at—liberalism was forgotten.

Vietnam thus fragmented an ideological group whose bonds originally had nothing to do with war and peace. This was by chance. But not by chance and apart from the war issue (and more interesting than that issue), liberalism had serious problems of its own. For the trend of self-destruction, begun in 1964, continued in 1968. Liberalism gathered more force in Chicago and thus, unnoticed, more peril.

The rule of 1964, that no state Democratic party could discriminate against blacks, worked in 1968 to bring to Chicago, for the first time, blacks in every Southern delegation. (This, like Abernathy's presence, was little noticed.) And there was another liberal victory. When McCarthy staged credentials fights to split the Humphrey delegates, he won few but got the convention to make a promise for the future. All delegates would be selected henceforth "through party primary, convention, or committee procedures open to public participation within the calendar year of the national convention." The convention authorized a reform commission to write new rules, by which this order would be carried out. Once framed, these rules would have the effect of putting an unprecedented number of minority delegates on the convention floor—a grand victory for liberalism, the culmination of twenty years of liberal struggle in Democratic conventions. By securing this promise for future conventions, more than by his protest against the war, McCarthy was truly a liberal. He was truly liberal in another respect, the respect in which liberalism undercut itself, for though the 1968 resolution spelled the acme of liberalism, that acme would also be its nadir. The acme was egalitarian measures backed by power; the nadir, rigidity and quotas and fragmentation. This was becoming a recurring problem for the liberals. Their success was more unbearable than their frustration.

The commission authorized by the convention to reform the party met several times in 1969 and under the guidance of George McGovern and Harold Hughes and, later, Congressman Donald

Fraser issued a set of guidelines. Now, these three men opposed the Vietnam War and for that were called liberals, though none had participated in the liberal battles in the 1940s and 1950s, in either the party or the Congress. They were more properly liberals by dint of their support for greater minority participation in the party, a position in which they distinguished themselves from older liberals only by the power they had to make that goal a reality now. Their staff, who wrote most of the new rules, was young—Eli Segal, Ken Bode, Robert Nelson, Gary Hart, Richard Stearns. These men distinguished themselves not only by their age but also by their bent. They had seen many Great Society programs fail, were suspicious of old liberals, labor, bosses, and all those who plotted in back rooms the course of the party. They also hated the Vietnam War. They interpreted the convention's authorization as a mandate to make the people displace the leaders as the masters of the party. In Model Cities and community action programs, as we have seen, this impulse to include the voiceless people in policymaking was a trend of the burgeoning liberalism of the 1960s. If the commission had stopped there, it would have executed its liberal duty. But it did not. The dynamism of liberalism was not one to check itself, and the reformers went on to require, on November 18, 1969, that all state Democratic parties take "affirmative steps to encourage . . . representation of minority groups on the national convention delegation in reasonable relationship to the group's presence in the population of the states." In November of 1971, Fraser warned state parties that fulfillment of this quota requirement would, in Miami in 1972, be a condition of seating.[29] He no doubt regarded this step as the Great Society planners regarded several of their programs, as a coercive measure, necessary to attain a liberal end; but it was, like those programs, a threat to liberalism itself. It was the prescription of a mathematical representation of blacks (and others), regardless of the people's desire or instinct, enforced by party machinery and backed by law. It was the exaltation of power and also of coercion, of minority rights and also, considering the ethnic groups left out, of the denial of rights, of the people's importance and of an individual's utter insignificance. It was a liberal's nightmare.

The political nightmare followed this ideological one already underway. Most liberals felt anguish during the 1968 convention, but in 1972 they felt detached, amused, and contemptuous. Southern Democrats reacted in unison with big city bosses, the most important of whom, Richard Daley, the convention unseated. "The political men are here all the time," said one Southerner, "and the activists come every four years," the latter of course not having the experience or interest required for the successful conduct of politics.[30] Jim Rowe went over to his state delegation, that of Montana, to visit old friends and found instead young people, American Indians, and a black woman recruited from an air force base to meet the quota. He asked, "Where the hell did these people come from," then blamed the "damn fool rules" and Donald Fraser and mourned the passing of the bosses. Congressman James O'Hara from Michigan said the convention was demographically the most representative ever, politically the least.[31] Labor and city machines and state organizations for thirty years had written the liberal platforms and elected liberal candidates; in 1972, by a combination of the new rules and McGovern's effective campaign, they were excluded from presumably the most liberal convention ever held. Something was amiss.

Much was. O'Hara blamed affirmative action and quotas. They were based on the assumption, implicit in the Great Society, that government owed a special debt to special groups, that the general public could be excluded from some services—transportation, health benefits, rent supplements—and left to the whims of the market. This belief sprang from liberalism's concern with civil rights, for once the liberals saw that equal rights were not all that was needed, the next step to compensatory action and special treatment was easy and logical. It was, however, to the bulk of liberals—men like O'Hara and Rowe and labor leaders—wrong. It was unfair. It was also restrictive, rather than liberating, and this brought liberals in Miami to their second criticism—coercion. Quotas like busing were compulsory. Liberalism had intended to broaden and open—to break down segregation and discrimination—but it ended in closing and tightening. It began to arouse the public spirit with its moral vision, one of rights and equality, but that spirit could not survive a quota of black or young or female bodies. Such compulsion, thought O'Hara, was tantamount to totalitarian government. Such was the displeasure of battle-worn liberals.[32]

Yet there was even more amiss. Liberalism was in other ways responsible for its own embarrassment. Not only had it started this inexorable and painful trend toward coercion and quotas, long ago and unforeseen, but it also inspired the fragmentation of its own power base. It was liberalism after all that had called upon blacks to act and seek political rights; once they did, liberal leaders were no longer needed. Nor were they longer wanted. Not only blacks sought their own leaders but so did blue-collar whites: once the liberals' backbone, by 1972 grown suspicious of a party and a leadership that embraced black militance, busing, and affirmative action, issues that could not move white labor, not as civil rights had, except to anger it. The liberal alliance was splitting up. Blacks, labor, women, homosexuals, young people, and Indians, all came out from under the liberal wing, where they had been nourished on a belief in rights and self-expression. They arose to speak for themselves. They dissolved their ties to the liberal alliance: they did not need them. They wanted other things. Fresh delegates besieged the platform committee in 1972, demanding planks in support of marihuana and abortion, the appointment of women cabinet members, equal rights for women and homosexuals, and the legalization of all sexual activities. The mood of the supplicants eliminated collaboration, reminding one of Stokeley Carmichael's regard for women, whose only position in SNCC, he said, was on their backs. The liberals of 1972 carried liberalism so far that they quit being liberals.

Soon after defeat in November, the lesson learned, the party recanted. The convention's peremptory decisions, such as the credentials committee decision to disfranchise the citizens of California and Cook County, had proved ill-advised. The Democratic party had extended its liberalism in the very years when even tempered liberalism was distasteful to most Americans. But ideologies do not follow calendars, they follow their internal rhythm; and the Democrats, responding to the urgent call of reform and rights, strained the party's alliance until it broke. Then the reformers fell quiet. In the year after the election the Democrats wrote new guidelines. Adopted by the national committee on March 1, 1974, these stated that the state and national parties were open to all people, that it was incumbent upon them to adopt affirmative action policies, but that, "This goal shall not be accomplished either directly or indirectly by the Party's imposition of mandatory quotas at any level of the delegate selection process or in any other Party affairs." They further ordered that composition of delegations "alone shall not constitute prima facie evidence of discrimination, nor shall it shift the burden of proof to the challenged party." Affirmative action, in these guidelines, meant not the prescription of color or sex but educational and publicity "efforts to encourage participation and representation" of minorities in the Democratic party—a far cry from 1972.

But the nation had moved far and the Democrats were catching up.[33]

Black Power

The town of Cambridge, Maryland, rests on the banks of the Choptank River, which carries rainwater one way into the great Chesapeake Bay and brings the other way, back to the people of Cambridge, oysters, crabs, and fish. Ten thousand people live in the town, one third black, the rest white. Some fish, others farm. Nearly all are poor. In 1967, on a hot July night, a crowd gathered in town and waited: H. Rap Brown was to speak at seven o'clock. Brown was late; the crowd grew, and it waited—"standing around being black," as one put it. At ten, H. Rap Brown appeared. He climbed onto a car and harangued the crowd: "You have rats in your houses, don't you?" (It was true.) "You have rats in your house and who owns your house? Who owns it? The white man! You have rats and the white man owns your house!" (Also true.) "But you can't get rid of the rats. He got rid of the buffalo. He got rid of the Indians. He can make napalm. But he can't get rid of your rats." (Also true.) So he began, and so he went on for two hours, mannered, reckless, and irrefutable. He pointed to the elementary school across the street, a decrepit building, whose basement cafeteria flooded knee-deep when it rained; mothers came to take their children home to feed them. "That school," he pointed from his roof-top dais, "That school—it's dirty, it's got rats. You want a new school?" (They did.) "Take some kerosene and go burn that school down. They'll give you a new one. Burn that down and you'll have a new one." Again he was right—for they burned down the school, then got a new one but not before other things had burned, for it was a windy night, and the embers jumped to the tops of other buildings and burned them down, too, a church and several blocks of houses and stores, including those of Hansel Greene, the town's leading black merchant. H. Rap Brown left and Cambridge began to rebuild itself. Hansel Greene, two days later, shot himself. Black Power moved on.[34]

It began, this anger, when slavery began, but in modern times, when blacks were free and cities crowded them together, it took on a new quality, one of pride and self-assertion. This pride was a sign of progress for blacks, who for so long had been instructed to believe they were inferior, but it was also a sign of trouble.

There was risk in this pride, just as there was danger in being an unproud people. For sixty years the leaders of the black community had been troubled by a dilemma. They found that if they stressed the special virtues and the separation of their race, they forfeited the support and benefits of white society; but if they failed to stress their blackness, they lacked the identity and unity a people need to succeed. It was a problem continuously impinging on the civil rights movement, and, by the 1960s, on the liberal movement as well.

Historians have perhaps unduly emphasized the split in the civil rights movement between those, like Booker T. Washington, who sought economic gains and those, like W.E.B. Dubois, who sought civil rights. For the more enduring and troublesome split has been in the black identity itself. Are they blacks or are they Americans; and which one are they first? It first appeared not as a split between Dubois and anyone else but as a split contained within Dubois, a man divided against himself. In 1909, he and others founded the National Association for the Advancement of Colored People, hoping to win for black people the political and economic benefits that all Americans enjoyed. His aim was a color-blind nation; he believed America could become one. And to this end he supported the nation's effort in World War I and called upon blacks to serve in the armed forces; supported the political parties; and opposed black nationalism. He—and Washington before him and Martin Luther King, Jr., after him—did not reject America but rather wanted blacks to share its opportunity, to share the American dream.[35]

The events of the 1920s changed Dubois, or rather they led him to speak thoughts he once had suppressed. The American Dream, it was revealed, was not for blacks: the Klan arose and claimed five million members; Harding ran for president as an avowed racist; and, most important, the Harlem renaissance arrived. Writers and artists—Jean Toomer, Langston Hughes, Claude McKay, Aaron Douglas, Zora Neale Hurston—celebrated the uniqueness of black culture. They groped for an identity and a past of their own—a difficult search, for slaveholders had deliberately stripped black people of these, taken away their names and history, and given them instead an inglorious past spent in servitude. But the difficulty only made the search more fervent and led the blacks to an ancient past; they skipped over the American blight and discovered Africa. There they found a people and past to be proud of, a new buoyancy and dress and music—the New

Negro. Africa gave them something of their own, something un-American, which was perhaps the most important benefit derived from the renaissance, for so much had been wrong in the American Negro past—and important for the trouble it caused the civil rights movement. For if blacks were a special and glorious race, they did not need, and should not want, to integrate with whites. If anything, they needed to reject white America and its culture, in order to preserve their own. It was this realization that disturbed Dubois after the 1920s, that led him to resign from the NAACP in the 1930s and to condemn the pursuit of integration, which served no purpose but to abuse "a little child as a battering ram." Rather blacks should instill in themselves and their children a sense of pride in black skin.[36]

If Dubois was torn, Marcus Garvey was not. He came to Harlem from Jamaica in 1916 and recounted the tales of Nat Turner, the Zulu warriors, and the daring Toussaint L'Ouverture. There was no doubt in his mind what direction blacks should take: they should return to Africa, the "redemption" of which was his goal. He founded the Universal Negro Improvement Association, which collected more money and enlisted more members than any black group ever has, then or since. He formed a black steamship company to link blacks together worldwide; named it the Black Star Line; sold stock to blacks only; adopted as its flag the red, black, and green. He began the Negro Factories Corporation to foster black business. In 1920 he held a convention of blacks, drawing delegates from twenty-five countries, and addressed them, all 25,000, in Madison Square Garden. Then he held parades in Harlem, and reviewed the African Legion and the Black Cross Nurses. In short, Garvey organized a formidable black movement, and he did so by declaring that blacks had nothing to expect from America, that only in Africa could blacks be free and equal, and also by exalting the special qualities of black people and insisting upon their separation from whites. The darkness of his skin was a matter of pride to Garvey. He harangued audiences about the necessity of racial purity, spoke of his suspicion of light-skinned blacks, and praised the Ku Klux Klan—for the Klan, like Garvey, feared miscegenation. In turn, the Klan praised Garvey, at one time dedicated a racist pamphlet to him, and invited him to Georgia, where Garvey went, in 1922, and met the imperial giant of the Klan, with whom he discussed the back-to-Africa movement and how the Klan might help it. Dubois denounced Garvey as "either a lunatic or a traitor," and Garvey denounced Dubois and the

NAACP. Their activities, he said, would lead to "amalgamation" and the dilution of the black people's blood.[37]

Garvey was deported in 1927, but the ideal of separateness remained, and so did the dilemma. With his appeals to racial pride Garvey had done more to arouse and organize black people than anyone ever had, and it was just such an aroused people that could win for blacks equality and civil rights. Dubois and others realized this, realized that perhaps they were mistaken to harbor a patient faith in the ultimate wisdom and kindness of American whites. Black pride brought results. But the trouble lay in the racism and rejection of American society that seemed the inevitable accompaniment of this pride. Blacks were caught. If they had no pride, they had no identity or organization and could put no pressure on whites to reform society; but with the identity and pride, they might no longer care for the reforms, or for the whites' society. It was an unending problem for Dubois and the civil rights movement, though not for Garvey, nor for the man who more than anyone else took his place.

In the 1930s, Adam Clayton Powell, Jr., began a romance with Harlem that did not end till he died. He organized boycotts, worked hard for the FEPC and the antilynch law, but Harlem loved him for other reasons. He was ostentatious, and he was brash. He attacked his own party, the Democrats, denounced Presidents Roosevelt and Truman, called Southern congressmen "fascists" and fellow black Congressman Dawson "Uncle Tom" and "house Negro." He was absent often from Congress, even on the day the 1957 Civil Rights Act reached the floor for final approval. He tacked the Powell amendment—a proviso barring federal funds from discriminatory programs—even to liberal bills, such as the school construction bill, often thwarting their passage. He antagonized labor. When he became chairman of the House Labor and Education Committee, replacing Graham Barden, a Southern Democrat unfriendly to labor, George Meany, who Powell implied was a racist, greeted the change with, "Terrible!" He frequently offended A. Philip Randolph and Roy Wilkins, who condemned his black nationalism and inflammatory rhetoric. He moved most of his belongings to Puerto Rico, where he threw himself into politics, opposing the popular Muñoz Marín, demanding statehood for Puerto Rico. In 1956, he endorsed Eisenhower for president. By all these adventures, Powell made it clear that he was his own man, not the tool of Democrats or liberals, whose cause he seldom helped, and for this Harlem loved him. It loved him, too, for his style. Like many congressmen he went on junkets and put his wife and girlfriends on the government payroll; unlike most he did not hide it. In a House committee room he got into a fist fight with a fellow Democrat. He neglected his taxes. In 1962, while the Eighty-seventh Congress was winding up its business, Powell took off for Europe on the *Queen Mary* in the company of two women and frolicked in gondolas in Venice and the Lido night club in Paris, where he was entertained by nude showgirls. The trip took a month, paid for by the government. The dam broke. Senators and Congressmen denounced him, and the *New York Times* said that the people of Harlem had been duped long enough. But Powell defended himself by pointing out that Estes Kefauver was also at the Lido that night, and with more guests; and two months later nearly 70 percent of duped Harlem gave him their vote. Powell had not campaigned.[38]

Powell was the lone representative of Black Power before that combination of pride and hostility became a mass movement: this was his success. His was a mission for black people only, out of the mainstream of the civil rights movement, the growing liberal ideology, and national politics. He spoke to the urban blacks and shared their anger. In March 1963, he denounced the NAACP and the Southern Christian Leadership Conference and the famous civil rights leaders. He implied Adlai Stevenson was a racist and told blacks not to heed Robert Kennedy's plea for caution. He told a crowd in Englewood, New Jersey, that he would return to Europe on another junket: "They tried to stop me, but I'm going again . . . the luxury flight to Paris . . . with lots of relatives . . . at the government's expense." Someone yelled, "First class," and he yelled back, "Yes. First class!"[39] By 1963, this bellicose mood was spreading among blacks, who increasingly resented the disparity between the liberals' promises and the conditions of life. In 1962, James Baldwin taunted Joe Rauh in Arthur Schlesinger, Jr.'s house; he regarded white liberals as worse than white supremacists. In the spring of 1963, Baldwin and several other black artists and intellectuals, in a meeting with Robert Kennedy, made no effort to hide their contempt for Kennedy and his brother's administration. They talked of sending arms to embattled blacks in the South; they laughed at the mention of Martin Luther King, Jr. Meanwhile Powell was allying himself with Malcolm X, King was pelted with eggs in Harlem, and James Meredith was booed in Chicago.[40]

The spirit of combativeness found release in violence. It was not just the conditions of living that brought racial violence to fifty cities from 1964 to 1967 and left sixty-three people dead within two weeks one year: Powell and others gave blacks a way to interpret those conditions. They told them that blacks were a proud and powerful people, and that the racial problem in America was a white problem, that the humiliation of centuries could be redeemed in a night of fire. Black Power emerged, at once a reaction and an explanation, a movement and an ideal. In May of 1966, Stokeley Carmichael spoke of it, and King and Wilkins promptly dissented. The next month James Meredith began his walk across Mississippi; a sniper shot him with a shotgun—seventy pellets into his neck, back, and legs—and Carmichael took his place to lead the march and talked again of Black Power. Cleveland and Chicago, the next month, erupted in riots. One year later Carmichael published a book, *Black Power: The Politics of Liberation in America,* and in it he explained his purpose.

"Black people," he wrote, "must redefine themselves, and only they can do that." This was bland, but then he grew bold: "The goal of black people must *not* be to assimilate into middle-class America, for that class—as a whole—is without a viable conscience as regards humanity. The values of the middle class permit the perpetuation of the ravages of the black community. The values of that class are based on material aggrandizement, not the expansion of humanity. . . . *This class is the backbone of institutional racism in this country.*"[41] Black Power, then, implied the corruption of the American people. Blacks must act for themselves: "The power must be that of a community, and emanate from there. The black politicians must start from there. The black politicians must stop being representatives of 'downtown' machines. . . . The goal of black self-determination and black self-identity— Black Power—is full participation in the decision-making process affecting the lives of black people, and recognition of the virtues in themselves as black people." This led him (and others) to an analysis of American history that stressed the importance of ethnic groups and ethnic solidarity. He wrote, "There is no black man in this country who can live 'simply as a man.' His blackness is an ever-present fact of this racist society, whether he recognizes it or not. It is unlikely that this or the next generation will witness the time when race will no longer be relevant." He attacked integration as a scheme to "abolish the black community," liberals as racists, and the Democratic party and organized labor as captives of an endemic "Anglo-conformity." Blacks should wrest control of institutions from the hands of the "professionals" and "experts" and "bureaucrats" that ignored the needs of the people. Federal programs he regarded as pointless, for, he concluded, only blacks could fend for themselves, and they would do this only by achieving a revolutionary mentality and a share of power.[42]

These attitudes, broadly shared if not articulated, impaired liberalism in several ways. There was the matter of timing. Just when the liberals brought civil rights to the forefront of the nation's conscience and managed, with difficulty, to pass the first substantive legislation since Reconstruction, Black Power appeared. In the month Johnson convened a national conference on civil rights and called for compensatory action for blacks, Stokeley Carmichael walked across Mississippi proclaiming the corruption of America. In the year liberals campaigned hard for Model Cities and answered the angry protest against militants and busing, the ghettos rioted; then Carmichael said, "American pluralism quickly becomes a monolithic structure on issues of race," and scoffed at Johnson for saying, "We shall overcome." Timing could not have been more precise. At no other time could this indictment of America have been less true, but coming when it did, it provoked a backlash that improved its accuracy. At the tense moment of uneasy success, white oppression dropped from sight and the civil rights movement itself became the debated issue.[43]

But timing was not the only problem. Liberals implied, by exercising power to apportion money and integrate the races, that the people themselves were flawed, incapable of equitably treating one another; and by so implying they provoked a reaction, growing already in 1966, that said the people were good, better than the government presumed, better indeed than the buses and quotas that coerced them. Black Power appeared and made the liberal implications explicit, said the middle class was corrupt and America was racist. Such an attack was not what liberals needed; they needed to mute their militant tone, their call for power, their emphasis on race. But instead they got more condemnation, which stirred up more commotion, riots and backlash, all of which hastened the liberals' reappraisal of their own precepts and confirmed their detractors' belief that the problems of society might, after all, best be left alone.

This exaggeration of liberal criticism was anathema, and in this way Black Power did to liberals and civil rights in the nation what the reformers did to liberals in the party. Their effect was similar in another way in their accent on ethnicity. When Black Power emphasized the value of race, just as when quotas treated the races differently, white people felt not more compassion but more distance; and they grew to have less in common with a group that stressed this distance, stressed the racism of Democrats and labor, the only allies the civil rights movement ever had. Where other tendencies of liberalism were unwitting, Black Power worked, fully conscious of its efforts, to split the liberal identity. And it was fully successful.

But it did even more. It not only made whites feel remote from blacks and their problems but also incited in them a search for ethnicity, a self-celebration of their own. This celebration worked against blacks in several ways, the most obvious being that though blacks cherished their heritage there were more whites to cherish theirs (and disparage others'). But its effect was also subtle. The ethnic revival lent a certain legitimacy to the long established, and previously deprecated, practice of discrimination. It became acceptable, suddenly, to defend the "ethnic purity" of one's neighborhood, and acceptable also to depict people by racist descriptions for comic effect. Television revived a sort of minstrel theater, though with greater variety, having as its characters not just blacks but Orientals, Jews, and Polish and Hispanic Americans. In defense of these characters, producers said they were a sign of racial tolerance, of the ability to laugh at oneself and also at the vulgarity of stereotypes. But it is likely that they were also a sign of a new tolerance of racism, and that they made people laugh for the same reason the minstrel had in the nineteenth century: one was pleased to note the difference between oneself and the races defamed; and those who laughed at characters of their own ethnicity were probably, as before, laughing to keep their distance from what they feared they were.[44]

The ethnic revival was illiberal in other ways. It obscured social problems by deflecting attention from the issues of race and poverty and drawing it instead to the superficial differences bequeathed by ethnic ancestry.[45] More specifically, it deflected attention from blacks. White ethnics believed the government helped blacks at the expense of themselves and demanded equal attention (as television had given them equal time). They said that they too should be the beneficiaries of affirmative action.[46] But on the whole they had little faith in government, and thought it the captive of a civil rights ideology. They called, therefore, for smaller government. Michael Novak proclaimed "the politics of cultural pluralism, a politics of family and neighborhood, a politics of smallness and quietness"; attacked social planning, and said, "The enemy is concentrated power." Nathan Glazer said that the sense of a debt to blacks had become a pathology for both blacks and whites, that busing was a dangerous threat to "group maintenance," and that the liberals had created an ideology of "brute power."[47] Thus did the ethnic revival employ in its defense charges already lodged against the programs of the Great Society and the Democratic party, for liberalism itself was the enemy and blacks the certain, if sometimes unintended, victim.

The ethnic revival of the late 1960s and early 1970s was thus illiberal, even though ethnicity in the past often had played a liberalizing role. The Irish, Italians, Jews, and other immigrants won their place in American society by emphasizing their ethnic bonds and helping those of their own group. They built their own churches, community centers, saloons, theaters, schools, and used these as a bridge to American society, a path to success and assimilation.[48] The revival of ethnicity, however, was not in the least comparable to this activity by the immigrants. These grandchildren had succeeded, did not need ethnicity to survive, and one can only conclude that their ethnic revival, having nothing to do with the rigors of assimilation, was the product of an exclusionary and racist reaction. Blacks on the other hand had never formed a community, never created their own institutions, never become assimilated—the experience of slavery having denied them the requisite tools—and Black Power was their belated attempt, similar to that of the immigrants, though more radical, to achieve solidarity and by it gain access to power. There is, then, a line, a fine one perhaps, distinguishing the ethnicity which is a liberalizing and worthy tool, helping to break down the barriers of discrimination, from the ethnicity which is put in the service of exclusion. The line is drawn between those who have been accepted and those who have not. Blacks have not, and their attempt to succeed by drawing together was a worthy one, long overdue. Yet ironically it was this assertion of pride by blacks that inspired the dangerous white ethnic revival. Once again they fell behind, by trying to get ahead.

The mission of Black Power entailed a final bit of irony. After the early 1960s, the liberal increasingly had called upon oppressed people to speak and act for themselves. The blacks conspicuously did so. Carmichael denounced the "old 'do-nothing,' compromise-oriented political parties," and said it did "no good to enact an anti-poverty program calling for 'maximum feasible participation of the poor' and then saddle that program with old City Hall and bureaucratic restrictions. . . . the people must be much more involved in the formulation and implementation of policy." This was hard for liberals, for the Black Power attack mirrored precisely the conservative reaction to liberalism: the people knew best. The people themselves, said Carmichael (echoing Strom Thurmond and prefiguring the white ethnics and Pixie Palladino), had the "experience and wisdom to govern."[49] They were sovereign, and the power of the government, imposed arbitrarily from above, must be thwarted. For some this was reason to resist busing and quotas; for Black Power it was reason enough to overhaul society: from either stance, liberal precepts would not do. They were pinned against the wall.

Few of these relations of Black Power to liberalism were apparent at the time, fraught as the time was with fear, which went far to discredit the liberals' aims. But fear is not a simple emotion. The white backlash would not have been so overwhelming had blacks alone seemed fearsome; other things were, too. Black Power strengthened the sentiment that the people were better than the liberals said. It deepened ethnic divisions, incited a reactionary ethnic revival, helped split the liberal coalition, and affirmed the suspicion that race was assuming a disproportionate position in American politics. It questioned the liberals' power and yet, in its ill-timed venture, called for more power, hateful and avenging. It shared points of success and failure with liberalism. It placed the blacks in the vanguard of radicalism, alone. It made people mean, small, and bitter.

And it did one thing more. Black Power raised the perennial question of revolution: Where does it stop? What was the debt of society to blacks?—a debt of rights?—money?—respect?—integration?—miscegenation?—or guilt and self-destruction? Carmichael had asked, "Can whites, particularly liberal whites, condemn themselves?" Was this the measure of debt and the end of revolution? It was an unsettling question. Did one choose the moment when the revolution exhausted itself and conclude this was its purpose? In France this would be the Napoleonic dictatorship or perhaps the revived monarchy. Or did one say that the true purpose lay somewhere before the irrational forces of revolt got the upper hand, say in 1792, when the king was alive, the constitution made, and the republic proclaimed? Liberalism, too, had raised this question for itself. Did the purpose lie in quotas and busing or somewhere before, in the 1964 and 1965 Civil Rights Acts; in compensatory action and rent supplements or before, in *Brown* and equal opportunity? Revolutions are impetuous; they do not have intelligence. But men and women do. And when the furor is over, they think on what they have done. Yet given the dilemma of the civil rights movement, torn as it was between identity and invisibleness, it is hard to see what else the blacks might have done, or what the liberals might have done. Their common task was formidable—to overcome the effects, past and present, of American prejudice. Blame can hardly be reckoned.

ELEVEN

LIBERALISM REASSESSED

By the end of the 1960s the liberals had about them the depressing sense of inevitable failure. To achieve their goals they had gone to certain lengths and provoked a reaction from the right and the left, each of which disliked the liberals' treatment of race and use of power. This reaction hid another, less apparent, source of the liberals' trouble, one which today may seem surprising. The liberals, as they knew only too well, never had been a powerful force, commanding a wide consensus. In retrospect, one imagines that the liberal Establishment dominated the nation in the 1960s, controlling Congress and public opinion, but in reality the liberals were a rather small group, who succeeded, just barely, and for a few years only, to pass a few bills. A short review of those years will show that though liberalism was a vigorous ideology, it never had broad support. Its years of success were few and difficult.

When they were over, the reassessment of liberalism began. The questions the liberals had asked seemed unanswerable, and the answers they had given made them uneasy. They reflected and wondered, into the 1970s, at what they had wrought. They wrestled with an ambivalence, intrinsic to American liberalism and as old as the republic; they, too, they found, always had doubted power. Even at the height of their success, they had been a little unsure of themselves, and now, out of office, when they— not just the left and the right—questioned the premises of their thought, liberalism truly unravelled. Vietnam and Nixon pulled at the strings a bit, made their parting rents. But liberalism unravelled on its own, and what some had mistaken as a quilt of consensus became loose and idle string.

A Narrow Margin

Those who in the 1940s and 1950s had opposed the liberals in the Democratic party and in the nation did not, in 1960, go away. The Virginia Commission on Constitutional Government, created by the state assembly, published an essay (first printed in the *Journal of the American Bar Association*) the year John Kennedy was elected; its purpose was to attack equality. "It is inequality," wrote R. Carter Pittman, "that gives enlargement to religion, to intellect, to energy, to virtue, to love and to wealth. Equality of intellect stabilizes mediocrity. Equality of wealth makes all men poor. . . . Equality of love stultifies every manly passion, destroys every family altar and mongrelizes the races of men. Equality homogenizes so that cream does not rise to the top." Pittman went on to attack Thomas Jefferson and say, "Slavery is the result of levelling. In the fruitless effort to achieve equality short of slavery the peaks must be bulldozed into the valleys to make a level plain."[1] So powerful was the persistent Southern ideology, filled as it was with old and tortured syllogism, that John Kennedy, as we have seen, dared not send civil rights bills to Congress for fear of jeopardizing his tax cut and test ban treaty. He failed to establish the department of urban affairs and the youth conservation corps; other social programs went underfunded. Richard Russell organized successful filibusters in 1961 and 1963 against efforts to change Rule 22, and in 1962 to defeat the bill outlawing state literacy tests. In 1963, 70 percent of white Americans disapproved of the civil rights march on Washington, which could not have been more peaceful or patriotic. Kennedy may have caused a new day to dawn for liberalism and civil rights, but the light was dim indeed.[2]

Under Johnson came the liberals' day at last, but it did not last long. In 1964 they won the Economic Opportunity Act by making two concessions to conservatives. Participants in the poverty programs would sign affidavits swearing that they did not support the violent overthrow of the government; and governors could veto programs—VISTA, Job Corps, community action, work-training, adult education—as they saw fit. These restrictions, designed primarily to appease the South, became in 1965 the center of a heated debate in Congress. A compromise emerged in which the veto on VISTA and Job Corps remained; and as for the other programs, the governors could veto them too, and the director of OEO could, if he chose, override the veto. There were other hints of liberal weakness at the outset of the Great Society. After Johnson passed legislation for medical care, education, and voting rights, he met resistance. In September 1965, the House rejected his bill for home rule for the District of Columbia, and in October, the Senate refused to invoke cloture on the filibuster against repeal of the Taft-Hartley section 14b (which permitted states to pass right-to-work laws). Two days later the House voted against appropriating funds for the rent supplements program. When the administration proposed the new department, one of urban affairs, some wanted to name it the department on cities, to call attention to the special problems of race and poverty in America's cities; but they relented when the housing lobby insisted on including the word "housing" and when the Congress made clear it did not want its attention to be so called. It became the Department of Housing and Urban Development. Such were the limits to the liberals' success at the start of the Great Society.[3]

In 1966, Johnson sent his message on the cities to the Hill, and the response came back—one of dismay. Model Cities ran into trouble immediately, stumbling on the issue of race even before it got to Denver. After lengthy hearings and debates, the Congress finally passed it, in the fall of 1966 (by the rather close vote of 22 against and 38 for in the Senate, 126 to 142 in the House), but by then it was a changed bill.[4] It prohibited the secretary of HUD from requiring busing as a condition of the program; it got half the funds Johnson had asked for; and it got a new name. From the Demonstration Cities and Metropolitan Development Act, the administration changed it to the Model Cities program, fearing that the first name, with the word "demonstration," would cause people to associate the program with the demonstrations and race riots that filled the cities the summer before. Not all congressmen were mollified. One warned his colleagues that if they voted for "this scheme. . . . you are voting for forced busing, school pairing and redistricting." He, a Republican from New York, called it the "most far-reaching civil rights bill . . . that the White House has ever proposed," and tried to amend the bill so as to exclude from its benefits "subversive . . . black power . . . or any other racist organization."[5]

Nineteen sixty-six was a year of uncertain achievement for other Johnson programs. Funds for rent supplements, denied in 1965, were denied again by a vote of 14 to 13 in the Senate Appropriations Committee but then at last were granted, approved in the House by only eight votes. Congress put ceilings on the salaries of administrators and the numbers of enrollees in OEO programs and also cut Job Corps down to a fraction of the number of people it was intended to help. But the broadest hint of liberal stalemate came in the field of civil rights. The 1964 Civil Rights Act had authorized the attorney general to file suit in civil rights cases only after the individual claiming an infringement sent him a complaint. This condition greatly limited the role of the federal government, and in 1966 the administration sought legislation that would eliminate it and also assure nondiscriminatory jury selection, open housing, and the protection of civil rights workers. A hail of diluting amendments rained down on this bill. Twice Mansfield tried to invoke cloture on debate and twice he failed. He adjourned the Senate, the bill died, and Eastland gloated: "The civil rights advocates," he told the press, "who hope to force an interracial society have been completely routed." It would not be long before "we can start the fight to repeal those vicious measures" of the last two years.[6]

Civil rights had reached a slump. In 1966 a poll showed that 75 percent of American whites believed that blacks were moving too fast. And in 1967 Congress again refused Johnson's request. He resubmitted the same bill in February, whereupon Sam Ervin, chairman of the Senate Judiciary Subcommittee on Constitutional Rights, insisted on holding hearings to postpone action. He denounced every section of the bill and refused to report it until the following year.[7]

Racial animus also hurt rent supplements in 1967. Congress funded the program but only after it also passed a rider which gave communities the option to refuse the supplements. Its purpose was to protect suburbs and other towns from the integration of classes and races, the program's original intention.[8] The poverty program also ran into trouble that year. Congress, altered by the loss of forty-seven Democrats in the 1966 election, passed an appropriation for OEO only after passing the Green amendment, stipulating that public officials or OEO should administer the programs, not the poor. Thirty-five Senators voted to transfer Head Start to HEW from OEO, an attempt to begin dismantling the latter. Thirty voted to abolish Job Corps. Forty-one voted (against forty-five) to give governors a veto on migrant programs. The House cut the overall poverty budget to $1.7 billion, a cut which, along with the Green amendment, permitted passage of the bill. Congress also attacked welfare programs, refusing to extend Medicare to 1.5 million disabled people and requiring all adult recipients of Aid to Families with Dependent Children to enroll in work-training programs, including mothers, compelled to put their children in day care centers, so they would be free to learn a skill. The new law put a freeze on the number of recipients the government would support, and other bills cut federal aid to such a point that now it is impossible to judge the efficacy of the programs. Johnson asked $40 million for rent supplements, Congress gave $10 million; he asked $662 million for Model Cities, Congress gave $312 million. Yet that these two programs were kept alive at all in 1967 was considered by one congressman "a great victory for the Administration."[9]

In 1968 the great housing act passed, owing to the recent riots, the hard work of professionals, and good luck—and not to a sense of commitment.[10] For Model Cities, the administration asked for $1 billion and Congress gave $625 million; for rent supplements, it asked $65 million and Congress gave $30 million. Upward Bound, the college preparatory program, moved out of OEO and into HEW by authority of Congress. And on civil rights, though the open housing law was an enormous liberal success, there were troubles that tempered the elation. Three times the Senate failed to invoke cloture to cut off the Southern filibuster, until on March 4, 1968, cloture was sustained by a vote of 65 to 32, the exact two-thirds vote required—and only then after a compromise that Senator Mondale, its author, described as a "miracle." It had taken two months to pass the open housing provision, but in one day, by a vote of 82 to 13, the Senate adopted an amendment offered by Senators Thurmond and Long which prescribed criminal penalties for the crimes of traveling across state lines or using interstate facilities, such as a telephone, to incite riot and for manufacturing or teaching the use of firearms or explosives for use in civil disorder. These the Senate passed in a hurry.[11]

Two months later the Poor People's Campaign rallied only 50,000 people in front of the Washington and Lincoln Memorials—one-fifth the number of those who came for civil rights five years before—and for eight weeks 3,000 people lived in the shantytown of mud, known as Resurrection City, until the Department of Interior would no longer extend their permit. They left with little stir. Four months later George Wallace, on the ballot in fifty states, won forty-five electoral votes, the largest number of votes ever won by a third party candidate, excluding Theodore Roosevelt. Wallace won 9.8 million votes, or 13.6 percent of the vote.[12] And Nixon won the presidency. The wind had left the liberals' sails, what wind they had had.

The Liberals' Doubt

But long before it left them, the liberals had doubts of their own. They had doubts about power, even as they amassed it.

They displayed their doubt in little ways. In 1952, during the fight over the loyalty oath at the Democratic convention, Joseph Rauh had scrupled at imposing the liberals' oath on Southern delegates, believing it a dangerous act to coerce the conscience of any man. In 1957, during the desegregation crisis, when after three years of studied inaction Eisenhower caught a whiff of the liberal meaning and ordered troops to Little Rock, Adlai Stevenson said on national television that force and troops were not the answer to segregation. In the New Frontier, John Kennedy frequently combatted the bureaucracy of his own government, which he regarded as immovable and inept.[13] And several times he withheld his endorsement of the proposed change in Senate Rule 22. He knew the Western and Southern senators would turn on him if he backed the change, but he knew, too, that a liberal state without a check on a simple majority might fast become illiberal. A month before he died, he spoke to Amherst College in honor of Robert Frost; his theme was power.

> The men who create power make an indispensable contribution to the nation's greatness, but the men who question power make a contribution just as indispensable . . . for they determine whether we use power or power uses us. . . . When power leads man toward arrogance, poetry reminds him of his limitations. When power narrows the area of man's concern, poetry reminds him of the richness and diversity of existence. When power corrupts, poetry cleanses.

In little ways, a contradiction tore at these men from the first.[14]

Sometimes it caused the liberals, once they reached office, to diffuse power, even as they created it. In the Model Cities and community action programs, they divided power among federal, state, municipal, and neighborhood agencies, and gave to these units control over planning and federal money. As we have seen, this diffusion led to trouble—to confusion, protest, and to a white backlash against the newly empowered poor and minority people. One critic, Theodore Lowi, has argued that it was this abdication of federal responsibility, this inability of the government to exercise power, that made the programs so unworkable.[15] He may be right. But as we have also seen, it was their unprecedented use of power that earned the liberals the people's hatred. To call for more power would not have appeased the people, neither the minorities nor the conservatives. Clearly, the liberals were in a dilemma, provoking reaction whether they diffused or collected power, and however one assesses their decision, the point is that they tried a little of each, that they too had doubts about power.

These doubts led them also, without conservative prodding, to limit the scope of their own legislation. The 1964 Civil Rights Act explicitly stated (in Title IV) that it did not authorize officials or courts to order racial balance in schools by busing. Title VI of the act, proscribing discrimination in federally assisted programs, stated that it did not intend to require equal employment, and Title VII, the employment section, stated that the act did not outlaw seniority, merit systems, or ability tests in employment, and in no manner intended to require quotas in hiring or training.[16] The liberals were fully aware, even at this apex of their success, that communities and employers had rights, that quotas could be more restrictive than liberating, that their aim after all was not to hedge people about but to free them.

This ambivalence about power acquired new meaning for liberals when Nixon took office. Prompted by their election defeat, by the dissolution of the Democratic coalition, by recession and inflation, and also by the sense that their creed had somehow failed them, they searched for the clue to their failure; and many found it in power, about which they long had had their doubts, and which now they began to oppose. This shift in attitude was not sudden or complete, nor was it the result of mere political calculation. It was an earnest, gradual, and uneasy reassessment of liberal doctrine, which entailed also the reassessment of liberal means—the federal government and its cumbersome bureaucracy, the use of busing and affirmative action. Social problems lost some of their importance as budget problems gained. And the problem of race, of the inequity between the races, almost dropped from view.

When Colonel Harland Sanders complained that his company "just got too big to control" and his chicken got greasy, no one was surprised; he was a Southern entrepreneur come back to the fold.[17] Nor was it surprising that Senator Eastland should have opposed the Environmental Protection Agency and the Occupational Safety and Health Administration (OSHA) for tampering with private enterprise, nor that his aide, Cortney Pace, should have mocked their efforts. For these were men marching to an old Southern rhythm. Pace was raised in Pace, Mississippi, founded by his father, who was born in 1855 and recalled the time he hid in the woods to keep two mules from Sherman's marching army. Cortney's grandfather limped till his death from a Civil War shot lodged in his leg. Older Paces fought the British in the Revolution and still older ones the Indians in Virginia. The oldest one in memory, Richard Pace, arrived in Jamestown in 1611, the nephew of an aide to Henry VIII. And now their descendant, Cortney Pace, the senior administrative assistant on Capitol Hill, told of the ants that walked from Brazil to the South and ravaged the crops. The farmers poisoned the ants, and the EPA, far from the ants, prohibited the poison. He told of a benevolent businessman in Mississippi who went about giving his employees a gift—pavement on the parking lot—until an agency of the government ordered him to paint white stripes on the asphalt and then another ordered yellow stripes, for only yellow stripes glisten in the dark. This was what came of doing a good turn—government oppression, begun in the New Deal when the "government learned the advantages of the alphabet" and built a network of agencies.[18] None of this, in a Southerner, was surprising.

But in a New Dealer and Fair Dealer, one who had advised Johnson and Humphrey and helped create the "alphabet agencies," it was. On the wall of the front office of his law firm hung a portrait of a youngish Franklin Roosevelt, for whom he served as special assistant, but deeper within, James Rowe gave his verdict: "Too goddamn many programs." He was close to Lyndon Johnson but thought the president overreached himself. "Landslides," he said, "are always bad for a President. Roosevelt got in trouble after 36, Johnson after 64, and Nixon after 72. There is a danger in it, and Johnson didn't see it when he tried to outdo Roosevelt. Mansfield saw it at the time. The country couldn't absorb so much." Neither could the liberals. They were disillusioned.[19]

One was Richard Goodwin, a young speechwriter for Kennedy and Johnson, and the author of the "Great Society" speech. Several years after concluding his public service, he wrote *The American Condition* in which he execrated the size of corporations and deplored the loss, since the Middle Ages, of a sense of community. But bigness in business was not his only target; bigness in all its forms was anathema. Now calling himself a radical, Goodwin said that were it not for big business he would favor decentralized government and the return of power to local communities and the people. They—the people and their values—were not the problem in American society; rather it was power.[20] Ted Van Dyk, a Humphrey advisor, also changed his views. He created a stir in Democratic circles in the early 1970s by favoring the reorganization and reduction of government bureaucracy. It was his belief that the people rejected Humphrey in 1968 largely because they "were convinced that, in the wake of the exhausting Johnson years, Humphrey would mean more New Deal/Fair Deal/ New Frontier/Great Society government activism." He proposed that the Democrats adopt a new approach. He called for the reorganization of departments so that "constituent groups would be forced to deal with new departments—often in competition with other groups—concerned with the overall public interest rather than that of a narrow sector." He favored zero-based budgeting and praised Governors Dukakis and Brown of Massachusetts and California as new politicians who questioned federal programs. Jerry Brown also impressed Anthony Lewis of the *New York Times,* who summarized Brown's political message as, "less is more," and cited a Brown statement: "I don't think," said Brown, "that one person or ten or a thousand can alter things that much. I have a more limited view. . . . If people would have a bit more tolerance for what they can do, what government can do and what life can be, then they'd be better off."[21]

Such tolerance would not make a slumdweller better off, but perhaps that was the point. Government had replaced him as the subject of debate; and oblivious of him the reassessment of liberalism sped on. Marshall Kaplan, a specialist in urban affairs, studied the Model Cities program and concluded that federal departments and agencies hindered the program's success; later he condemned "bureaucratic imperialism." The Medicaid program of New York, others pointed out, was the largest in the country, riddled with corruption, and according to Senate investigators, led by a Democrat, sunk to its abject condition because of the mayor's "ultraliberal welfare philosophy."[22] From the high aims of "social welfare" to the opprobrious "welfare mess" the liberals moved in rapid succession.

These words were symbols—politics is largely a matter of symbols—by which liberals communicated their sudden distrust of big government. There were others, employed by such liberals as James O'Hara. A Democrat from Michigan, elected to Congress in 1958, he chaired the liberal Democratic Study Group and fought hard for the open housing act of 1968, but by 1976, when he ran for the Senate, his emphasis had changed. His campaign brochure began, "He doesn't promise you a rose garden," and went on to assert that he was not one of those "great political promisers," that he concentrated his efforts on "inflation, an overblown bureaucracy, unemployment," that "ordinary people can come up with sound ideas on how government ought to run," and that he combed every bill to spot the "money-wasting boondoggles, administrative overlaps and other defects." In his conclusion O'Hara said, "Who's really running this country, anyway? Elected officials or the bureaucrats who too often enlarge and expand the laws they are supposed to enforce?" One need not stress the opportunism of O'Hara's tergiversation; there is more to ideology than ruse. O'Hara, like so many others, changed his emphasis because it now seemed wrong; the liberals had, in the prevailing view, gone too far in their reliance upon government, so they renounced their allegiance and responded to the summons of new slogans. The slogans were in fact old, but they seemed new, as they swept across the North, leaving George Wallace to complain that "all the other candidates are now saying what I've been saying all along," that he had "no positions of my own left": Thus failed the man who had coined that invincible phrase—"Send them a message!"—and succeeded too well.[23]

Views were changing. Liberals not only criticized the federal bureaucracy—so much that O'Hara suggested the government abandon several of "the goddamn departments" and Van Dyk that they be reduced—but also revised their attitude toward the budget. The Brookings Institution, which served liberals out of office much as Paris bookstores served Spanish Republicans after the Civil War, sponsored several economists who altered their emphases. Charles Schultze, director of the Bureau of the Budget under Johnson, later concluded that defense outlays, which had been declining, would have to rise and social welfare outlays, which had risen, would continue to rise but at a slower rate than in the past quarter century. (This prediction concurred with President Ford's, though Ford called for a slightly higher defense outlay.)[24] At the same time, Arthur Okun, his colleague at Brookings and Johnson's chairman of the Council of Economic Advisers, wrote of the perils in saddling enterprise with so many government restrictions and transfer payments that the incentive to produce might disappear. Okun wrote, "Capitalism does have something to do with freedom. It is impressive that no nation with a fully centralized economy has ever had a free press or a free election." He took care to point out that businessmen often used this argument to attack a regulated economy but went on to say he saw no "substitute for the prizes and penalties of the marketplace" and to propose that the best way to reach an equitable welfare policy was by "modifying and strengthening democratic capitalism" and by avoiding "the collectivized economy proposed by the left [which] would be bureaucratic and inefficient." This analysis was not startling; but the circumstance of its appearance was. Okun had worked hard in the Great Society and had gazed with others into the chasm of social inequity which it exposed; now he had concluded that the answers did not lie in radical overhauls or adamantine bureaucracy but rather in some new attempt at an old design, to propitiate the majority of Americans so they might without disruptive protest transfer some money to the poor. Robert C. Wood, Johnson's under secretary of HUD, arrived at a similar view. In his 1972 book, *The Necessary Majority,* he wrote of the need to engage the majority's interest in solving the crisis of the cities. These men—both of them thoughtful and conscientious public servants—did not turn their back on the Great Society. On the contrary they searched to improve it, and in searching they laid emphasis on caution, on the dangers of expectations and on the demands of the marketplace. This caution was a new thing for liberals.[25]

Others considering federal expenditures changed not just their emphasis but also their direction. The issue was revenue sharing, a complex one which cut across party lines. Walter Heller, chairman of the Council of Economic Advisers under Kennedy and, for a while, under Johnson, proposed the plan to Johnson. Governors were enthusiastic; it would give them more flexibility in the use of federal money. Labor, mayors, and liberals preferred categorical grants, which the federal government made for specific projects, retaining control over the money. Johnson, in 1966, rejected revenue sharing and stuck to categorical grants. But by that year Congress was taking on a conservative bent, and it stipulated that several programs—the Comprehensive Health Planning and Services Act and in 1968 the Crime Control and Juvenile Delinquency Acts—should be funded by block grants, a device similar to revenue sharing, which gave the money to state officials who used it as they saw fit. The momentum for revenue sharing picked up. Its popularity went up as the liberal ideology waned, until Nixon was able to announce the Second Great American Revolution and pass revenue sharing with little difficulty.

But revenue sharing was not a strictly conservative plan. It appealed to the sentiment that people, communities, and states should run their own affairs and spend their tax dollars as they wanted, that the federal power to engineer society should be replaced by the power of the people. Walter Heller was no conservative; he was the first to elaborate the plan. Paul H. Douglas, the nemesis of Senate moderates and conservatives, recommended revenue sharing in his report on urban problems, submitted in December 1968. Cortney Pace and Herman Talmadge looked upon Governors Brown and Dukakis with favor because they, too, supported revenue sharing. Douglas Costle, who studied the Model Cities program, agreed that local and state governments were more capable of responding to the people than the federal government. He favored revenue sharing. Ted Van Dyk wondered if "Nixon was not right . . . in using revenue-sharing as a disguised means of stopping the growth in federal grant programs," and whether "we Democrats still really believe that tight federal guidelines should be attached to revenue-sharing funds on the basis that federal bureaucrats can make better judgments about their use than local elected officials." In 1967, when Congress was heavily Democratic, block grants, which ten years earlier had amounted to nothing, came to $15 billion, or fully one-third the money appropriated by categorical grants. Revenue sharing was discovering its liberal constituency. And the liberals discovered in yet another way their affinity with their liberal ancestors.[26]

The busing issue made that affinity even stronger. The South of course had an old position. Forcible integration, a step to miscegenation, was unnatural and might lead to war, said one of the old guard. Before integration, the races had lived in peace, said Cortney Pace, who explained that the town of Pace was 85 percent black: "We never locked our doors. Blacks and whites lived right alongside each other. And they loved my Daddy. When he died whites couldn't get to the graveside for the blacks, and one big nigger woman, standing by the grave, cried over and over"— he mimicked a wail— " 'Captain Jim is dead, Captain Jim is dead!' " Federal coercion destroyed this alleged harmony, and Southern politicians and mobs, as we have seen, put up a resistance, which in the end only strengthened the liberals' case. Then the South refined its argument, accepted *Brown* as the law, and said only that it was misinterpreted, that the law called not for assignment of children by race but for the opposite, nondiscrimination in school systems. The government had begun to engineer society. Thus refined and tempered, the Southern argument persuaded even Boston, which for a century, from Sumner to Kennedy, had vilified the South, and which suddenly erupted in racial violence. The South then asked, said Pace with a rasping laugh, "How does that shoe fit?"[27]

The shoe fit rather tightly—so tightly that busing prompted many in the North to agree with Edmund Wilson (in his essay on Alexander Stephens, vice-president of the Confederacy) that there was in each of us an unreconstructed Southerner.[28] For it was not just Boston Italian and Irish families who opposed school busing but also liberals. James Rowe, Ted Van Dyk, Richard Goodwin, and James O'Hara were liberals of the 1960s who complained in the 1970s not only of big government but also of school busing. They said the real problem was the economy, which could not be repaired by forcible integration. Senator Joseph Biden, one of the "new liberals" of the 1970s, voted liberal on defense and foreign affairs, but also offered an amendment to an education bill outlawing busing. A lawyer in Wilmington, Delaware, where federal judges ordered cross-district busing, said that Nixon might "still get quite a few votes around here," on account of his Court having prohibited such busing between suburbs and cities. Some blacks, too, spoke up against busing and affirmative action, saying that special and tasteless treatment resulted when liberals, wedded to a crusade, did not know when to stop. Intellectuals lent the antibusing sentiment scholarly adornment. Edward Banfield and Daniel Patrick Moynihan argued that the problem of the black in America, derived from heritage, was irremediable by state action and that anyhow statistics proved his lot was improving and could only be jeopardized by special treatment. Nathan Glazer, in *Affirmative Discrimination,* said that *Brown* eliminated segregation in schools, that further efforts to give preferential treatment to blacks and efforts to disrupt natural residential patterns could lead only to white resentment and racial friction, and that blacks, whose root problems lay in education and shiftlessness, could not be helped by special consideration that put them in places where they were bound to fail.[29]

Now the point of all this is not to suggest that one view is right and another wrong. (The reader surely can do that for himself, and no doubt he already has.) The point is rather that in appraising the recent past, the liberals reconsidered their liberalism. Intellectuals, liberal politicians, officials of Democratic administrations—many found that their ideology had driven them to lengths they now regretted. Not only had programs failed; they had entailed a use of power that the liberals now found unavailing, disruptive, and coercive. They looked with new amity on the people and their liberty to act and be left alone. They did not make a volte-face, an outright repudiation of their past. They did not need to. Liberalism, like any ideology or mood, could be vitiated by a subtle gesture, and such a gesture the liberals made. By qualifying their previously unqualified support of civil rights and by questioning federal power, they struck at the symbols of their creed, at the fervor and the logic of the liberal quest. Its spirit was dead.

By no means did liberals suddenly become racist and reactionaries; but their reflections lent support to racists and reactionaries. On several issues, they found common cause with Republicans and Southerners, the white ethnic revival and the opponents of busing and Washington. The suspicion of federal power was perhaps what all these people had most in common. Washington became a bad town, so bad that even Southern conservatives, like Otto Passman, the Louisiana congressman, could not survive the resentment of power that he and other Southerners had tried so long to foster. (He lost his seat of fifteen terms to a man who campaigned against Washington.) It did not matter to anyone that the federal government had not grown in the last thirty years nearly so fast as the population or state governments, for in the reaction to liberal programs and thought a new mythology arose, or rather an old one revived; and mythologies do not pivot on facts. Government might be smaller and the Great Society have been untested—all the same, not ten years after the height of the liberal success, the ADA had trouble bringing new people into its ranks. Young people no longer yearned to devise ways by which federal power might extirpate social injustice. Instead (a survey found), both conservatives and liberals (as defined by their position on welfare, civil rights, and Vietnam) equally distrusted big government in 1968; and by 1972, liberals distrusted it more.[30] A revolution in attitudes had occurred, the beneficiaries of which included nearly everyone but the blacks and those few who still clung to the verities of postwar liberalism.

What came to replace liberalism was not so much an ideology as an attitude, one that belonged to an older liberalism. It held, as one old liberal put it, that "we all have rights," and that government power must benefit the majority of the people. To the American mind, this thought was not shattering: no one ever had doubted it. But as a reaction to liberalism, in the context of a declining liberal creed, which after all had championed power and the importance of special rights and special people, it was indeed shattering. The majority emphasis implied no minority emphasis; revenue sharing meant the loosening of federal control. Most people, liberals included, considered the government incapable of solving social problems and were tired of its trying—tired of federal coercion and tired of civil rights. They went on to new battles, so swiftly changing their views and so utterly dismissing liberal ideas that the liberals of the 1960s appeared, only ten years later, as the curious relics of a distant past.

Vietnam and Nixon

There were two additional and obvious forces behind the demise of liberalism—Vietnam and Nixon—so obvious that if one is not careful he will miss the guile of history. For these also had an insidious, unintended effect, inscrutable at the time, abetting the liberal ideology in its act of self-destruction. Let us see how.

But first the obvious. One week toward the end of December in 1965 Robert Wood presented to the president the report of his task force on urban affairs, recommending massive expenditures for the Model Cities it proposed. The same week the president received a military report, recommending the assignment of 500,000 troops to Vietnam. Neither group of planners knew of the others' efforts, but Johnson knew all.[31] He went ahead with both. In January he gave the State of the Union Address, and proposed a four-year term in the House, slum rehabilitation, anti-pollution programs, prison reform, open housing, help for depressed rural areas, a department of transportation, anticrime programs, a highway safety act, consumer protection, the reorganization of the federal government, the SST, campaign laws reform, repeal of Section 14(b) of Taft-Hartley, home rule for Washington, the Teacher Corps for city slums, and rent supplement appropriation. Then he sent 360,000 troops to Vietnam. Congress wondered which Johnson wanted to do—build the Great Society or fight the Vietnamese—and there ensued, as one administration liberal put it, a sapping of liberal energy.[32]

Just when the Great Society had focused the attention of the government and press on the problems of poverty and race, it divided that attention and presented an issue of more pressing urgency. And not only attention, for Vietnam split the money, too. Of the surplus in 1966, HUD received roughly one-third of what it had anticipated. When the fan deck on the carrier *Enterprise* broke down, the cost of repairs amounted to one-half of the Model Cities budget.[33] Johnson did not comprehend this problem, though he felt its burden. He thought he could do almost anything with government—and he almost did. But the people were another matter.

The people divided on Vietnam, and here we enter the inscrutable territory. The Vietnam War was not a social issue, not a liberal issue, but rather an issue of foreign policy, which in recent history has not cut a dividing line between reformers and the established power, between liberals and conservatives. The Spanish-American War, the two World Wars, the Korean War—these wars were not fought and supported by one ideological group and opposed by another. Not since the Mexican War of the 1840s, and before that the War of 1812, had a foreign matter divided Americans as neatly as their own ideological squabbles did. In the recent past, liberals and conservatives alike feared the Communist challenge to democracy and alike endorsed the policy of containment. So when Johnson escalated the war, in 1965, 1966, and 1967, it was not a conservative escalation; and when resistance grew, it was not a liberal resistance. The war issue, as things turned out, would help erode liberalism, but it was itself barren of liberal or conservative meaning.

That it was so barren was apparent in the pro- and antiwar factions, which bore no resemblance to the postwar liberal and conservative coalitions. The congressmen who began and led the antiwar movement were not notable liberals. Most were new to national politics and had not fought in the liberal battles of the 1940s and 1950s. Wayne Morse, who was one of the only two senators to dissent from the Gulf of Tonkin Resolution in 1964, was the exception. He was a liberal on labor rights and the only such liberal to have both served in Congress since the 1940s and early joined the protest against Vietnam—and even he was an erratic liberal, especially on civil rights, having sided with Richard Russell in 1960 to keep Johnson from introducing a voting rights act. Ernest Gruening, the other dissenter, was too new to the Senate to have established a liberal record. He came when Alaska joined the Union and engaged his interest mainly in American

Samoa, lead-zinc subsidies, and the space communications monopoly. These were the two dissenters in 1964.

In 1965 and 1966 opposition grew, and it was led by those who are famous for their liberalism now but not so then. In February 1965, after the bombing of the North began in earnest, George McGovern and Frank Church made speeches against the war and called for negotiations. McGovern had arrived in the Senate in 1963, in the House in 1957. Church, elected in 1956, had served longer but was not an outspoken liberal. He was part of Johnson's network in the Senate, helping out the majority leader in exchange for favors, even cosponsoring the jury trial amendment, in 1957, which weakened the civil rights bill. In this he resembled Vance Hartke, an Indiana moderate, elected to the Senate in 1958, who also formed a part of Johnson's Senate coterie. Hartke early opposed the war, turning against his former master. Eugene McCarthy was next. Elected in 1958, he had no civil rights record, perhaps because he came from Minnesota (though so did Humphrey), but made something of a record for his turnabouts. In 1960 he went to Los Angeles committed to Johnson, and in 1964 he strove again to be Johnson's running mate. He was John Connally's favorite over Humphrey, whom Connally regarded as too liberal, but Johnson did not choose McCarthy, who thenceforth, for three years, let loose a continuous and venomous attack not just on the Vietnam War, but also on the character of the one he had served. Gaylord Nelson and Stephen Young then joined the opposition, the one new to the Senate in 1963, and the other elected to the House off and on since the 1930s and in the Senate since 1959. Young was renowned for his mastery of civil defense spending. J. W. Fulbright, by 1968, was investigating the Tonkin Resolution and like most Southern senators had voted against most civil rights legislation. Before 1968, these were the only congressional opponents of the Vietnam War who might be considered as having been liberals, and they were not, as we have seen, among those who led the liberals' postwar struggle.

The supporters of the war were a mixed group. Through 1968, most Republicans supported the war; so did Southern Democrats, Richard Russell proposing that Congress affirm the president's authority to wage war in Vietnam. But many liberals did, too. Robert Kennedy backed the administration until his 1968 campaign, though he expressed doubts in early 1966. Chairman of the ADA John Roche supported the policy, and Arthur Goldberg, who made his career as a labor lawyer, defended it in the

United Nations. Before him, Adlai Stevenson at the UN, like all older liberals, never doubted the policy of containment and favored (until his death in 1965) military action in Vietnam, if negotiations failed.[34] Averell Harriman, who with Kefauver (who died in 1963) had forced his party time and again to face the civil rights issue, went around the world explaining the war effort. And Paul H. Douglas, the inimitable liberal ideologue, defended on the Senate floor the war and the man he had so often opposed on civil rights. Johnson, who had denied Douglas Senate perquisites and committee seats, said that his campaign for reelection in 1966 was the most important one that year. But Douglas, seventy-four years old, lost; and Johnson lost a formidable defender. But he kept the other renowned liberal of the Senate, Hubert Humphrey, who consistently defended the war policy as vice-president and then as presidential nominee, through November 1968.

For the first several years, then, the war issue would not sit comfortably in the ideological milieu of the previous quarter century. But soon, as the war protest grew and mingled with other protest movements, it built an ideology of its own. Students demonstrated, in colleges and in Washington, not for civil rights or labor rights or other social needs but against a foreign war and the draft. A new world of mythology materialized, with a new axis separating ideologies, one which replaced the North-South axis and cut its way not through regions but across the land, conjuring new villains and heros. Liberalism faded in this new configuration of ideology, not because it opposed or favored the war in Vietnam but because it and its opponents were shuttled out of the way.

But as it was shuttled, liberalism took a few final blows, the first of which was the inevitable deflection of attention from liberal issues. Never from the 1950s to the 1970s had there been a high correlation between domestic and cold war issues in the public mind.[35] It was no surprise, then, that when the war issue rose in importance it did not bring with it a rising concern in social problems. The two matters were unconnected in the public mind—and in the mind of the protestors as well. They did not draw from, nor did they contribute to, an awakening social conscience. If anything the protest movement did the reverse. Of the 15,000,000 young men that won exemptions and deferments during the draft years, most hailed from privileged backgrounds, and on that account—because of their schools, their resources, or their objecting consciences—won the deferments and exemptions.[36]

Far from probing the social divisions of America, the protest movement thus seemed to have taken advantage of them. More commonly it ignored them, as we have seen in the Democratic convention of 1968; but whether ignored or exploited, social inequity was not a concern of the protest movement, which was, like previous reform movements, powered by moral outrage. Like the abolitionists and Prohibitionists, the protestors harnessed their energy in service to a righteous cause and saw no other issue but the hated war. They were nearly blind to the liberals' world.

What little they saw of it, they disliked, thus making liberalism not only obsolete but a deliberate target of the protest movement. For the protest's distinguishing mark was none other than the dangers of power. Fulbright in Congress saw an executive branch encroaching upon the rights of Congress, and the students wrote songs about the "power of the people," love, and peace. They ridiculed Johnson and Nixon for their solemnity, their high office, their arrogance. All manner of authority was mocked, a mockery damaging to the liberal idea that in the government was vested the power, and upon it fell the duty, to act in peremptory ways to protect the people. Like the protest against busing and quotas, even like the black power movement, the antiwar protest awakened a new interest in the people's rights, their common sense, their ability to challenge senseless power. The awakening was profound; the interest lingered after the war. The Congress curbed the war powers of the president and aborted an administration effort to involve the United States in Angola. Frank Church led the Senate investigation of the CIA, which, he felt sure, had acted arbitrarily, against what the people would have wanted. Outside Congress, the consumer and ecology movements engaged the attention of ordinary people. They did not seek power, nor did they ask that the federal government exercise power to benefit a deprived minority. This was not their aim. They wanted instead to curb power, assert themselves as masters of their lives; and for this they were called liberals. They were in fact a new people rising en masse out of the forgotten liberals' remains.

Thus vanished the world in which liberalism made sense. A new one took its place as the people assaulted power. But the war gave its final blow to liberalism when it, like black power, then divided the people.

It would seem that the war split workingmen from the liberal groups—from blacks and young and intellectuals—and made them conservative, patriots and hard hats fighting flag burners and long-hairs. This was what seemed to happen, but in fact what happened was rather more complicated. The splintering of the liberal coalition had occurred earlier and on account of liberalism's internal problems; the war sped the process along. The attention the liberals gave to the poor and the blacks, as we have seen, was repulsive to many who thought rights were one thing and preferential treatment quite another. Laboring men, many of them descended from immigrant families, had fought for their rights and helped blacks win theirs, but no one ever gave Italians, Jews, or Poles rent supplements. They reacted badly. Liberalism, as we have seen, had another self-destructive component: In stressing the rights of peoples it urged them to claim power for themselves, and when they did, increasingly belligerent, labor did not like it. Most Americans did not. Already in the 1964 convention, militant blacks were splitting the civil rights movement, and labor and liberals were rejecting their demands. Vietnam, then, was not a catalyst but rather an accelerating force. It threw in the issues of patriotism and life styles, and helped the liberals drive themselves apart from one another. But the war did not drive them apart; rather its singular effect was in what it drove them toward.

For it drove the liberals into false positions. Working men and women, proud of their country and also of the material advantages they won so hard, associated the war protest, young people's hedonism, Black Power, and the challenge to middle-class values with liberalism. It was an easy misperception. Liberal policies, after all, had nurtured the ideal of self-expression. The Democratic party, moreover, the cradle of liberalism, turned out ever greater numbers of antiwar leaders. Like most people, labor responded to images and impressions rather than facts, and, perceiving several threats to American society, mingled them, attacked them, and called them "liberal." The ones labor attacked were not, as we have seen, liberals at all but rather the successors to the liberals, antipower people who eschewed the tag, preferring to call themselves by their own names—yippies, hippies, doves, Afro-Americans, or, simply, people. These, for their part, engaged in their own erroneous labeling. They associated all their opponents with one group, equally monolithic, and called it the Establishment, the power structure. This included hard hats, Democrats and Republicans, Hubert Humphrey and Richard Nixon, liberals and conservatives, army men and corporate executives, a gathering that never sat well together except in the addled minds of those who felt themselves rebelling. A war between the myths ensued.

The myths ripened when people took on the characteristics of the thing they were called. Once their cast of mind was set, they voted accordingly—not according to their interest. Labor voted for Nixon, not for the liberal Humphrey, their choice under other circumstances. For a few years they did not bristle at the name "conservative" but in time they regained their faith in liberalism, for they would always need the government's protection of labor rights. In 1976 the Ford administration proposed to weaken OSHA, the Occupational Safety and Health Administration, and labor protested vehemently. No other group did, for who among the "liberals" that emerged from the peace and youth movements ever had heard of OSHA? Many old liberals, those of the New Deal and Great Society, had heard of OSHA and in rethinking their liberalism condemned it along with the growing bureaucracy. The hard hats of the Vietnam era reappeared to take their place among the few consistently liberal advocates.

But that was not seen and so did not matter. The nation saw polarization, which it lamented, though the truth was worse. There were many groups, when Vietnam falsely made them two. And the two it made had nothing in common with liberalism: one group blamed the liberals for having started the war and another for having opposed it. The liberals had done neither. They merely had arrived and begun to run into trouble of their own just when Vietnam arrived, a war that rendered them and their trouble obsolete, their power ignominous, and their issues forgotten.

●　　●　　●

Richard Nixon had several problems, of which the most conspicuous was his personality. He was contentious and liked to attack, and unlike Johnson, who always looked for consensus, he sought the points of social division. His Supreme Court nominees were "judges who share my philosophy that we must strengthen the peace forces against the criminal forces in America"—the liberals, by implication, relished crime—and students he once called "bums." But Nixon's personality was not his problem alone, for it soon became a burden to liberals as well. Because of his image and style, the trappings of his presidency, he seemed but the last in a long line of presidents who built the government into an engine of power, arrogance, and secrecy. This superficial affinity with liberalism hurt the liberals more than his policies did. For Nixon was disgraced. When he fell from power, he took his final and ironic swipe at liberalism and made it—with himself—a thing of obloquy.

One does not need to tarry on the simple ways by which Nixon attacked liberal programs. What policies he took were illiberal (though they could do little damage to an ideology already disheveled). Many programs he did not kill outright but rather starved of funds; they did not die, only withered. From OEO he removed several programs, and from it and Model Cities he withheld funds. He put limits on budget requests from HUD and other departments. And he impounded funds. But the momentous act of his domestic policy was revenue sharing, which greatly impaired liberal programs and also the liberals' confidence. His plan was to turn back to the states in block grants $500 million in 1971 and increase the flow to $5 billion by 1976. But even Nixon did not foresee the speed of the liberals' decline; it sped apace regardless of him, so fast that by 1976 Congress had appropriated $15 billion and planned $25 billion by 1980. And the Senate, strongly Democratic, asked for $41 billion. It did not matter that the Government Accounting Office found that local government discriminated against minorities in its use of the revenue; or that most of the money went to white middle-class areas and little to the old Model City areas. Services to the poor were cut; money for crime control and building went up. All this did not matter because all this was the point—to help, as one former HUD official put it, the "have-some" have more. New Federalism, Nixon said, was the Second American Revolution, to rival the first; and insofar as it reversed the tide since the New Deal of federal categorical grants, it was, as he hoped, an enduring change. But it was not all Nixon's work, for the liberal concerns had died. Nixon did not kill them; he exploited their demise.[37]

On school busing Nixon was no more innovative. The mood of the country made possible his Southern strategy (which worked as well in the North); his strategy did not create the mood. In 1969 he took pressure off the South by preventing HEW from cutting off funds from noncomplying school districts, though the 1964 Civil Rights Act ordered differently. Two years later, the Supreme Court decided in *Swann* that busing was a sanctioned means to remedy segregation. Nixon said it was the law of the land. But soon he reversed himself, said he would not grant funds for court-ordered busing, and proposed that Congress prohibit such funding in the future. In 1972, he attacked "massive busing" on national television and announced his intention to send Congress legislation limiting it. Those people who had felt through the long 1960s that blacks and the poor got more attention than they merited now found an ally in the White House, and they might also have felt relieved when he said, one year later, that America's urban crisis was over. How many believed him? How many cared not to believe him? The issues had dropped from sight.

Gerald Ford also found the country's mood congenial to his view of government. In 1974, he said that, though desegregation was the law of the land, he had "consistently opposed forced busing to achieve racial balance as a solution to quality education." The language was ambiguous, and besides, the Court never had ruled that racial balance was the goal of busing. No matter: no one marched on Washington. He proposed legislation to limit the definition of illegal segregation and the duration of busing. Two years later, Ford still complained of "forced busing," said he considered asking the Court to review its *Brown* decision, said he had opposed busing since 1954. He was of course mistaken. *Brown* did not consider busing, nor any of the means to integrate schools. To such an extent did the symbol of busing grasp and blur men's minds.[38]

Ford continued his appointer's policies in other ways. In the late 1960s, HEW had cut federal funds from 200 public school systems for having discriminated against minorities, yet in the years between 1969 and 1976, it cut funds in only one comparable situation. Federal regulatory agencies, except for the Federal Trade Commission and several others, fell into the hands of friends of the industry to be regulated. Ford recommended changing HEW rules so that a federal contractor would have to receive $15 million rather than $1 million before having to pass a preaward affirmative action review. In 1974 the president issued an executive order calling for "inflationary impact reports" before a federal agency required industry to conform to safety, environment, or other standards. Labor and even the President's Council of Economic Advisers complained that one agency, OSHA, was rendered ineffective as a result. One union, filing a civil suit, argued that the president used these reports to avoid taking action unpopular with industry. But Ford found his defense. Avowing his desire to "throw OSHA into the ocean," the president said he had ordered the agency to start treating "citizens as friends, not enemies"—a gentle reminder that the people were the purpose of government.[39]

The Supreme Court of Nixon and Ford also reflected the

nation's new mood. It struck down a congressional statute extending the minimum wage to state and local employees. It held that a
school district, once it had rearranged its school system and
assignments, did not have to continue rearranging them to maintain racial balance. It upheld a case of reverse discrimination and
said that the 1964 Civil Rights Act applied to whites as well as
blacks (and also, as we have seen, upheld zoning laws and the
integrity of school districts, when these were challenged by civil
rights lawyers). These were familiar issues—labor and civil rights—
but they were framed differently now, turned upside down. The
achievements of the past, the Court believed, needed qualification.
Justice William Rehnquist, writing for the majority in the minimum wage decision, said that Congress could not use the commerce
clause "so as to force directly upon the states its choices as to how
essential decisions regarding the conduct of integral governmental
functions are to be made," for such "assertions of power" would
"allow the national government to devour the essentials of state
sovereignty." This, in 1976, was the first time since the New Deal
that the Court had struck down a piece of major social legislation,
and it did so with the reasoning of Taney and Calhoun.[40]

The Court was moving with Nixon, and Nixon with the people,
all against the liberals. But a less obvious threat to the liberals was
Nixon's personality. He was paranoid, devious, and insecure. And
he loved power. Propelled by this personality, he moved in one
crucial regard away from the people and made his government imperial, awesome, and frightful, when the liberals already had made
it suspect. He took the substance of liberalism out of government,
but then he adorned his administration with its style, arrogance,
and omniscient power.

When Lyndon Johnson left the White House its staff numbered
208; seven years later it was 522. Nixon enlarged it. He liked "Hail
to the Chief" and plumed guards and trumpets. He referred to
himself in the third person and, if not, then in the plural first,
seldom as "I," except when he was beseeching, as when, toward
the end, he said, "I am not a crook." These were idiosyncracies
of his character. They drew him into the Watergate scandal.

In the summer of 1973, in the Watergate hearings, dark se-
crets were told. The government had conspired to keep itself in
power. It had bribed people, bugged others, and burglarized a few;
it had sold high office to high bidders; it had lied to the people.
The president's campaign staff had been warned to close its blinds
in the Washington office, lest the "opposition" take photographs

from windows across the street.[41] They had shredded their documents and taped their conversations, then erased the tapes. Several officials went to jail, including the president's closest advisors; the president resigned. Several people died. What did it mean?

The message was simple and old. In the crisis that led to the American Revolution the colonists had spoken of power, its "encroaching nature," "the hand of power," "like the ocean, not easily admitting limits to be fixed in it." Opposite it they had set their liberty, which they considered the concern only of the governed, not of the governors, and which they thought might be protected if the people realized that "a deep-laid and desperate plan of imperial despotism" was making designs upon them. The events of the 1760s and 1770s confirmed their suspicions; they became convinced of a conspiracy; they blamed a cabal of ministers, then the king himself.[42] The process repeated itself in the 1970s. Many long had thought, for different reasons, that the government was becoming tyrannical. Nixon's role in the Hiss case and then, as president, in the Calley case and Cambodia bothered some, mostly those who thought he was the conspiring sort. Others resented the power that bused their children and spent their money on social programs. Watergate confirmed both in their suspicions. Nixon had in fact conspired; and the government acted secretly, sometimes illegally, against the people's interests. First the attack fell on his aides, those in the White House who ran the government, and then on Nixon himself. A fear had come true, the government was bad, a new one was made.

And who should be the hero? It was no coincidence. Southerners had always been legalistic in their arguments. They felt persecuted by the North and became defensive, fell back on the law and extolled the careful words of the Constitution. They opposed Roosevelt's effort to pack the Court, an effort they thought equivalent to tyranny. Two of them and four other conservatives had sat on the Select Committee to investigate Senator Joseph McCarthy. They relied, as anyone must who would thwart the designs of the future, on the complex rules of the Senate and House. Rule 22 was meant to protect a minority from the passions of a simple and rash majority, and it often saved the South. When Southerners opposed busing and affirmative action they were careful to base their argument on law: *Brown*, a decision they detested, ruled against assignment by color, they piously reminded the advocates of busing.

It was no coincidence, then, that the hero of Watergate was

one of these who always upheld right over power, Sam J. Ervin, Jr., honored by a popular ballad and several books and by 200 of his former colleagues in Congress, who gave him a party and the Distinguished Service Award of Former Members of Congress— this man who signed the Southern manifesto in 1956, which attacked the *Brown* decision; who tried to weaken the voting rights bill in 1960, already pitifully weak; who denounced every section of the open housing bill in 1967 and delayed its reporting until 1968, when he again denounced it and tried to attach to it a crippling amendment; who ten years before was the hero of only the South, renowned as a leading strategist of the segregationists in Congress, when liberals like Humphrey, Johnson, and Kennedy, if not the heros, were the leaders of all the nation. To such a point had liberalism fallen that the drama of Watergate, the most stirring and unsettling national experience since the death of President Kennedy, unleashed the nation's affection for a homespun Southerner, whose record did not matter, and made a villain of a man who had proved that government conspired in ways more crude and pernicious than people had ever believed but lately had come to suspect. Nixon was perhaps as much the victim of liberalism's decline as liberalism was the victim of Nixon's paranoid mind and eventual disgrace. At any rate, they both went into hiding and a segregationist went to glory.

TWELVE

THE POSTLIBERAL WORLD

To judge the liberals it is well to remember what came before them and to look at what came after.

We have seen that American liberalism was born in the Revolution, and that owing to the circumstances of its birth it acquired certain sentiments—a dread of power and a faith in people and property—that pervaded American political thinking from the late eighteenth century well into the twentieth. These ideas served the liberals well, so long as the issues were familiar, but when the issues changed, involving race and class, and when the power that oppressed came not from a coercive state but instead from an acquisitive or prejudiced people, then these ideas served to limit the range of liberal activity. Obsessed with property, the liberal would not have it controlled or given away; fearful of power, he would not use it to aid the dispossessed. Rather the liberal placed a patient, abiding faith in the people. As a consequence, both the good and the bad of our past may be laid at the feet of the liberal. To some extent, the brutal cast of the Civil War arguments, both Northern and Southern, the long privation of sharecroppers and urban workers, slavery, segregation, and all manner of discrimination—to some extent, the very denial of rights was complacently accepted and even justified by the American mind because of its peculiarly liberal bent.

On occasion, racism helped, lending incongruous support to the ideas of liberalism. It spared men the trouble of demanding power, for first it had spared them the trouble of analyzing society, as Americans, convinced of a minority's racial and moral inferiority, attributed their unequal status to their low position on the Darwinian ladder. And racism did more. It perverted the antislavery movement and split the Populist movement. It—and liberalism itself—prevented the Jacksonians from leading the antislavery crusade and hence from surviving. It helped end the Reconstruction era and also the era of the Progressives. The sources of this racism do not concern us here, though it is worth noting that the denial of rights to the black man was sometimes the necessity of the white man's prosperity, and even a necessity, economic and psychological, of his rights and his liberal belief. And certainly, whatever its source, racism was linked to liberalism, in the sense that prejudice and a faith in property and fear of power were sentiments which together and repeatedly limited the striving of earnest and humane men, compelling them to channel their reforming instinct into moral causes of a sometimes shallow, desultory, and even reactionary nature.

In the twentieth century, events began to embarrass this thought. The most dramatic event was the depression. Property was not so sacred (or worth much either) and big government not so bad: these were the hints one might derive from the depression and the New Deal response. Yet, as we have seen, the New Deal did not make an ideology, did not compose new articles of faith of the reforms it undertook; nor did it challenge the people's racism. Instead it addressed the preeminent need—the security of the people, threatened by depression, then by war—and it was left to Truman to catalyze the Democrats, enunciate an ideology of big government, and attack head-on the racism of America. He failed in Congress, but considering the weight of history against him, it was no surprise. The transformation of liberalism was begun.

Though just begun, it had of course been impending for some time. The immigrants had come and asked for an equal chance; blacks had moved North and the civil rights movement emerged; cities had grown, and so had industry, and with it the threat to labor. The Northern Democrats responded to this change, to the needs of labor and the arrival of blacks and immigrants, precipitating a party struggle; for meanwhile the Southern Democrats changed not at all. In the last years of the New Deal tension had mounted between these two wings of the party, but it was only after the New Deal, the war, and Roosevelt's death, when Truman took the side of the new liberals, that the Southerners rebelled and the struggle emerged. The differences were considerable. The Democrats fought over federal power, business regulation, labor rights, and civil rights, of which civil rights, for several reasons became the test issue. To the South, white supremacy was the

central myth in a series of myths that composed its powerful
identity. To the North, blacks were the most deprived of several
groups of people that gave the Democrats votes and a moral mission. But civil rights also derived its importance from the fight
over federal power, which alone could protect the blacks and labor
and regulate an industrial economy, and which to the South stood
as a threat to free enterprise and states' rights. Thus it happened
that the struggle to define liberalism was fought by the Democrats, and that they fought most often about civil rights.

There was perhaps no doubt as to the outcome of this fight—
not in the wake of a war against Hitler, not after blacks had moved
to the North, and not after *Brown*. But the Democrats did not
behave as if the matter were foreclosed. They fought with tenacity.
And in any case, what mattered was not the suspense of the fight
but the fight itself, the influence it had on the party. It took on
transcendent importance, impinging on every Democratic decision
from the 1940s to the 1970s; every candidate had to reckon with
civil rights and try to advance his career by helping one side or
the other. Civil rights and the party—the fate of each—were linked.

Allied with the ADA, the CIO, and the NAACP, two men—
Harriman and Kefauver—did more than anyone else to help civil
rights. For they, more than anyone else, stood to benefit from the
civil rights fight. They hoped that by initiating platform and
credentials fights with strong civil rights demands they might split
conventions and thus advance the liberal cause as they advanced
their own. Occasionally they (and others) slid: Harriman tried to
appease Johnson in 1956; Kefauver told Tennessee one thing and
the party another; and Paul Butler promised the South he would
ignore civil rights. But these were minor and hidden incidents in
the careers of men who pushed the party (and therefore the nation) as no one else did, save the Supreme Court, to adopt an
enlightened view of civil rights. They were incidents that merely
attested the implacable force of the civil rights issue.

Adlai Stevenson also benefited from the civil rights struggle,
and also, in his own fashion, contributed to it. In many ways, he
was not a born leader. Though he had rare talents—charm, intelligence, eloquence, and the ability to conciliate opposing sides—
he often preferred to educate rather than lead, to explain rather
than take a stand (at least on civil rights); and he disdained demagoguery, which was the politician's way of responding to popular
pressure. Stevenson hated being pressured. Because of these traits,

he was twice the party's compromise candidate, the only man acceptable to both liberals and Southerners. Under other circumstances, had his party not been torn by struggle, he, a moderate and cautious man, might never have been appealing to his party; and in this sense his success owed something to the civil rights fight. Yet Stevenson also was necessary to the party, and in this sense its liberal transformation owed something to him. Without him to unite the Democrats, to appease both sides and compose their differences, they might have split apart or not changed at all. He did not lead the change, often opposed it, but he preserved the party as it changed beneath him; and with his party he changed too.

Johnson performed a similar role in the Senate, though more aggressively—extending promises and threats to both sides, keeping the Democrats together as they passed the first civil rights bill since Reconstruction. Both he and Stevenson tended the wounds of the party and permitted the liberal tide gradually to swell—until it overwhelmed them. Kennedy, the beneficiary of this liberal surge, turned it to his advantage. No more capable than the others of avoiding the civil rights issue, he avowed to the liberals his support of *Brown,* got their support in turn, and won the nomination. When he did, the triumph of the liberals was complete.

Thus after fifteen years of struggle did the Democrats espouse a new ideology at last. It inspired, in the New Frontier, a new approach to domestic problems, an approach which in the Great Society governed thinking and determined policy. But as soon as it did, as soon as the liberals followed the logic of their ideology, they failed. Just when civil rights had seemed to liberate liberalism, freeing it of the restraints imposed by free enterprise and racist beliefs, enabling the liberals to explore the social origins of inequality and invoke federal power—a turn in the road at last—they provoked an implacable reaction, as if they had liberated nothing but the abiding hatreds Americans always had.

Perhaps underlying a network of failures there was a single cause; the problems exposed required solutions more drastic than liberalism could provide. Community action programs, Model Cities, busing, affirmative action, job training, housing laws, rent supplements, food stamps, and all manner of services—the liberals tried many things. Had any one of them succeeded in reducing the poverty and segregation of blacks, there would have been no liberal failure and no liberal reappraisal. But none did; the slums continued, even grew worse. Their eradication would require programs of even greater size and power and cost; yet even the programs the liberals framed aroused deep resentment. For the moment, then, the solution was beyond their reach.

The resentment itself, however, was the greater failure. Having raised the sensitive issue of race, the liberals provoked a mighty reaction. Blacks and others, in the Democratic party and in the streets, condemned American racism, thus further antagonizing the conservative critics of liberalism, and, even worse, they reiterated the conservatives' central complaint—that the government was oppressive. They demanded power for themselves, and the conviction grew that the people, whether in the ghetto or in the suburb, were the better judges of their own affairs than were the officials in power. Of all the threats to liberalism, this conviction was the most serious. For since the 1940s, and through the long struggle in the Democratic party, the liberals had pinned their hopes on federal power, looking to the government as the provider and protector of disfranchised groups. Now they saw that power condemned—not only by intransigent Southern racists, but by the middle class everywhere, and by the poor in city slums. The core of liberal belief came under attack, and the liberals were stunned. The better they achieved their postwar goals—the more power they used and the more emphasis they placed on civil rights—the worse was the abuse they suffered. The more they succeeded, the more they failed.

This irony, inexorably embarrassing their ideology, just as inexorably broke up the liberal coalition. Liberals had espoused the cause of threatened groups—labor, blacks, and immigrants—and asked that they be protected and endowed with rights and a voice in the nation. They succeeded; these groups became so endowed. And as they did, the liberals became a burden to them. Liberals controlled the party and government and blocked the path of not just blacks but new subject groups, arising by the end of the 1960s to protest their own denial, patiently borne till then. Distrusting the liberals, blacks, students, Indians, women, and others claimed power for themselves; and still others, labor and white ethnics, dismayed by the liberals' abdication, left the coalition. The bonds broke apart, and the coalition dissolved.

There was thus something inescapable about the liberals' plight, something which, when they faithfully pursued the logic of their ideology, achieving its goals as they went, led them to certain disaster. One is tempted to say it was the ideology itself, a creed far in advance of the people, one designed, in fact, to correct the people. If this was the case, then the enigma was not why liberalism failed, but why it had any success at all.

Its success, as we have seen, was in the Democratic party. There it was defined and supported by an alliance of liberals, labor, and machines—groups whose clients were the workingmen, immigrants, and blacks, and who therefore were always more liberal than the public. It was they who gave the critical support to the civil rights fight in the Democratic party, working for strong platforms, especially in 1948. Had these platforms been submitted to a national plebescite, it is likely they would have lost. But they were not; the people did not vote. Instead the voters were the labor leaders—the Hillmans, Murrays, and Reuthers—and the bosses—the Arveys, Finnegans, DiSalles, Flynns, Lawrences, and Baileys. These were the men who backed the ideas the liberals proposed and gave to postwar liberalism its first success. Its second was when, after being imposed upon the Democrats, liberalism was imposed upon the nation, this time by a Democratic administration which, because of Kennedy's death and Goldwater's candidacy—and not because of popular approval of liberal thinking—had won a huge mandate.

This is a fact of some importance, this manner of the liberals' success, for in time they lost the support of these large organizations. Liberals had a way, as we have seen, of overthrowing their own leaders; but more importantly, these organizations declined in influence, and they did so because, having helped those they set out to help, they were no longer needed. Prosperous workers listened less closely to the calls of labor leaders; the immigrants prospered and became assimilated in society, no longer needing the machines, which, moreover, were replaced by state and federal governments as the dispensers of welfare. Other changes reduced the influence of the machines. Education raised the people's understanding and lowered their tolerance of precinct captains. Television and open primaries brought the candidates to the people, giving them, more than they had had before, the power to choose. And finally machines suffered from the general decline in party influence. In the 1950s, people let the parties do their thinking for them, only 20 percent identifying themselves as Independents. By the 1970s, only 26 percent identified themselves with either party, and a full 40 percent declared themselves Independents.[1] The power to persuade had diminished.

Without that power, the liberals were in trouble. Shorn of

party and union and machine strength, they threw themselves on the people—to no avail. Never having derived their strength from a groundswell of popular outrage, never having been a grass-roots movement, the liberals stood alone—and not just alone but besieged as well. Far from having been a people's movement, the liberals had set themselves against the people and tried to correct their ways. They had made of government a countervailing force, only not, as in the New Deal, a force against the banks and utilities, but, as in the Great Society, a force against a wholly new enemy, the people—their prejudice, their choice of schools and neighborhoods. This was an awkward villain for a democratic government to behold, and an untenable one for the liberals, once they lost the support of the large organizations.

It was no wonder, then, that what came to replace liberalism was a series of grass-roots movements. The busing and Black Power movements were perhaps the first; they attacked liberalism directly (though from different sides). Next came the opponents of the war and of Nixon, opponents who may have been indifferent to liberal programs but who, by attacking the symbols of power, further eroded the premises of liberal thought. These events, the crises of the war and of Nixon, served perhaps as the transition from the liberal to the postliberal world, from the time when popular movements sprang up against liberal power to the time when they sprang up against all forms of power and liberalism was obsolete. Power, in the new climate of opinion, was perfidy—presidential power, war-making power, taxing power, nuclear power. The people were what mattered. What affected them, the majority of citizens, became the dominant issues. Campaign contributions and disclosures, a free press and "the people's right to know," CIA plots and secrecy in government, consumer products and the dangers of cigarette smoke, pollution and nuclear waste—these were the new issues. They might engage the interest of the average citizen but not the special interest of the few that were deprived. They were narrow issues, incapable of sustaining a coalition, and did not derive from a party principle. Their supporters might adhere to either party or to no party at all. For parties and coalitions were unnecessary; these issues aroused quick and fleeting support. The people were enough.

This attitude was not a retreat from left to right but a new definition of the left, not a new conservatism but an old liberalism revived, shorn of its twentieth century wings, guided by one thought—the importance of the people. It was neither hostile nor friendly but rather indifferent to the liberal issues, and thus it ignored civil rights and labor rights. It might make demands of big corporations, but not as liberalism had—not to break up monopolies or protect workers or give blacks an equal chance—but to prohibit the companies from polluting the atmosphere or marketing products hazardous to one's health. In the politics of consumerism, as this attitude might be called, the claims of all the people were higher than the claims of special people, rich or poor.

The first beneficiary of this mood was Jimmy Carter, who in 1976 spoke of the "decency of the people" and the troubles in Washington. He eschewed definite positions—an idiosyncracy not just of his character but of the politics he practiced. For the politics of consumerism is not an ideology but rather an attitude, a sentiment, though a strong one; it has not adopted a program yet, or a clear constituency, except as it appeals to everyone. And it may be that one of its principles is to have no fixed principles or party program and to follow instead the wandering inclinations of the people. If that is the case, it will not become an ideology and will not last, but will serve instead as the pause before some event—an explosion in the cities, a foreign war, a depression—gives the parties new direction.

In the meantime, it is a sentiment which, like all political myths, requires people to ignore many facts. One is the need for a large federal government. The large bureaucracy, indispensable to all, is deplored by all. The South especially has deplored it, for years, but has needed it too. For two centuries the South tried to link the Gulf of Mexico to the Tennessee River, until at last, in June 1976, the old alliance of Southern leaders and the military bureaucracy produced a promise of $1.5 billion to complete the canal. Without federal aid, the many rural and poor counties of the South would have no money for their dams, schools, libraries, hospitals, water supply, sewage disposal, and housing projects.[2] Southern Congressmen vote for large defense appropriations, lobby for the location of military installations in their languishing districts, and support lavish pensions for military personnel, which when combined with civil service pensions comprise 30 percent of the annual budget—and yet they lament the growth in government.

The relation of facts to the mind is ambiguous. Fully 75 per-

cent of the budget is uncontrollable, going to pensions, unemployment, social security, and debt service. Defense and all else split
the remaining 25 percent, of which roughly three-quarters go to
defense and one-quarter, or roughly 6 percent of the annual
budget, goes to the departments, agencies, and the Army Corps
of Engineers.[3] These are facts. But it is in the 6 percent that
government's detractors find the waste, sprawl, and incipient
socialism. Such is the way of the mind. Since 1946, federal employees have decreased as a percentage of the population, and
federal costs have grown less than state government costs—but
facts do not always count. Federal power is abhorred.

Not everyone abhors it. Civil rights organizations, the League
of Women Voters, the ADA—a handful of unreconstructed liberals
point out that only 1.6 percent of revenue sharing funds go to
social services and 1.15 percent to health care, the rest to law
enforcement, fire protection, street repair, and environmental
protection. This, they say, is unfair. The problems in city cores—
poverty, unemployment, segregation, land values, and housing
costs—are so large that only the federal government, its laws and
money and planning, can treat them.[4] They say convergent
accidents, not unworthiness, spoiled the liberal experiment. The
Great Society depended on expanding economic resources; the
war and then recession contracted them. As states collected less
revenue they demanded more in block grants from the government. Prosperity, they say, will return the initiative to the federal
government. The riots of the 1960s were another accident. They
panicked Congress, which forgot the experimental purpose of
poverty programs, hurriedly appropriated money, and converted
prototypes into entrenched agencies. These soon atrophied, became bureaucratic, until Nixon, the final accident, came to power
and cut the funds off. The great liberal experiment was aborted;
it should be tried again.[5]

These liberals have a point. We have dwelled on the failures
of liberalism, but its successes were many. And they endure. Thirty
years ago Washington was a segregated city, the poor went unnoticed and the blacks discriminated against, and there were few
people, let alone laws, to challenge these conditions. Today the
poor and the minorities command a place in the national mind,
in the press and in the laws. For liberalism broke with precedent
and established the federal government as the guarantor of civil
rights. Even the programs, though leaving the slums intact, al-

leviated the misery somewhat. Community action programs failed in raising the standard of living but gave the poor access to policy-makers and departments. Menacing in their hostile quiet, riots their only voice, the poor were stirred by the programs, and they made the government listen.[6] The food stamp program aroused little resentment—it subsidized agriculture and the retail business—and helped feed hungry people. In 1965, it and welfare raised a third of the poor out of poverty. From 1961 to 1969, they re-duced the number of people with incomes less than the poverty level from forty to twenty-four million. And from 1965 to 1976 transfer payments further halved the percentage.[7] This was not a record of failure, nor was the civil rights record, nor the change in awareness, all of which suggests that we live in a world profoundly shaped by liberalism.

It may be that the liberals changed the world so much that it no longer had a place for them, and that this is why they vanished. They achieved their goals of the 1940s and 1950s—strong unions, a medical insurance plan (though not so bold as Truman's proposal), federal aid to education, federal power projects, and civil rights. They did not, of course, eradicate poverty and slums. But the liberals came to these concerns only after they had come to power and found that more than legal equality was necessary. Not having worried about these problems during their years of struggle, the liberals were ill-prepared to meet them, just as they were ill-prepared to handle the ferocity of Black Power and the antiwar movement. They gave way to others—but only after accomplish-ing what, in the 1940s, they had set out to do. It was a record of partial achievement, in the judging of which one might take into account an old theory. The theory holds that politics in American history swings on a pendulum, that liberal reform and conservative reaction alternate their sweep every twenty years. The liberals' fate suggests that the theory be modified. The swing was not irrational or haphazard, nor was it their failure that in-duced the liberals to give way to conservatives—it was instead their success. For success, whether Jacksonian or Progressive or liberal, endures and frames the rules of a new stage of contention and calls into being new battles and new men to fight them. It may be that the rate of liberal success is high in America, higher than in Europe—where across generations parties may espouse the same tiresome platforms—and that it explains the swing of the pendulum. In its most recent swing, the liberals vanquished the foes that had ignited their wrath, then, lacking those foes, they lacked also their cause. The world went on, changed by them, without them.

In any case, the effects of liberalism endure. Its success made the South more like the North, its failure the North more like the South. The Democratic platforms, the *Brown* decision, the boycotts and sit-ins, the federal troops and civil rights acts, all this changed the South. Since 1964 Southern politics has revolved less and less around race, so that today segregation is an untenable position for a statewide candidate.[8] In the ten years after the 1965 Voting Rights Act, the registration of blacks in the South jumped from 2 to 3.5 million; Republicans and Democrats competed for their votes as never before in a competition which President Hayes saw 100 years earlier as the only hope of the South. In 1964 Goldwater won five Deep South states that had not gone Republican since Reconstruction. The exclusive grasp of the Democratic party, guardian of white supremacy, was broken for good.[9]

Blacks quickly became a force in the South, electing, as one surprised member of the old guard put it, "three nigger mayors in Mississippi."[10] Later that state sent a delegation to the 1976 Democratic convention, half-black and half-female, including Ross Barnett, Jr., the son of the governor who had fought Kennedy over Meredith in 1962 and had led his all-white delegation out of the convention two years before. In 1976, Ross, Jr., said the New South had arrived and hugged Aaron Henry, a black leader of the MFDP in 1964. That fall Henry campaigned for Jimmy Carter with John Stennis, himself changed by the rapid pass of events. "Let me just say one thing about this integration," Stennis said in Biloxi, "I'm against it, always have been and always will be, but it's a fact. I'm not a fool. It's a fact. It's there"—hardly the reflexive battle-cry of a fevered and romantic people. It could not be. Ole Miss had 475 blacks; fourteen years before it had taken 6,000 U.S. Army troops (in addition to federal marshals and the National Guard) to integrate one. In 1975 the school's football star, the "Colonel Rebel," was a black athlete, chosen by popular vote, escorted by the homecoming queen, a white.[11] Even the tenacious George Wallace succumbed and, for the first time in ten years, flew the American flag atop the state capitol in Montgomery and pardoned the remaining *Scottsboro* defendant. The New South may indeed have arrived, for the issue that had made it always old was at last passing away.

But the race issue passed away not absolutely, for nothing does. Racial tension was endemic to the North, but in the absence of a pronounced caste system it had slumbered, except for vicious white and black riots in 1919, 1937, and 1943. Then the legislation of the 1960s, the riots, the busing issue, affirmative action—the unfocused sense that blacks received undue attention—all produced a sharp backlash. Northern whites resented busing no less than Southern whites.[12] And suburbs pled the case of community control, manipulating their zoning, to keep the poor out. Regional distinctions blurred; the sections of the nation approached each other on the issue of race. At the same time they joined in emphasizing the autonomy of their smaller parts, their towns and neighborhoods, perhaps to stress their identity, precisely because in this era of communications—when the televisions of New York broadcast the same images as those of Alabama and Utah—and of federal power—when the writ of Washington ran large in Louisiana—there was the sense growing that local nuance and character were dying.

As liberalism split the regions apart, its decline brought them together. But it is an uneasy reunion. The liberals, defeated, are defensive. So too are the old guard Southerners, who display Confederate flags in their Senate offices, a large one in the front office for Eastland, a small one in the interior for Talmadge. They look back over thirty years and say they knew all along it was a rear-guard fight against liberalism, the government, civil rights, and socialism. They are wistful.[13] Something is gone. But do they need to be so wistful? Though they lost something, they also gained—the fellowship of the nation, denied them when they stood alone. For the unravelling of liberalism laid bare several threads that traced their way back to the nineteenth century and beyond, threads that the South had held tight and safe between its fingers since. Now they no longer stand alone. The nation joins them and senses that the romance of the South had more than one legacy, not just the blood and meanness of Selma, but also legality and defense of minorities (however loosely construed), order and character and the lone people who will not be coerced. This is where the liberals brought themselves and the nation. This is where they ended.

They began in the same place, during the eighteenth century. In opposing the British crown, Americans concluded that power was bad, the people good. But then they had to frame a government, a power that would not be bad, that the people would not have to fight. They struggled with this problem for years, until the delegates solved it in 1787—and grandly made it worse. They placed sovereignty in the people, who never again would oppose the government because now it was their agent, the guardian of their rights. But by being so constituted, the government was morally invested with almost limitless power and hence with the potential for coercing the people. It did not coerce many people, as things turned out, until after the New Deal, for men had restrained it, themselves restrained by a persistent faith in property, fear of power, and racist beliefs. But, armed with the ideology of civil rights, the liberals broke these restraints and tried a daring experiment. They defied the contradiction, as Henry Adams had called it, implicit in democratic power. Never before had leaders defied it, not even in the Civil War, that event of utmost coercion, for then only Lincoln and a handful of others understood their purpose to be democratic. But the liberals did; they coerced the people who for so long had coerced the blacks. When the nation responded poorly to their demands, the liberals emphasized more and more the power, and implied the people were sometimes bad. There was the problem. For infusing all strains of liberalism, underlying all democratic government, is the conviction that the people must be good.

And yet—here was the larger problem—the people were, as the liberals implied, not always virtuous. They were racist. Since the Revolution this racism had rendered pale and artificial the articles of liberal doctrine—the faith in the virtuous people and property and small government, otherwise a set of reasonable and humane beliefs—for some men were decidedly unvirtuous, and others were their victims. Moreover this racism was intractable. It fell beyond the scope of liberalism to affirm or deny, sometimes sustaining, other times wrecking liberal movements, but never itself susceptible to liberal analysis. It could only be uprooted if liberals assaulted the people's racism, instead of extolling their virtue, and if they resorted to federal power and deserted the concepts of state and local autonomy—if they recast their liberal belief. This task the postwar liberals undertook, and if they succeeded only partially, becoming caught in the contradiction of democratic power, the fault lay less with them than with the legacy they struggled against.

NOTES

Chapter One

1. On the origins of European liberalism, see Guido de Ruggiero, *The History of European Liberalism* (Boston, 1959), especially pp. 1-151.

2. See Isaac Kramnick, *Bolingbroke and his Circle: The Politics of Nostalgia in the Age of Walpole* (Cambridge, Mass., 1968); J.G.A. Pocock, "Machiavelli, Harrington, and English Political Ideologies in the Eighteenth Century," *William and Mary Quarterly* 22 (1965).

3. Bernard Bailyn, *Ideological Origins of the American Revolution* (Cambridge, Mass., 1967), pp. 1-93.

4. Gordon S. Wood, *Creation of the American Republic, 1776-1787* (Chapel Hill, 1969), pp. 125-255.

5. Ibid., pp. 257-389.

6. Ibid., pp. 469-564.

7. Bailyn, *Ideological Origins,* p. 160.

8. James Sullivan, *Land Titles in Massachusetts* (Boston, 1801), pp. 348-50. Here I part with those, such as Gordon Wood, who say that the Constitution resolved the conflict between the people and power. It seems that it was resolved only in theory, that in practice it continued, and that it did so because the notion of the virtuous people long survived the Revolution.

9. Henry Adams, *The United States in 1800* (Ithaca, 1955), p. 83. This book consists of the first six chapters of Adams' *History of the United States of America during the First Administration of Thomas Jefferson* (New York, 1889-91).

Chapter Two

1. For the ideological dispute of the 1790s, see Joseph Charles, *The Origins of the American Party System* (New York, 1961).

2. Thomas Jefferson to Gideon Granger, August 13, 1800, in Andrew A. Libscomb and Albert Ellery Bergh, eds., *The Writings of Thomas Jefferson,* Definitive Edition, 20 vols. (Washington, D.C., 1905), 10:166-70; Thomas Jefferson to Spencer Roane, September 6, 1819, ibid., 15:212-16.

3. Margaret L. Coit, *John C. Calhoun: American Portrait* (Boston, 1950), p. 97.

4. Arthur M. Schlesinger, Jr., *The Age of Jackson* (Boston, 1945), p. 34.

5. The argument here, that the Jacksonians elaborated the liberalism of Jefferson by adding to it a little class analysis, follows Schlesinger, *Jackson*, pp. 18-44.

6. Ibid., pp. 81, 91, 505. For differing views in the debate over the composition of the Jacksonian alliance or the details of its ideology, see Bray Hammond, *Banks and Politics in America from the Revolution to the Civil War* (Princeton, 1957); Lee Benson, *The Concept of Jacksonian Democracy: New York as a Test Case* (Princeton, 1961); and of course Schlesinger, who opened the debate. My purpose is restricted to showing the continuing usefulness of the revolutionary thought—the symbols of power and people—in the time of Jackson.

7. Coit, *Calhoun,* pp. 251-52.

8. Ibid., pp. 4-5.

9. Ibid., pp. 95-96, 97, 111, 112-13, 114-15, 116-17, 132.

10. Ibid., pp. 144-46, 166-68, 182-91, 211-13, 264-66; Schlesinger, p. 106.

11. David Brion Davis, *The Problem of Slavery in the Age of Revolution, 1770-1823* (Ithaca, 1975), pp. 164-212.

12. Coit, *Calhoun,* pp. 292, 294, 451-55, 388; Richard Hofstadter, "John Calhoun: The Marx of the Master Class," in *The American Political Tradition* (New York, 1948), pp. 68-92.

13. Coit, *Calhoun,* p. 437; William W. Freehling, "Spoilsmen and Interests in the Thought and Career of John C. Calhoun," *Journal of American History* 52 (1965), 25-42; Coit, *Calhoun,* p. 436.

14. Edmund Morgan, *American Slavery, American Freedom* (New York, 1975); George Fitzhugh, *Sociology for the South, or the Failure of Free Society* (Richmond, 1854), p. 26; Coit, *Calhoun,* pp. 251, 493, 501.

15. W. J. Cash, *The Mind of the South* (New York, 1941), pp. 62-65.

16. Ibid., pp. 76-77.

17. For the abolitionists' argument, see John L. Thomas, ed., *Slavery Attacked: The Abolitionist Crusade* (Englewood Cliffs, N.J., 1965); Dwight Lowell Dumond, *Antislavery Origins of the Civil War in the United States* (Ann Arbor, 1959), pp. 37-50.

18. Eric Foner, *Free Soil, Free Labor, Free Men: The Ideology of the Republican Party Before the Civil War* (London, 1970), pp. 149-85.

19. Ibid., pp. 11-39.

20. Ibid., pp. 73-102.

21. Ibid., pp. 181-82.

22. Ibid., pp. 90-91.

23. Ibid., pp. 195-200.

24. Ibid., pp. 267, 269, and 261-317.

25. George M. Fredrickson, *The Inner Civil War: Northern Intellectuals and the Crisis of the Union* (New York, 1965), pp. 65-79.

26. Ibid., pp. 80-112, 184-98.

27. Edmund Wilson, *Patriotic Gore: Studies in the Literature of the American Civil War* (New York, 1962), p. 97. See also Wilson's essay on Lincoln, pp. 99-130.

28. Benjamin P. Thomas, *Abraham Lincoln* (New York, 1952), p. 469.

29. Ibid., p. 268.

30. "O Captain! My Captain," line 12; and "Respondez!", lines 20-21.

31. Thomas, *Lincoln*, p. 402.

Chapter Three

1. Kenneth M. Stampp, *The Era of Reconstruction, 1865-1877* (New York, 1967), pp. 135-45.

2. Richard Kluger, *Simple Justice: The History of Brown v. Board of Education and Black America's Struggle for Equality* (New York, 1976), pp. 57-66; Stampp, *Era of Reconstruction*, pp. 140-41.

3. Stampp, *Era of Reconstruction*, pp. 124-29.

4. Ibid., pp. 188-94.

5. Ibid., p. 191.

6. Ibid., pp. 190-91.

7. Samuel Lubell, *White and Black* (New York, 1964), p. 15.

8. C. Vann Woodward, *Origins of the New South, 1877-1913* (Austin, 1951), pp. 179-80.

9. Ibid., p. 205.

10. Ibid., p. 211.

11. Ibid., p. 212.

12. C. Vann Woodward, *The Strange Career of Jim Crow* (Oxford, 1966), pp. 98-99.

13. Woodward, *New South*, p. 361.

14. Woodward, *Jim Crow*, pp. 116-17.

15. Woodward, *New South*, p. 321.

16. Ibid., pp. 342-43.

17. Ibid., pp. 350-51.

18. Ibid., p. 333.

19. Louis Hartz, *The Liberal Tradition in America: An Interpretation of American Political Thought since the Revolution* (New York, 1955), 228-31.

20. Richard Hofstadter, *The Age of Reform: From Bryan to FDR* (New York, 1955), pp. 131-73; Hartz, *Liberal Tradition*, pp. 240-43.

21. George E. Mowry, *The Era of Theodore Roosevelt and the Birth of Modern America, 1900-1912* (New York, 1958), pp. 85-105.

22. Oscar Handlin, *Al Smith and His America* (Boston, 1958), pp. 34-35, 39ff, 53ff, 62; John D. Buenker, *Urban Liberalism and Progressive Reform* (New York, 1973), pp. 27ff; J. Joseph Huthmacher, *Senator Robert Wagner and the Rise of Urban Liberalism* (New York, 1971), pp. 3-37; Nancy Joan Weiss, *Charles Francis Murphy, 1858-1924: Responsibility in Tammany Politics* (Northampton, Mass., 1968), pp. 14ff.

23. Hartz, *Liberal Tradition*, pp. 240-43; Buenker, *Urban Liberalism*, pp. 80-117; Theordore J. Lowi, *The End of Liberalism: Ideology, Policy, and and Crisis of Public Authority* (New York, 1969), p. 94.

24. Buenker, *Urban Liberalism*, pp. 42-44. Buenker's book is devoted to proving this point—that urban immigrant leaders were an important part of the reform movement. In correcting the impression that the machines were only corrupt and had no redeeming virtues, Buenker has performed a worthy service. His book, persuasively argued, is rich in detail. I believe he has made a mistake, however, when he says (pp. 205-06) that the machines' contribution to liberalism was similar to the Progressives'. Huthmacher, whom Buenker follows, also fails to distinguish carefully between the Progressives and the urban leaders, and instead says they are both of the "Progressive Era," which was "the first phase in the evolution of modern American liberalism" and the precedent for the "New Deal, Fair Deal, New Frontier, and the Great Society." (31) This is to misstate the case. In raising the issue of ethnicity, the machine politicians gave to liberalism a wholly new concern, which would become a central concern of the Fair Deal and New Frontier and Great Society— though not of the New Deal. Hence to speak of the urban leaders as the first spokesmen of a "twentieth century liberalism" is excessively to reduce a complex matter. And to so speak of them in connection with the Progressives is a mistake. For the significant point is that although they backed much Progressive reform the machine politicians were essentially different from the Progressives. They differed not only in the style of politics but also in their motivation and their concerns—in their fight against Prohibition and for minority rights and unions. In these fights they broke new ground—and were opposed by Progressives. Thus to do justice to the machines—which in other respects Huthmacher and Buenker have admirably done—does not require one to promote them to the level of the Progressives, which in some ways is more of a demotion.

25. Handlin, *Al Smith*, pp. 18-20; Weiss, *Charles Murphy*, p. 90; Buenker, *Urban Liberalism*, p. 208.

26. Hofstadter, *Age of Reform*, pp. 272-328; Buenker, *Urban Liberalism*, pp. 226ff.

27. Eric Foner, *Free Soil, Free Labor, Free Men* (London, 1970), pp. 226-29; Handlin, *Al Smith*, pp. 117-20; Buenker, *Urban Liberalism*, p. 171.

28. Handlin, *Al Smith*, pp. 78-79; Hofstadter, *Age of Reform*, pp. 289-92; Buenker, *Urban Liberalism*, pp. 167-70, 172ff, 186, 188-89, 226ff.

29. Handlin, *Al Smith*, pp. 78-82; Buenker, *Urban Liberalism*, pp. 194, 195.

30. Handlin, *Al Smith*, pp. 46-47, 115, 123, 126-35; Kluger, *Simple Justice*, pp. 90-91, 108.

Chapter Four

1. Oscar Handlin, *Al Smith and His America* (Boston, 1958), pp. 186-87.

2. Louise Venable Kennedy, *The Negro Peasant Turns Cityward* (New York, 1968), p. 43.

3. Ibid., pp. 44, 46, 47.

4. C. Vann Woodward, *The Strange Career of Jim Crow* (Oxford, 1966, p. 114.

5. C. Vann Woodward, *Origins of the New South, 1877-1913* (Austin, 1951), p. 368; Chicago Commission on Race Relations, *The Negro in Chicago: A Study of Race Relations and a Race Riot* (Chicago, 1922), 75-105.

6. Kennedy, *Negro Peasant*, pp. 23-31; Gunnar Myrdal, *An American Dilemma* (New York, 1944), p. 183.

7. Kennedy, *Negro Peasant*, pp. 32-34; Chicago Commission, *Negro in Chicago*, p. 79.

8. Myrdal, *American Dilemma*, p. 183; Kennedy, *Negro Peasant*, p. 74.

9. Samuel Lubell, *White and Black* (New York, 1964), p. 54.

10. Myrdal, *American Dilemma*, pp. 493-95, 503-04.

11. Philip M. Hansen, "Demographic Factors in the Integration of the Negro," in *The Negro American*, eds. Talcott Parsons and Kenneth B. Clark (Boston, 1966), p. 75.

12. Myrdal, *American Dilemma*, pp. 493-95, 475.

13. Arthur M. Schlesinger, Jr., *The Politics of Upheaval* (Boston, 1960), p. 426.

14. Myrdal, *American Dilemma*, pp. 503-04; William E. Leuchtenburg, *Franklin D. Roosevelt and the New Deal, 1932-1940* (New York, 1963), pp. 185-87.

15. Richard Kluger, *Simple Justice* (New York, 1976), p. 117.

16. Arthur M. Schlesinger, Jr., *The Coming of the New Deal* (Boston, 1958), pp. 385-96, 407-19; see also Herbert Harris, *Labor's Civil War* (New York, 1940).

17. Lubell, *White and Black*, p. 37.

18. Arthur Ross and Herbert Hill, eds., *Employment, Race and Poverty* (New York, 1967), p. 421.

19. Lubell, *White and Black*, p. 60.

20. Arthur Goldberg, *The AFL-CIO Merger* (New York, 1957), pp. 197-98.

21. Ibid., pp. 197-98.

22. Richard J. Stillman, *Integration of the Negro in the U.S. Armed Forces* (New York, 1968), p. 34; also for the importance of the war, see John Hope Franklin, "The Two Worlds of Race: A Historical View," in Parsons and Clark, *The Negro American*, pp. 62-63.

23. Woodward, *Jim Crow*, p. 128.

24. Stillman, *Integration of the Negro*, p. 34.

25. Ibid., pp. 22-29.

26. *New York Times*, May 18, 1954.

27. Interview with James Rowe. (Hereafter interviews will be cited as _____ interview.)

28. George Brown Tindall, *The Disruption of the Solid South* (Chapel Hill, 1972), p. 47.

29. Ibid., p. 27.

30. Myrdal, *American Dilemma*, p. 474.

31. James T. Patterson, *Congressional Conservatism and the New Deal: The Growth of the Conservative Coalition in Congress, 1933-1939* (Lexington, Ky., 1967), pp. 21, 28.

32. Tom P. Brady, *Black Monday: Segregation or Amalgamation . . . America Has Its Choice* (Winona, Miss., 1955), pp. 37, 62, 49, 45.

33. W. J. Cash, *The Mind of the South* (New York, 1941), pp. 273-89.

34. Patterson, *Congressional Conservatism*, p. 54.

35. Ibid., pp. 59-78.

36. Kluger, *Simple Justice*, pp. 105-54.

37. Lubell, *White and Black*, pp. 68-69.

38. Ibid., p. 67; Patterson, *Congressional Conservatism*, p. 43; Harry S. Ashmore, *An Epitaph for Dixie* (New York, 1958), pp. 100-01.

39. Patterson, *Congressional Conservatism*, pp. 95-98, 128-32, 136-40, 150-51, 156, 191-205, 232, 323-24, 257.

40. Ibid., pp. 23, 45; Cash, *Southern Mind*, pp. 420, 389ff; Patterson, *Congressional Conservatism*, p. 128-32.

41. Myrdal, *American Dilemma*, pp. 515, 1015.

42. Schlesinger, *Politics of Upheaval*, pp. 430-31.

43. Handlin, *Al Smith*, pp. 138-43, 151-53, 159-66.

44. Schlesinger, *Politics of Upheaval*, pp. 430-38; J. Joseph Huthmacher, *Senator Robert Wagner and the Rise of Urban Liberalism* (New York, 1971), pp. 171-74, 238-42, 274-75; Kluger, *Simple Justice*, p. 166.

45. Rowe interview; Louis Hartz, *The Liberal Tradition in America* (New York, 1955), pp. 259-83; see also Frank Freidel, *FDR and the South* (Baton Rouge, La., 1965).

Chapter Five

1. Rowe interview. For a more detailed account of the events leading to Truman's nomination, see Robert J. Donovan, *Crisis and Conflict: The Presidency of Harry S Truman, 1945-1948* (New York, 1977), pp. ix-xvii.

2. Pace interview.

3. Alonzo L. Hamby, *Beyond the New Deal: Harry S. Truman and American Liberalism* (New York, 1973), p. 44.

4. Donovan, *Crisis and Conflict*, pp. 30-31; Hamby, *Beyond the New Deal*, p. 46.

5. *To Secure These Rights: Report of the President's Committee on Civil Rights* (New York, 1947), pp. 87-95, 140-41.

6. Ibid., see text pp. 53-59; also John Morton Blum, *V Was For Victory: Politics and American Culture During World War II* (New York, 1976).

7. Hamby, *Beyond the New Deal*, p. 49.

8. Alfred Steinberg, *The Man from Missouri* (New York, 1962), p. 262; Rosenman said to Ickes that he thought Truman braver than Roosevelt on several issues, among them health insurance. Donovan, *Crisis and Conflict*, p. 125.

9. Allen J. Matusow, *Farm Policies and Politics in the Truman Years* (New York, 1970), pp. 55-64.

10. Donovan, *Crisis and Conflict*, pp. 243-45; Richard Kluger, *Simple Justice* (New York, 1976), p. 250.

11. *To Secure These Rights*. The following summary is from this excellent report of 1947.

12. Ibid., p. 5.

13. Barton J. Bernstein and Allen J. Matusow, eds., *The Truman Administration* (New York, 1966), p. 105.

14. Hamby, *Beyond the New Deal*, pp. 189-90; Donovan, *Crisis and Conflict*, p. 335; Kluger, *Simple Justice*, 253, 558-61.

15. Richard J. Stillman, *Integration of the Negro in the U.S. Armed Forces* (New York, 1968), pp. 36, 38.

16. Ibid., p. 40; C. Vann Woodward, *The Strange Career of Jim Crow* (Oxford, 1966), p. 137; Bernstein and Matusow, *Truman Administration*, p. 110.

17. Donovan, *Crisis and Conflict*, pp. 411, 333-34.

18. Steinberg, *Man from Missouri*, pp. 303-04; Kluger, *Simple Justice*, p. 300; Susan M. Hartmann, *Truman and the 80th Congress* (Columbia, Mo., 1971), p. 153.

19. Estes Kefauver Papers, University of Tennessee Library (Special Collections), Knoxville, Tennessee, Series 3, Box 25, Civil Rights File: *Congressional Record* Clipping, 84th Congress (hereafter cited as EK Papers, Series, Box, File); Hartmann, *Truman and the 80th Congress*, p. 153.

20. Stillman, *Integration of the Negro*, p. 39.

21. Bernstein and Matusow, *Truman Administration*, pp. 108-10.

22. Woodward, *Jim Crow*, p. 141.

23. Steinberg, *Man from Missouri*, p. 272.

24. Donovan, *Crisis and Conflict*, pp. 107-115, 163-73, 34-44, 51-64.

25. Hamby, *Beyond the New Deal*, p. 83.

26. Donovan, *Crisis and Conflict*, pp. 208-18 (on the rail strike). It should be noted that some liberals later found grounds to criticize Truman for his loyalty program. To consider the merits of his program is beyond the scope of this book, but it is perhaps neccssary to explain why civil liberties in general is not relevant to this study. It is not because it was not relevant to the transformation of liberalism in the postwar years; though civil rights— it is partly the purpose of this book to show—was relevant to that transformation. The two issues were vastly different. Civil rights advocates turned to the equal protection clause of the Fourteenth Amendment; civil liberties advocates turn to the First Amendment. Civil rights involved the deprivation of a racial minority, civil liberties the deprivation of everyone, or someone, who was not defined by class or race. And, what was of greatest importance, civil rights invoked the power of the federal government, but civil liberties was hostile to government power. It was the role of government, indeed, that the Democrats fought over. The liberals, through the 1940s and 1950s and 1960s, wished to make government the protector of outcast people—sick, old, poor, and minority—as they had made it protect the rights of labor in the 1930s; and they were opposed in this by the Southern Democrats: Hence the struggle in the Democratic party. Civil liberties was not in the least

germane to this struggle. If anything, it pointed in a direction opposite from the one toward which the Democrats were moving. Moreover, it should be noted that although the two matters of civil rights and civil liberties seem connected in some people's mind, such a connection did not exist in the public's mind during the 1950s. (Norman H. Nie, Sidney Verba, and John R. Petrocik, *The Changing American Voter* (Cambridge, Mass., 1976), pp. 132-33.) Nor did it exist in the mind of Adlai Stevenson and many Southerners, who, willing to defend at length the Bill of Rights, had trouble with the civil rights issue.

Thus civil liberties, certainly central to the founding ideas of liberalism, implied a different conception of government from that implied by civil rights and was not central to the transformation of liberalism and therefore is excluded here from consideration.

27. Daniel Yergin, "Harry Truman: Revived and Revised," *New York Times Magazine* (October 24, 1976), pp. 40, 80-93. Truman also mentioned the violence on December 5, 1946, when he announced the appointment of the civil rights committee and explained its purpose. *To Secure These Rights*, p. vii.

28. The following two paragraphs are based on Rowe's memorandum, written for Truman in late 1947. Rowe was kind enough to give the author a copy.

29. Steinberg, *Man from Missouri*, p. 310; Donovan, *Crisis and Conflict*, p. 404.

30. Rowe interview.

31. Unpublished notes of Joseph Rauh. Rauh, a participant of six Democratic National Conventions (and a labor and civil rights lawyer), has written a short memoir of his experiences and been kind enough to give the author a copy.

32. Democratic National Committee Papers, John F. Kennedy Library, Waltham, Massachusetts, Box 94, 1948 Credentials Committee Report, pp. 58, 95-96. (Hereafter cited as DNC, Box, subject, page.)

33. Ibid., pp. 199-202; Rauh notes.

34. Rauh notes.

35. Ibid., Rauh interview.

36. Rauh notes; Rauh interview.

37. DNC, Box 94, 1948 Convention Proceedings, Fifth Session, July 14, 1948, pp. 359-71.

38. Rauh notes; Rauh interview.

39. DNC, Box 94, 1948 Democratic Platform Folder.

40. Ibid., Convention Proceedings, Sixth Session, July 14, 1948, pp. 436-37.

41. Ibid., p. 502; Rauh notes; Harry S. Truman, *Memoirs* vol. 2: *Years of Trial and Hope* (Garden City, N.Y., 1956), p. 183.

42. Hartmann, *Truman and the 80th Congress*, pp. 189-90.

43. Hamby, *Beyond the New Deal*, pp. 251-53.

44. Ibid., pp. 277-92.

45. Ibid., see Part Two.

46. David Mayhew, *Loyalty Among Congressmen: The Difference Between Democrats and Republicans, 1947-1962* (Cambridge, Mass., 1966); Hamby, *Beyond the New Deal*, p. 511. For a view of Truman's troubles and a convincing refutation of the revisionists, see ibid., pp. 505-516.

47. *The New Republic* was the magazine. Hamby, *Beyond the New Deal*, p. 485.

48. Rauh interview.

Chapter Six

1. There is little doubt that the liberals' victory at the 1948 convention took everyone by surprise. Interviews with Talmadge, Pace, and Rauh.

2. Norman H. Nie et al., *The Changing American Voter*, (Cambridge, Mass., 1976), pp. 14-73, 156-73.

3. John Bartlow Martin, *The Life of Adlai E. Stevenson*, 2 vols. (Garden City, N.Y., 1976-77), 1:30.

4. Walter Johnson, ed., *The Papers of Adlai Stevenson* (Boston, 1972), 1:248-49.

5. Martin, *Stevenson Life*, 2:351.

6. Adlai E. Stevenson Papers, Firestone Library, Princeton, New Jersey, interview with Arthur M. Schlesinger, Jr., conducted by John Bartlow Martin, R6, p. 135. (Hereafter cited as AES Papers.) The Adlai E. Stevenson Papers are located in four places. The papers of the governorship are in the Illinois State Historical Library, Springfield; of his UN years in the Department of State archives in Washington, D.C., and in the chancery of the U.S. Mission to the UN in New York; and the rest, including his personal papers, in Firestone Library, Princeton, New Jersey. In the course of writing his biography of Stevenson, *The Life of Adlai E. Stevenson*, John Bartlow Martin made copies of many of these papers, and he has included these, along with his own memorandums on the 1952 and 1956 presidential campaigns, in his own archive, which he deposited in the Library of Congress. I had access to this archive, and anyone wishing to consult the Stevenson Papers cited here should therefore visit the Library of Congress collection. These same papers, though organized differently (and excluding Martin's own memorandums), can be found in the Firestone Library.

Martin also interviewed many people during his research, and I had access to the transcripts of those interviews (which are deposited in the Martin Papers at the Library of Congress). Only a few of the citations in this book are to these interviews, which are cited here as part of the AES Papers. By contrast, my own interviews are cited simply as _____ interview.

7. AES Papers, speech, New York State Democratic Convention, August 28, 1952.

8. Ibid., letter to Alicia Patterson, July 16, 1951, G16, p. 73.

9. Ibid., television transcript, November 4, 1951, S1, pp. 1-23.

10. Newton Minow, longtime friend of Adlai Stevenson (later chairman of the FCC under Kennedy) said this. Perhaps, said Minow, Stevenson was

concerned with civil rights during his days at the Navy Department, though Minow, not then acquainted with Stevenson, cannot be sure. Letter to author, June 2, 1978.

11. AES Papers, interview with Jacob Arvey, R5, p. 147; Rauh interview; Pace interview.

12. AES Papers, memorandum by John Bartlow Martin, 1952 campaign, M4, p. 92; Dorothy Fosdick to AES, June 14, 1952, G9, pp. 152-60.

13. Democratic National Committee Papers, Box 94, 1948 Convention Proceedings, Sixth Session, July 14, 1948, p. 541.

14. AES Papers, speech, Brooklyn, Ill., September 6, 1948, S29, p. 203.

15. Jonathan Daniels to author, June 3, 1978. Daniels was a friend to both Stevenson and Truman.

16. *Chicago Tribune,* October 1, 1948; October 25, 1948.

17. For the business opposition to the FEPC, see AES Papers, C111.

18. AES Papers, S21, 35; C111, p. 98; City Club's Race Relations Committee letter to AES, C111, pp. 7-8; 57-62.

19. Ibid., speech, Gettysburg, November 19, 1951, S1, pp. 146-49; speech, Waldorf-Astoria Hotel, January 21, 1952. Illinois Congressman Sidney Yates put the speech and a *New York Herald Tribune* January 22 editorial praising Stevenson into the *Congressional Record Appendix,* January 24, 1952, pp. 476-77.

20. *New York Times,* November 19, 1948; AES Papers, Ralph Bunche to AES, August 2, 1951, C131, p. 4; memorandum from E. E. Reynolds to George E. Allen, June 12, 1952, C104, p. 49; Harold Ickes to AES, July 23, 1951, C43, pp. 234-35; James Farley to AES, January 30, 1952, S10, p. 92; John B. King to AES, January 23, 1952, S10, p. 94. See also Martin, *Stevenson Life,* 1:517-18.

21. Jack Anderson and Fred Blumenthal, *The Kefauver Story* (New York, 1956), pp. 24-25; Martin, *Stevenson Life,* 1:42.

22. Interviews with Talmadge, Pace, and Rauh. Rauh says that this is the view many liberals had of Kefauver then and that perhaps some have changed their mind since, in recognition of his liberal achievement.

23. Anderson and Blumenthal, *Kefauver Story,* p. 72; Estes Kefauver Papers, University of Tennessee Library, Series 1, Box 11, File 16.

24. Estes Kefauver Papers, University of Tennessee Library, Series 1, Box 25, Voting Record File; Series 1, Box 10, Civil Rights Folder 1; Series 1, Box 10, Folder 11.

25. Ibid., Series 5e, Box 3, Anti-EK Folder; EK to John S. Hilson, June 8, 1951, Series 1, Box 10, Folder 11; EK speech, March 18, 1949, Series 1, Box 11, Folder 2.

26. Ibid., EK to Edward Roybal, May 6, 1952, Series 5e, Box 33, Issues Folder.

27. Ibid., EK to S. V. Dowtin, October 29, 1958, Series 1, Box 12, Segregation Folder 2.

28. Ibid., constituent to EK, June 18, 1957, Series 1, Box 10, Folder 12; ibid., constituent to EK, June 19, 1957.

29. Ibid., Donohue memorandum, Series 5g, Box 10, Civil Rights Folder.

30. Several stories about Kefauver have come to this author's attention, but considering their intimate nature it would be tasteless to print them. Moreover, it was Kefauver's reputation, not the activities themselves, that is important here.

31. EK Papers, EK memorandum to himself, undated, Series 5e, Box 33, Presidential 1952 Folder.

32. Ibid., Series 5e, Box 31, Civil Rights Folder; Margaret Truman, *Harry S. Truman* (New York, 1973), p. 526.

33. George Ball, "Flaming Arrows to the Sky," *Atlantic Monthly* (May 1966), pp. 41-45; Martin, *Stevenson Life*, 1:523.

34. Paul T. David, Malcolm Moos, and Ralph M. Goldman, *Presidential Nominating Politics in 1952* (Baltimore, 1954), 1:63, 61; M. Truman, *Truman*, p. 532.

35. Jonathan Daniels to author, June 3, 1978. Daniels was one of several emissaries Truman sent to Stevenson in the spring of 1952.

36. AES Papers, Arthur Schlesinger, Jr., to AES, April 1, 1952, C106, p. 198; April 8, 1952, C106, p. 200.

37. Martin, *Stevenson Life*, 1:549.

38. AES Papers, Schlesinger to AES, April 16, 1952, C106, p. 199; speech, July 9, 1952, S32, pp. 144-58.

39. David et al., *Nominating Politics*, 1:135.

40. DNC, Box 97, 1952 Platform Committee Hearings, July 17, 1952, pp. 316, 260, 361; July 21, 1952, pp. 1, 267-69.

41. Ibid., July 17, 1952, pp. 305-14; July 19, 1952, pp. 874-86; July 17, 1952, p. 255.

42. David et al., *Nominating Politics*, 1:131-32; 1:111.

43. Ibid., 1:111; Rowe interview; David et al., *Nominating Politics*, 1:112.

44. Democratic National Committee, *The Democratic Platform: 1952* (Washington, D.C., 1952), pp. 43-44.

45. Rauh interview.

46. DNC, Box 7, Credentials Committee Proceedings, July 22, 1952, pp. 268-310; David et al., *Nominating Politics*, 1:129.

47. DNC, Box 7, Credentials Committee Proceedings, July 22, 1952, p. 11; David et al., *Nominating Politics*, 1:130.

48. DNC, Box 7, Credentials Committee Proceedings, July 22, 1952, p. 315; David et al., *Nominating Politics*, 1:130-31.

49. David et al., *Nominating Politics*, 1:133.

50. James F. Byrnes, *All in One Lifetime* (New York, 1958), pp. 413-14.

51. David et al., *Nominating Politics*, 1:139-40; 142-43.

52. Ibid., 1:112-13, 147; AES Papers, Arvey interview, R5, p. 155.

53. David et al., *Nominating Politics*, 1:123.

54. Rowe interview.

55. Pace interview; Rauh interview.

56. AES Papers, Hermon Dunlap Smith to his daughter, July 28, 1952, C77, p. 111.

57. *Wall Street Journal,* July 27, 1952; July 26, 1952.

58. David et al., *Nominating Politics,* 1:128.

59. Martin, 1:596-97; *New York Herald Tribune,* July 25, 1952.

60. AES Papers, memorandum from Arthur Schlesinger, Jr., to AES, undated, C163, pp. 17-18. Schlesinger told Stevenson of the liberals' discontent.

61. Ibid., speech, St. Louis, October 9, 1952; Martin memorandum to himself, 1952, M3, p. 124.

62. Ibid., speech, Harlem, October 27, 1952; Martin memorandum to himself, M4, p. 128; *New York Times,* September 3, 1952.

63. AES Papers, speech, Richmond, September 20, 1952; speech, Nashville, October 11, 1952; Martin memorandum to himself, M4, pp. 38-43.

Chapter Seven

1. *Chicago Sun Times,* January 1, 1954.

2. John Bartlow Martin, *The Life of Adlai E. Stevenson,* 2 vols. (Garden City, N.Y., 1976-77), 2:101.

3. DNC, Box 116, DNC Meeting Proceedings, December 4, 1954, p. 61.

4. John Brademas to author, June 2, 1978.

5. Adlai E. Stevenson Papers, Firestone Library, Princeton, N.J., interview with Jacob Arvey, R6, p. 3.

6. Democratic National Committee Papers, John F. Kennedy Library, Waltham, Mass., Box 116, DNC Meeting Proceedings, December 4, 1954, pp. 34-46; AES Papers, interview with Jacob Arvey, R5, p. 178.

7. Estes Kefauver Papers, University of Tennessee Library, Knoxville, Tenn., Series 5g, Box 1, Butler Folder, April 7, 1955; Rauh interview; AES Papers, interview with Jacob Arvey, R6, p. 3.

8. EK Papers, Series 1, Box 41, Democratic Party Folder.

9. AES Papers, interview with Arthur Schlesinger, Jr., R10, p. 50; speech, Miami Beach, March 6, 1954.

10. Ibid., interview with Arthur Schlesinger, Jr., R10, pp. 32-33.

11. Arthur Ross and Herbert Hill, eds., *Employment, Race and Poverty* (New York, 1967), pp. 403, 404.

12. Rauh interview.

13. James F. Byrnes, *All in One Lifetime* (New York, 1958), p. 418.

14. Richard Kluger, *Simple Justice* (New York, 1976), pp. 294, 580, 708, and see his Appendix for text of the decisions.

15. John Emmet Hughes, *The Ordeal of Power* (New York, 1963), p. 201; Dwight Eisenhower, *The White House Years: Waging Peace* (Garden City, N.Y., 1965), p. 150; Carl M. Brauer, "The Kennedy Administration and Civil Rights," unpublished Ph.D. dissertation, Harvard University (1973), pp. 2-11; C. Vann Woodward, *The Strange Career of Jim Crow*

(Oxford, 1966), p. 163.

16. Woodward, *Jim Crow,* pp. 168, 139.

17. AES Papers, release, May 27, 1954.

18. Ibid., AES to Millard Tydings, July 15, 1955.

19. Ibid., Jonathan Daniels to AES, April 5, 1955; AES to Jonathan Daniels, April 8, 1955; Jonathan Daniels to author, June 3, 1978.

20. AES Papers, Harry Ashmore to AES, December 14, 1954.

21. Ibid., Chalmers G. Davidson to AES, July 18, 1955; AES to Chalmers G. Davidson, July 22, 1955.

22. Confidential but reliable source.

23. AES Papers, interview with Arthur M. Schlesinger, Jr., R10, p. 158.

24. Ibid., reported in memorandum by W. M. Blair, an aide to AES, June 24, 1955.

25. Arthur Goldberg, *The AFL-CIO Merger* (New York, 1957), pp. 198-99, 201-02.

26. EK Papers, Series 10, Box 5, Speech Folder, June 12, 1954; Series 5f, Box 17, Ten Big Lies Folder; Series 10, Box 5, Speech Folder.

27. Woodward, *Jim Crow,* p. 165; John Bartlow Martin, *The Deep South Says Never* (New York, 1957), pp. 11, 1-2.

28. William Graham Sumner, *Folkways* (New York, 1940), p. 63.

29. Edmund Wilson, *To the Finland Station* (New York, 1940), pp. 11-12.

30. Alexis de Tocqueville, *The Old Regime and the French Revolution* (New York, 1955), p. 72; *Democracy in America,* Vol I. (New York, 1945), pp. 310-34.

31. Gunnar Myrdal, *Asian Drama* (New York, 1968), I:5-38.

32. Pace interview; Talmadge interview.

33. Pace interview.

34. Tom P. Brady, *Black Monday* (Winona, Miss., 1955), pp. 7, 65, 45.

35. Ibid., p. 45, 1-2.

36. EK Papers, Series 3, Box 25, Civil Rights Folder of 84th Congress (where are collected clippings from *100 Congressional Record,* May 27, 1954, and the *New York Times,* May 28,1954).

37. Martin, *Deep South,* pp. 28, 37.

38. Talmadge interview.

39. Pace interview.

40. Martin, *Deep South,* pp. 38, 11, 21, 107.

41. Ibid., pp. 140-41; Woodward, *Jim Crow,* pp. 154ff.

42. Martin, *Deep South,* pp. 40-41.

43. Margaret Price, *The Negro and the Ballot in the South* (Atlanta, Ga., 1959), pp. 9-11, 15, 34.

44. Byrnes, *Lifetime,* p. 418; Martin, *Deep South,* p. 49.

45. EK Papers, Series 1, Box 11, Acts Folder; Kluger, *Justice,* pp. 744-46.

46. Woodward, *Jim Crow,* p. 153; Martin, *Deep South,* pp. 37, 54.

47. Woodward, *Jim Crow,* p. 156; Brady, pp. 74, 60.

Chapter Eight

1. Rowe interview.

2. Estes Kefauver Papers, University of Tennessee Library, Knoxville, Tenn., Series 10, Box 7, Speeches Folder; *New York Times,* February 5, 1956.

3. EK Papers, Series 5g, Box 9, Civil Rights Folder; Series 10, Box 7, Speeches Folder; Series 5g, Box 48, Issues Folder; Box 10, Civil Rights Folder.

4. *New York Times,* February 5, 1956.

5. Ibid., February 8, 1956. Later, when Stevenson abandoned "gradualism," his staff discarded those texts referring to it, fearing they might be used inadvertently. And today few references to gradualism remain in his papers.

6. Adlai E. Stevenson Papers, Firestone Library, Princeton, N.J., memorandum by John Bartlow Martin, M6, p. 154; Arthur M. Schlesinger, Jr., to Willard Wirtz, February 8, 1956, Q6, pp. 139-41; interview with Newton Minow, R8, pp. 92-93; memorandum by John Bartlow Martin, June 23, 1956, M6, p. 199.

7. EK Papers, Series 1, Box 10, Civil Rights Folder 10; see *Congressional Record,* 84th Cong., 2d sess., 104, pt. 4, March 12, 1956, pp. 4515-16.

8. AES Papers, memorandums by John Bartlow Martin, March 26, 1956, M5, p. 3; April 23, 1956, M5, pp. 5-6.

9. EK Papers, Series 5g, Box 10, School Desegregation Folder; Box 81, Civil Rights Folder.

10. AES Papers, memorandum by John Bartlow Martin, April 9, 1956, M6, pp. 120-21.

11. This passage is taken from Arthur M. Schlesinger, Jr.'s, diary. John Bartlow Martin, *The Life of Adlai E. Stevenson,* 2 vols. (Garden City, N.Y., 1976-77), 2:301-02.

12. Stuart Gerry Brown, *Conscience in Politics* (Syracuse, N.Y., 1961), 93.

13. AES Papers, memorandum by John Bartlow Martin, June 23, 1956, M6, p. 171; AES speech, Ministerial Alliance, Oakland, California, May 8, 1956, S47, pp. 46-48.

14. EK Papers, Series 5g, Box 10, Civil Rights Folder; Series 1, Box 10, Folder 11.

15. Ibid., Series 5g, Box 10, Segregation Folder; Box 16, EK Says Folder.

16. AES Papers, memorandum by John Bartlow Martin, MB, p. 179. According to the Stevenson staff's analysis, Stevenson carried Florida by about 11,000 votes, and Sikes's district was the only one he won big.

17. Ibid., Press Release of Kefauver, C25, pp. 194-95.

18. EK Papers, Series 5g, Box 82, Anti-AES Folder. In an analysis of the California vote by the Stevenson staff, AES won big with the farmers, old people, and blacks. See AES Papers, MB, p. 197.

19. EK Papers, Series 5g, Box 1, Butler Folder; Box 9, Civil Rights Folder; *New York Times,* May 14, 1956; May 15, 1956.

20. EK Papers, Series 5g, Box 16, EK Says Folder; AES Papers, memorandum by John Bartlow Martin, 1956, MC, pp. 11-12.

21. Arthur Ross and Herbert Hill, eds., *Employment, Race and Poverty* (New York, 1967), p. 406; AES Papers, Arthur M. Schlesinger, Jr., to AES, June 11, 1956, C7, p. 76.

22. AES Papers to Agnes Meyer, August 25, 1957; January 16, 1958; Adolf Berle to AES, June 7, 1956, C130, p. 7; AES to Berle, June 15, 1956, C130, p. 8; AES to Mrs. Franklin Roosevelt, June 8, 1956, C145, p. 80; AES to Arthur M. Schlesinger, Jr., June 8, 1956, C7, p. 75.

23. Ibid., Stephen Mitchell to Francis Nipp, October 17, 1966, Q4, pp. 226-27.

24. Ibid., Mrs. Franklin Roosevelt to AES, May 13, 1956, C7, p. 75; EK Papers, Series 1, Box 44, 1956 Folder.

25. EK Papers, Series 1, Box 44, 1956 Folder.

26. Confidential but reliable source.

27. Rauh notes.

28. Democratic National Committee Papers, John F. Kennedy Library, Waltham, Mass., Box 103, Platform Committee, August 9, 1956, 1:1825.

29. Ibid., Box 104, Platform Committee, August 10, 1956, 1,A-B: 2312-81; ibid., August 11, 1956, 2,A:2883-85; ibid., August 10, 1956, 1,B:2407; ibid., 2:2563.

30. Ibid., 2:2510, 2635, 2590; Box 105, Platform Committee, August 11, 1956, 1:3057.

31. Ibid., Box 104, Platform Committee, August 10, 1956, 2:2519, 2524-37.

32. Ibid., 2:2534-35.

33. Ibid., 2:2620-28; August 11, 1956, 1,A:2718-19; 1,B:2818-23; ibid., August 11, 1956, 1,A.

34. Democratic National Committee, *The Democratic Platform* (Washington, D.C., 1956), p. 43.

35. DNC, Box 105, Platform Committee, August 15, 1956, 1:3407; 2,B:3738, 3743.

36. DNC, Box 49, Convention Proceedings, August 15, 1956, pp. 329-30.

37. Rauh notes.

38. Rauh interview.

39. DNC, Box 49, Convention Proceedings, August 15, 1956, pp. 331-33; Diary of Arthur M. Schlesinger, Jr., August 19, 1956.

40. Diary of Arthur M. Schlesinger, Jr., August 4, 1956.

41. Rauh interview.

42. Diary of Arthur M. Schlesinger, Jr., August 4, 1956; EK Papers, Series 5g, Box 16, Platform Folder; Rauh interview.

43. AES Papers, Harry Truman to AES, August 19, 1956, C4, pp. 119-24.

Chapter Nine

1. Rowland Evans and Robert Novak, *Lyndon B. Johnson: The Exercise of Power* (New York, 1966). The following discussion of Johnson in the Senate is based on this work, where not otherwise noted. Theirs is an excellent study, the best so far.

2. Adlai E. Stevenson Papers, Firestone Library, Princeton, N.J., AES speech, Little Rock, September 25, 1956, S19, pp. 97-99.

3. Ibid., AES speech, Harlem, October 4, 1956, S19, pp. 165-68.

4. Ibid., Dowdal H. Davis to AES, November 7, 1956, C180, p. 107.

5. Rauh interview.

6. Margaret Price, *The Negro and the Ballot in the South* (Atlanta, Ga., 1959), p. 44.

7. Talmadge interview.

8. *New York Herald Tribune*, December 2, 1956.

9. AES Papers, AES statement, January 5, 1957, C167, pp. 94-95.

10. Ibid., AES on television, September 8, 1957, S48, p. 113.

11. Daniel M. Berman, *A Bill Becomes a Law: Congress Enacts Civil Rights Legislation* (New York, 1966), pp. 53, 82, 28.

12. Ibid., pp. 59, 125.

13. Rauh notes.

14. Arthur M. Schlesinger, Jr., *A Thousand Days* (Boston, 1965), p. 23.

15. Estes Kefauver Papers, University of Tennessee Library, Knoxville, Tenn., Series 1, Box 41, Democratic Party Folder.

16. Rauh notes; Rauh to author, June 19, 1978.

17. Rauh notes.

18. Democratic National Committee, *Official Report of the Proceedings of the Democratic National Convention and Committee* (Washington, D.C., 1964), p. 72; *Congress and the Nation, 1945-1964: A Review of Government and Politics in the Postwar Years.* Congressional Quarterly Service (Washington, D.C., 1965), p. 1629. (Hereafter cited as *CQ*, year, page.); Rauh to author, June 19, 1978.

19. Schlesinger, *Thousand Days*, pp. 39-40.

20. Democratic National Committee *Proceedings*, p. 98; Rauh interview; Rauh notes.

21. Schlesinger, *Thousand Days*, p. 41.

22. Ibid., pp. 848, 75; *CQ, 1945-64*, p. 1629.

23. The best source is Arthur Schlesinger, Jr.'s, memoir, *A Thousand Days*.

24. Allan Nevins, ed., *The Strategy of Peace* (New York, 1960), pp. 181-83.

25. Schlesinger, *Thousand Days*, pp. 603-08, 918-23.

26. Harold C. Fleming, "The Federal Executive and Civil Rights: 1961-1965," in *The Negro American*, eds. Talcott Parsons and Kenneth B. Clark (Boston, 1966), p. 383.

27. Schlesinger, *Thousand Days*, pp. 851-55.

28. Ibid., pp. 858-61.

29. Ibid., pp. 861-65.

30. Ibid., pp. 865-66; Pace interview. This was so even though the housing order covered only a small portion of the market. Fleming, "Federal Executive," p. 381.

31. Schlesinger, *Thousand Days*, p. 880.

32. *Public Papers of the Presidents of the United States: John F. Kennedy. Containing the Public Messages, Speeches, and Statements of the President. 1963.* (Washington, D.C., 1964), pp. 468-71.

33. Schlesinger, *Thousand Days*, 880-86.

34. *CQ, 1945-64*, pp. 1633-35.

35. Goodwin interview.

36. Evans and Novak, *Johnson*, p. 344.

37. Ibid., p. 349. Evans and Novak pointed out the similarity with Kennedy's phrase.

38. Daley said this to John Bartlow Martin.

39. Rowe interview; Rowe to author, June 1, 1978; Goodwin interview; Pace interview.

40. Schlesinger, *Thousand Days*, pp. 939-40n; Evans and Novak, *Johnson*, p. 379.

41. *CQ, 1945-64*, p. 1638.

42. *Congress and the Nation, vol. 2, 1965-1968: A Review of Government and Politics.* Published by Congressional Quarterly Service (Washington, D.C., 1969), p. 354. (Hereafter cited as *CQ*, year, page.)

43. *Public Papers of the Presidents: Lyndon B. Johnson. 1965.* (Washington, D.C., 1966), Book 1, p. 284.

44. Pace interview.

45. *CQ, 1965-68*, p. 362.

46. Ibid., pp. 378-88.

47. U.S. Department of Health, Education, and Welfare, Office of Civil Rights, *Higher Education Guidelines: Executive Order 11246,* 1972, interview with Kathy Hwang, Office of Civil Rights, Boston.

48. *Federal Register,* July 16, 1976.

49. U.S. Department of Health, Education, and Welfare, Office of Civil Rights, *Policies on Elementary and Secondary School Compliance with Title VI of the Civil Rights Act of 1964,* March 1968.

50. *CQ, 1965-68*, pp. 746-51; Wood interview; Goodwin interview.

51. *CQ, 1965-68*, pp. 185-226; Robert C. Wood, *The Necessary Majority: Middle America and the Urban Crisis* (New York, 1972), pp. 6, 50ff.

52. Wood interview; Douglas M. Costle, "Model Cities in Denver, Colorado: A Case Study," unpublished report, August 1969. This report was prepared as part of an evaluation of the Model Cities Program for the Department of Housing and Urban Development by Marshall Kaplan, Gans, and Kahn. (Hereafter cited as Costle Report.) See also Department of Housing

and Urban Development, "The Model Cities Program: A Comparative Analysis of the Planning Process in Eleven Cities," by Marshall Kaplan et al., 1970.

53. Goodwin interview. Goodwin, who wrote the speech, said he had not expected the phrase would become the slogan of Johnson's administration.

54. Wood interview; Wood, *Necessary Majority*, p. 34.

55. This is perhaps the most commonly held view of the Great Society.

56. Rowe interview.

Chapter Ten

1. Chicago Commission on Race Relations, *The Negro in Chicago* (Chicago, 1922), pp. 106-07, 113-15, 198, 221, 223-24.

2. Karl E. and Alma F. Taeuber, *Negroes in Cities: Residential Segregation and Neighborhood Change* (Chicago, 1966), pp. 1-3.

3. *New York Times*, August 12, 1976; September 16, 1976; August 23, 1976; November 3, 1976. Daniel Patrick Moynihan, "Poverty in Cities," in *The Metropolitan Enigma: Inquiries into the Nature and Dimensions of America's "Urban Crisis,"* ed. James Q. Wilson (Garden City, N.Y., 1970), pp. 367-85.

4. Moynihan, "Poverty in Cities"; Talmadge interview.

5. Thomas J. Ladenburg and William S. McFeely, *The Black Man in the Land of Equality* (New York, 1969), pp. 155-62.

6. Robert C. Wood, *The Nesessary Majority* (New York, 1972), p. 83.

7. *New York Times*, April 27, 1976; October 23, 1976.

8. Wood, *Necessary Majority*, p. 34.

9. Douglas M. Costle, "Model Cities in Denver, Colorado: A Case Study," unpublished report, August 1969. Unless otherwise indicated the discussion of Model Cities in Denver is from this report.

10. Wood, *Necessary Majority*, p. 49; Theodore J. Lowi, *The End of Liberalism* (New York, 1967), pp. 246-47.

11. Douglas Costle interview.

12. U.S. Commission on Civil Rights, *Fulfilling the Letter and Spirit of the Law: Desegregation of the Nation's Public Schools*, August 1976, pp. 6-13.

13. Palladino interview.

14. Ibid.

15. Ibid.

16. *New York Times*, March 8, 1976; *Fulfilling the Letter*, pp. 27-39; Palladino interview.

17. Melvin King interview.

18. *Fulfilling the Letter*, pp. 178, 182-83, 186-87, 218-19.

19. *New York Times*, April 19, 1976; November 20, 1977; August 6, 1978.

20. Lowi, *End of Liberalism*, p. 282; *New York Times*, April 19, 1976.

21. *Fulfilling the Letter*, p. 295.

22. Richard Kluger, *Simple Justice* (New York, 1976), pp. 355-56, 361-62, 420-21. On these pages Kluger summarizes the gist of the plain-

tiffs' arguments in *Brown*. It seems evident that urban segregation in the North (and South) is not comparable to rural segregation in the South, and that the remedies for one will not work as the remedies for the other. For an incisive analysis of this problem, see Oscar Handlin, "The Goals of Integration," in *The Negro American*, eds. Talcott Parsons and Kenneth B. Clark (Boston, 1966), pp. 659-77. His point is similar to Melvin King's (see above), that integration is not always a desirable goal.

23. *New York Times*, November 24, 1977; May 1, 1977; May 8, 1978.

24. *San Antonio Independent School District* v. *Rodriguez* (1973); *Milliken* v. *Bradley* (1974); *Arlington Heights* v. *Metropolitan Housing Corporation* (1977). For summaries and discussions of these cases, see Kluger, *Simple Justice*, pp. 770-73; *Harvard Law Review* 88 (November 1974), pp. 61-71; Gerald Gunther, *Cases and Materials on Constitutional Law* 9th ed., *1978 Supplement* (Mineola, N.Y., 1978), pp. 97-105. Whether or not integration was desirable (see above note 22), local districts, suburbs, and the Supreme Court have rendered it impossible. For how resistance to integration rises in accordance with economic status and racial homogenity, see Wood, *Necessary Majority*, p. 62.

25. *Fulfilling the Letter*, pp. 181-84, 293-313.

26. Norman H. Nie et al., *The Changing American Voter* (Cambridge, Mass., 1976), pp. 126-27, 246, 255. It may be of interest that the leader of the 1978 tax revolt, Howard Jarvis, announced, when tax reduction passed in California: "A new revolution. . . . The people is going to run the Government and the Government is not going to run the people." *New York Times*, June 9, 1978 ("A 'New Revolution' " by Tom Wicker).

27. Rauh notes. The following discussion of the Democratic National Conventions, unless otherwise noted, is drawn from these notes.

28. Pace interview.

29. Theodore White, *The Making of the President, 1972* (New York, 1973), pp. 18-47.

30. Pace interview.

31. Rowe interview; O'Hara interview.

32. O'Hara interview.

33. Democratic National Committee, "Delegate Selection Rules for the 1976 Democratic National Convention" (Washington, D.C., 1974).

34. Derrick Cephas interview.

35. Nathan Irvin Huggins, *Harlem Renaissance* (New York, 1971), pp. 34-35, 48, 142.

36. Ibid., pp. 52-83, 137-39; Kluger, *Simple Justice*, pp. 165, 170.

37. David E. Cronon, *Black Moses: The Story of Marcus Garvey and the Universal Negro Improvement Association* (Madison, Wisc., 1955), pp. 5, 50, 55, 60-67, 187-93.

38. Neil Hickey and Ed Edwin, *Adam Clayton Powell and the Politics of Race* (New York, 1965), pp. 135, 185, 212-19, 123, 219-26.

39. Ibid., p. 242.

40. Arthur M. Schlesinger, Jr., *A Thousand Days* (Boston, 1965), pp. 877-83.

41. Italics are Carmichael's. Stokely Carmichael and Charles Hamilton, *Black Power: The Politics of Liberation in America* (New York, 1967), pp. 37, 40-41.

42. Ibid., pp. 46-47, 54, 55, 62.

43. Ibid., pp. 7, 51.

44. See Huggins's discussion of the nineteenth century minstrels and their effect on the identity of both blacks and whites. *Harlem Renaissance,* pp. 244-301.

45. See articles by Irving Howe, "The Dangers in Ethnicity," *Washington Post,* June 19, 1977; and Orlando Patterson, "Hidden Dangers in the Ethnic Revival," *New York Times,* February 20, 1978.

46. *New York Times,* July 30, 1978. Speaking for the National Urban Coalition, its leader M. Carl Holman described the efforts to extend affirmative action to white ethnics as an attack on civil rights.

47. Michael Novak, *The Rise of the Unmeltable Ethnics: Politics and Culture in the Seventies* (New York, 1971), pp. 8, 250, 273; Nathan Glazer, "The Issue of Cultural Pluralism in America Today," in *White Ethnics: Their Life in Working Class America,* ed. Joseph Ryan (Englewood Cliffs, N.J., 1973), pp. 168-77.

48. Oscar Handlin, *Al Smith and His America* (Boston, 1958), p. 8; *The Uprooted* (New York, 1951), pp. 170-200. It was Handlin's detailed knowledge of immigration and the role of ethnicity in helping the immigrants to become assimilated that led him, in another essay, to oppose compulsory integration of blacks; for such integration would weaken, not strengthen, the community bonds and ethnic identity of blacks. See his "The Goals of Integration," in *The Negro American,* eds. Parsons and Clark, pp. 659-77.

49. Carmichael and Hamilton, *Black Power,* p. 182.

Chapter Eleven

1. R. Carter Pittman, "Equality v. Liberty: The Eternal Conflict," in *Historical Statements,* Virginia Commission on Constitutional Government (Richmond, 1960), pp. 22-23.

2. Robert C. Wood, *The Necessary Majority* (New York, 1972), p. 63.

3. Goodwin interview.

4. Wood, *Necessary Majority,* pp. 45-46.

5. *Congress and the Nation,* vol. 2, 1965-1968 (Washington, D.C., 1969), pp. 198-99 (Hereafter cited as *CQ,* year, page.).

6. Ibid., pp. 365-74.

7. Ibid., pp. 374-78.

8. Ibid., pp. 206-07.

9. Ibid., pp. 209-11, 766-76.

10. Wood, *Necessary Majority,* p. 51.

11. *CQ, 1965-68,* pp. 224, 377-88.

12. Ibid., pp. 776, 29.

13. For AES statement in 1957, see Chap. 9, n. 10; for Kennedy's troubles with the bureaucracy, see Arthur Schlesinger, Jr., *A Thousand Days* (Boston, 1965), p. 625.

14. Schlesinger, *Thousand Days*, p. 926. On the subject of the liberals' ambivalence about power, one is reminded of Henry Adams's statement in *The Education of Henry Adams,* 1st printed (privately) 1907, ed. Ernest Samuels (Boston, 1974): "During a million or two of years, every generation in turn had toiled with endless agony to attain and apply power, all the while betraying the deepest alarm and horror at the power they created," p. 497.

15. See Theodore Lowi, *The End of Liberalism* (New York, 1969), pp. 231-33.

16. *Congress and the Nation, 1945-1964* (Washington, D.C., 1965), pp. 1639-40 (Hereafter cited as *CQ,* year, page.).

17. *New York Times,* September 9, 1976.

18. Pace interview.

19. Rowe interview.

20. Goodwin interview; Richard Goodwin, *The American Condition* (Garden City, N.Y., 1974).

21. Van Dyk interview; Ted Van Dyk, "Fixing the Potholes: The Need for a New Democratic Domestic Agenda," *Democratic Review* (October-November 1975), 1:64-69. See also *Washington Post,* October 1, 1975; *New York Times,* April 12, 1976.

22. Marshall Kaplan, et al., "The Model Cities Program"; *New York Times,* April 12, 1976; August 30, 1976.

23. "O'Hara for Senate Committee" [Campaign brochure] (Mount Clemens, Mich., 1976).

24. *New York Times,* September 16, 1976; *The Budget of the United States Government: Fiscal Year 1977* (Washington, D.C., 1976), pp. 61-71.

25. Okun interview; See also Arthur M. Okun, *Equality and Efficiency: The Big Tradeoff* (Washington, 1975); and "Equal Rights but Unequal Incomes," *New York Times Magazine,* July 4, 1976; Wood, *Necessary Majority,* pp. 88-90.

26. *CQ, 1965-68,* pp. 164-165; Rowland Evans and Robert Novak, *Lyndon B. Johnson* (New York, 1966), p. 501; Talmadge interview; Pace interview; Costle interview; Van Dyk, "Fixing the Potholes," p. 68.

27. Pace interview; Talmadge interview; Pace interview.

28. Edmund Wilson, *Patriotic Gore* (New York, 1962), p. 435.

29. Rowe interview; O'Hara interview; Van Dyk interview; Goodwin interview; *New York Times,* May 29, 1976; August 8, 1976; Wood, *Necessary Majority,* pp. 11-19; Nathan Glazer, *Affirmative Discrimination: Ethnic Inequality and Public Policy* (New York, 1976).

30. Rauh interview; Norman H. Nie, et al., *The Changing American Voter* (Cambridge, Mass., 1976), pp. 126-27.

31. Wood interview.

32. Goodwin interview.

33. Wood interview.

34. John Bartlow Martin, *Life of Adlai E. Stevenson* (Garden City, N.Y., 1976-77), 2:801-02, 820-21, 838, 842-43. Martin makes clear what was unclear to many liberals at the time: that Stevenson never doubted the rightness of our containment policy, nor the reasonableness of military action, should negotiations fail.

35. Nie, et al., *Changing American Voter*, p. 124.

36. Lawrence M. Baskir and William A. Strauss, *Chance and Circumstance: The Draft, the War and the Vietnam Generation* (New York, 1978). Their book appeared just as this one was finished, and this author has not had time to study it. Their conclusions, however, appear sensible; they are what one might have suspected.

37. *New York Times*, April 19, 1976; Wood interview.

38. *New York Times*, May 28, 1976. Ron Nessen, the president's press secretary, corrected Ford the next day.

39. *New York Times*, March 4, 1976.

40. Ibid., June 26, 1976; *Wall Street Journal*, July 16, 1976.

41. "Report of the Activities of the 1972 Finance Committee to Re-Elect the President" (in possession of the Committee to Liquidate the 1972 Campaign, Washington, D.C.).

42. Bernard Bailyn, *Ideological Origins of the American Revoluion* (Cambridge, Mass., 1967), pp. 56, 144-59.

Chapter Twelve

1. Norman H. Nie, et al., *The Changing American Voter* (Cambridge, Mass., 1976), p. 49.

2. *New York Times*, June 22, 1976. A good example of such an area is Boone County, Kentucky, studied by a *New York Times* reporter. See the *Times*, May 29, 1976.

3. *The Budget of the U.S. Government: Fiscal Year 1980* (Washington, D.C., 1979), pp. 47, 560-61.

4. Robert C. Wood, *The Necessary Majority* (New York, 1972), p. 22.

5. Wood interview; Gwirtzman interview; Rauh interview; Goodwin interview. There may be many liberals that have not given up on liberalism; if so, they do not advertise their thoughts. A few do. See Elizabeth Drew, "Profile" (of Senator John Culver), *New Yorker*, September 11 and 18, 1978; John Bartlow Martin, "Reasserting Our Faith in Liberal Government," *Washington Post*, September 10, 1978. But in general liberals lately have not known where to stand on the issues of big government and expensive social programs. Recently Senator Edward Kennedy has made something of a test case out of national health insurance, an issue which engages the old pro- and antiliberal arguments and which should help the liberals make up their mind. (It should be noted that of those men interviewed and cited above some may have changed their views since the interviews, which were conducted in the spring and fall of 1976. It is likely, however, that they

still believe that in the last thirty years there have been only two years of substantial liberal success—1964 and 1965—and that this was hardly a fair test, or a long enough record, by which to judge liberal government.)

6. Costle interview; Wood interview. By the same token, as we have seen, the community action programs, by giving a measure of power to the poor, made conflict and confusion an inherent part of some OEO and Model Cities programs and also gave conservatives a reason to assail them.

7. Toni Morrison, "A Slow Walk of Trees (As Grandmother Would Say) Hopeless (As Grandfather Would Say)," in the *New York Times Magazine*, July 4, 1976, p. 103; and Robert J. Samuelson, "The View from the Battlefield of the War on Poverty," *National Journal* (March 3, 1979), Vol. 11, pp. 340-44.

8. Earl Black, *Southern Governors and Civil Rights: Racial Segregation as a Campaign Issue in the Second Reconstruction* (Cambridge, Mass., 1976).

9. Jack Bass and Walter DeVries, *The Transformation of Southern Politics* (New York, 1976), pp. 3-56; George Brown Tindall, *The Disruption of the Solid South* (Chapel Hill, 1972), pp. 64, 10. The transformation of the South was perhaps the most notable and enduring success of the liberals.

10. Pace interview.

11. *New York Times*, September 18, 1976; October 11, 1976.

12. Bass and DeVries, *Southern Politics*, p. 16. This comparison of views on busing is based on polls, which merely establish a point that is self-evident and that has been covered already in this book, pp. 201-08, 240-43.

13. Pace interview; Talmadge interview.

INDEX